History
in
the
Schools

History
in the
Schools
What Shall We Teach?

Edited by
Bernard R. Gifford

Macmillan Publishing Company
A Division of Macmillan, Inc.

NEW YORK
Collier Macmillan Publishers
LONDON

Macmillan Publishing Company
A Division of Macmillan, Inc.
866 Third Avenue, New York, N.Y. 10022

Collier Macmillan Canada, Inc.

Library of Congress Catalog Card Number: 88-9223

Printed in the United States of America

printing number
1   2   3   4   5   6   7   8   9   10

Library of Congress Cataloging in Publication Data

History in the schools.

   Includes bibliographical references.
   1. United States—History—Study and teaching—
United States.   2. History—Study and teaching—
United States.   I. Gifford, Bernard R.
E175.8.H57   1988   907′.1273   88-9223
ISBN 0-02-911701-1

Contents

Preface

In my initial public pronouncements, following my acceptance in 1983 of the deanship of the University of California at Berkeley's Graduate School of Education, I made much of the fact that I felt obligated to conduct a search for opportunities that would enable me to link more effectively "practice-sensitive researchers" within the Graduate School of Education to "research-sensitive practitioners" in elementary and secondary schools. I defined "practice-sensitive researchers" as those members of the faculty who had made a commitment to conduct systematically research designed to illuminate and clarify particular problems of educational practice, placing special emphasis on the concentrated search for new knowledge and understandings that could lead to improvements in teaching and learning in the classroom. Similarly, I had defined "research-sensitive practitioners" as unusually effective school district-based educators. What made these successful practitioners distinctive from other successful educators was their conviction that their special expertise was not simply the product of inspiration, fortune, or chance, but was, instead, the outcome of their systematic application of principles, rules, and insights that they had distilled and gleaned from purposeful observation, systematic reflection, and thoughtful experimentation.

To put my major goal more succinctly, I wanted to connect wisdom-seeking expert researchers with wisdom-seeking expert teachers. Moreover, I wanted to achieve this coupling within specific disciplinary, or content, areas. In concrete terms, this meant linking, say, history professors from the university with history teachers from the public schools. My emphasis on the importance of content area collaborations and investigations, versus research activities aimed at uncovering general insights about the broad process of teaching and learning, stemmed from my belief that the best way to engage discipline-oriented university faculty in practice-sensitive research was to start with a disciplinary problem. I had met very few professors of, say, mathematics who had indicated a strong interest in learning more about the general process of knowledge transmission from expert teacher to novice learner. On the other hand, I had met a fair number of talented mathematicians who had devoted considerable energy to uncovering and understanding the steps and procedures utilized by novice learners in acquiring particular mathematics knowledge and skills transmitted by expert mathematicians. Needless to say, my arguments about the relationship between scholarship and practice, as well as the importance of disciplinary knowledge, as a vehicle for bringing together researchers from the university with expert educators from the schools, generated considerable debate among faculty within the Graduate School of Education, and to a lesser degree, within the University of California as a whole.

In the midst of my thinking about what I intended to do as a new dean and how I might achieve my objectives, the opportunity to test my theories about the proper function of faculty in research-oriented schools of education was unexpectedly thrust upon me. In the summer of 1983, just as I was about to start my first full year as dean, I was invited to a meeting at the home of Ira Michael Heyman, chancellor of the University of California at Berkeley. Chancellor Heyman's other guest was Bill Honig, California's peripatetic superintendent of public instruction. Not only did Chancellor Heyman introduce Honig to me, he also initiated the conversation that unleashed the series of events that eventually generated the essays that appear within. And therein lies the origin of *History in the Schools: What Shall We Teach?*.

The conversation that proved to be so eventful centered on the quality of history instruction in the high schools, particularly the events leading up to the crafting of the U.S. Constitution. Chancellor Heyman, a professor of law before he moved into academic administration, had strong views on what the schools should be doing in the area of constitutional history. He presented his views, which grew out of his experiences as a frequent guest lecturer to high school classes in American history, to Honig and me with great passion and considerable insight. Bill Honig, also a lawyer, and a former student of Chancellor Heyman, turned to me at one point in the lively conversation and solicited my views on what I thought should be done about the problem of poor history instruction in the state's and nation's public schools. My first reaction to Honig's inquiry was to offer some general comments about the sorry state of the high school curriculum *in toto* and then to attempt to move the conversation away from me, in my capacity as dean and answer-finder, and back to generalities. After all, since I had not been formally trained in history, although an avid reader of all things having to do with the New Deal, what could I offer, by way of useful answers, to Honig's inquiry? Surely, I thought, Honig's question could not represent anything more than good manners, an attempt on his part to keep the conversation from becoming a closed debate between two lawyers.

Before I could act on my initial instincts, as well as on my analysis of Honig's motives, I was surprised to hear myself suggesting a means for answering the questions raised by Heyman and Honig. More specifically, I found myself suggesting that a conference be held, during which we would bring together knowledgeable historians, history educators, and expert teachers to examine empirically the issue of how well California's elementary and secondary schools were doing in the area of history teaching. If nothing else, I thought, the conference would give me the opportunity to test some of my ideas about the usefulness of bringing together those university-based historians most likely to be sensitive to the practice-related problems of history teachers in the schools, with those classroom teachers who would, in all likelihood, be most strongly committed to the centrality of good history teaching. A conference was not exactly what I had in mind when I had argued for stronger connections between practice-sensitive researchers and research-sensitive practitioners, but in this instance, especially in light of my own lack of expertise in history, it would have to do.

The rest of the story is, of course, history. The conference suggestion was met with immediate enthusiasm and offers of support from both Heyman and Honig. What eventually became the Clio Project was off to a promising start. However, even though the idea of a conference was off to a quick beginning, I knew enough about my own shortcomings to know that I required the advice and assistance of capable historians and history educators to make the conference more than just another gathering of complainers, which I was determined to avoid. Fortunately, I found the advice I needed (and made a good friend in the process) in Professor Sheldon Rothblatt, then chair of Berkeley's Department of History. Not only did Professor Rothblatt generously share with me his ideas on the aims of history instruction—in the process, piling my desk high with articles and books on the historical enterprise—he also recommended that I employ Dr. Paula Gillett, a recent Berkeley Ph.D. in history, and an extraordinarily committed history educator, to assist me in planning the conference and to run the Clio Project on a day-to-day basis. I had the good sense to follow Rothblatt's suggestions, learned a great deal from the materials he suggested that I read, and have had very few regrets since.

Having secured the moral and intellectual support of Heyman, Honig, and Rothblatt, I also needed to secure financial assistance from government agencies and foundations. Again, fortune was on my side, as I found this essential support relatively easy to secure. After minimum prompting, William Bennett, then chair of the National Endowment for the Humanities (NEH), provided the Clio Project with a chair's discretionary grant. Bruce Sievers, executive director of the Walter and Elise Haas Foundation, also came through with timely support. The support of NEH and Haas, along with modest grants from Chancellor Heyman, Superintendent Honig, and David P. Gardner, president of the University of California, proved to be more than adequate to conduct the conference. More important, the encouragement of all these individuals invited those of us involved in the Clio Project to think of the conference as just the beginning of a long-term effort to improve the quality of history instruction in the schools. And so we did.

And so it began. The August 1984 conference "History in the Public Schools: What Shall We Teach?" initiated the Clio Project, still one of the most ambitious university-based history instruction improvement projects in the nation. Some of the essays contained in *History in the Schools* owe their origins to the 1984 conference. Others were developed for presentation to subsequent Clio Project activities—including workshops for history teachers, sponsored by the NEH, the California State Department of Education, and The Ford Foundation, and held on the Berkeley campus in the summers of 1985 and 1986. The support and guidance of Peter Stanley, head of Ford's Education and Culture Program, has been especially helpful.

I have made it clear how much in debt I am to my colleagues at Berkeley for *History in the Schools*. I would be remiss if I did not mention the sacrifices my family made by permitting me to indulge without limit or complaint my passion for reading history, under the new pretext that what had previously been a time-consuming way to relax and withdraw from the present was now job-related and thus legitimate work. I am especially indebted to my son Nelson Bernard, age seven, to whom I dedicate this book in the hope that he will live to see the American Creed—so optimistically described by Gunnar Myrdal in his classic study of race relations in the United States, *An American Dilemma: The Negro Problem and Modern Democracy*[1]—transformed into the American reality. I harbor the same dreams for his older brother, Bernard IV, who works hard every day to make the Constitution a living document for people in legal difficulty, and also for Antoinette Grace, Nelson's oldest sibling, who works just as hard to blend the analytical approach of formal policy analysis with the spirit of freedom and opportunity for all, as contained in the Constitution. For Elizabeth Danielle, my youngest child, I harbor the most precious dream of all—hope that the day will come when neither race nor sex will prove to be an impediment to any of her ambitions and aspirations, or for that matter, the ambitions and aspirations of any child, of any race or gender.

In addition to being helped by colleagues in the university, I had the good fortune to have some first-rate administrative and editorial support: Regina LeRoy-Burrell and Cynthia Spears, with their usual speedy efficiency and good humor, typed this manuscript and its many drafts. Paula Yurkewecz coordinated the efforts on the final version, meeting tight deadlines. Ann Seabury and Matt Downey read each and every draft, offering me useful advice along the way. Nevertheless, as helpful as Ann's and Matt's comments were, I must admit that I have not always adhered to their good and wise advice. To them I offer my thanks and my apologies.

Finally, to the reader, I offer a set of fine essays, containing ideas that require more thought, additional clarification, and not a little debate. Let the debate begin!

NOTES

1. Gunnar Myrdal, *An American Dilemma: The Negro Problem and Modern Democracy* (New York: Harper and Row, 1944).

History
in
the
Schools

Introduction
Thinking about History
Teaching and Learning

BERNARD R. GIFFORD

More than five years have passed since the National Commission on Excellence in Education presented its landmark report, *A Nation at Risk: The Imperative for Educational Reform*.[1] When issued, the commission's report did not make for very pleasant reading, especially for members of the educational establishment. The commission—appointed by a secretary of Education who was a self-styled conservative and chaired by the president of the University of Utah, hardly a hotbed of radical sentiment for social change—portrayed the nation's public schools as being mired in mediocrity. What made *A Nation at Risk* especially notable was its style of presentation, as it stated its arguments in forceful and colorful language unusual for a staid governmental study group. The tone of the report was not what one expected from a conservative administration strongly committed to principles of local control of the schools and educational policy-making.

Long after our collective memory of the commission has faded, many of us will be able to recall some of its more pungent observations. Its comment that "the educational foundations of our society are presently being eroded by a rising tide of mediocrity that threatens our very future as a Nation and a people"[2] has been quoted in the mass media so often that it is now part of the nation's storehouse of popular political trivia. Others of the commission's overcharged statements also fall into this category, including its observation that "if an unfriendly foreign power had attempted to impose on America the mediocre educational performance that exists today, we might have viewed it as an act of war" and its conclusion that "we have, in effect, been committing an act of unthinking, unilateral educational disarmament."[3] Rhetorical excesses aside, the commission did a world of good by helping to launch within the educational community one of the most intensive periods of self-examination ever. Fortunately, the commission balanced its message of despair with a message of belief in the possibility of improvement and a sense that the time was ripe for real school reform. Many of us in the educational establishment took to heart the commission's message that the time was ripe for real school reform. The question we faced was, Where should we start?

High on our agenda in California was the improvement of history instruction in the schools. Our initial surveys and discussions with history educators indicated that the teaching of history in the schools was in sad shape. It seemed to need improvement in nearly every area that we examined. Some of its problems were symptomatic of what was wrong with American education in general. Instruction was excessively textbook driven; teachers lacked the resources they needed for professional development; graduation requirements, especially for prospective college students, were too low. But history also had its own problems. History is difficult to teach; its aims are ambiguous, its outcomes hard to measure. The narrative style of historical discourse is of marginal interest to a generation of students raised on television. But we realized that history is a valuable subject for these very reasons. Even if it lacks direct appeal to the television generation, history is by this very fact all the more needed as a corrective to the shallowness and provincialism of the present-minded. The sort of generalized wisdom and judgment that it fosters is an essential part of education, however difficult it may be to assess. We were convinced that the improvement of history instruction warranted the high priority we were giving it.

We were also concerned that the special needs of history would be overlooked in the larger movement to reform American education. Reflecting the themes initially presented in *A Nation at Risk*, much of the criticism of the schools articulated after 1983 hinged on the alleged failure of the schools to advance the scientific, technical, economic, and military aims of the United States. It is relatively easy to define these aims, to describe the competencies students need to fulfill them, and to decide what the schools must do to improve education in these areas. With history, the matter is altogether more complex. The crisis in history education has not come about through its failure to provide society with properly trained experts. Rather, the problem is that expertise in history is not perceived as important or useful to powerful constituencies. While history would doubtlessly benefit from the recent concern with the quality of education, some of the measures that seek to improve general education are likely to be a detriment to history. A narrow-minded, back-to-basics program may even exclude history as not being "basic." Greater time in the school day devoted to technical and vocational subjects may undercut the place of history in the curriculum. Preferential pay for science and mathematics teachers could further weaken the morale of history teachers and heighten student perceptions that history is unimportant. We saw the need to single out history as a subject with unique problems that demanded special attention within the broader movement for educational reform.

History as a school subject does have its advocates among educators, especially within the historical profession. Historians have become more concerned in recent years about the teaching of history both in the colleges and in the schools. This is reflected in the founding of *The History Teacher* and other teaching journals, the increasing number of sessions devoted to history teaching at professional meetings, and the growing participation of historians in NEH-funded summer institutes for those who teach in colleges and schools.[4] The Organization of American Historians' sponsorship of the *Magazine of History*, a journal begun in 1985 expressly for junior and senior high school teachers, is the most recent evidence of the profession's concern about the status of history in the schools. Individual historians have also risen to the occasion, teaching in summer institutes, serving as National History Day judges, and working with teachers on professional committees. But individual dedication is no substitute for the organized professional commitment necessary for historians to have any significant impact on the way history is taught in the schools. While the historical associations have tried to build bridges to the schools, they have not succeeded in mobilizing the professional or financial resources needed to revitalize the teaching of history. Moreover, research by academic historians has become so narrow and specialized that the generalist history now taught in the schools fails to excite academic interest. Finally, like other humanists, historians are suffering from a crisis of confidence. The diversity of world cultures and the diversity of cultures within America itself have severely limited the mastery historians once had over the universal dimensions of their subject, which now seems less about eternal values and wisdom and more about the values and wisdom of that fragment of humanity that falls within each historian's area of specialization. To respond effectively to the problems facing history in the school curriculum, historians need assistance from teachers and other educators who have the benefit of a more general perspective.

We called our effort to mobilize support for history in the schools the Clio Project, named after the muse of history. The project was initiated by the Graduate School of Education at the University of California, Berkeley, and the California Department of Education because of our shared conviction that the resources of that university ought to be more available to the state's schools. Early on we decided to make history the focus of our efforts. There was agreement on the serious nature of the problems confronting history in California classrooms, on the real possibility of finding some solutions, and on the need for close cooperation between ourselves, professors of history and education, local school districts, and, most important, school teachers.

The idea of bringing together a variety of resources and expertise has been basic to the Clio Project from the beginning. This approach was encouraged by the example of a number of other collaborative projects that have already proved successful: the CHEM study (started by Genn T. Seaborg, Nobel Prize winner in chemistry and a long-time activist for improvements in science instruction),[5] the Yale–New Haven Teachers Institute,[6] and University of California at Berkeley's National Writing Project,[7] for example. We felt that the Graduate School of Education should be more than a center for teacher training and scholarly research; it should actively reach out to the schools and make its many resources readily available to them.[8] Also, the Graduate School of Education seemed the obvious and appropriate institutional link between the university community—here, the Berkeley History Department—and the State Department of Education, local school districts, and school teachers.

The problems that confront history as a school subject are compounded by the failure of academic historians to become involved in an organized and sustained effort to support their colleagues in the schools. This neglect encourages a prejudice against school teachers in the university community, and consequently it both demoralizes the history teacher and weakens the position of history in the schools. Eventually this disregard will weaken the position of history in the universities as well. The problem has been recognized by the American Historical Association. In a 1983 report the AHA recommended establishing partnerships linking professors of history and education with school teachers. We are doing precisely this and have discovered that the problem is solvable. Many academic historians—not all or even enough, but many nevertheless—are concerned about the place of history in the schools. However, they need a vehicle through which they may express their concern. Clio is such a vehicle, and we have had good cooperation from many Berkeley historians in our efforts.

Clio has initiated a number of programs that attempt to improve the quality of history in the schools. Based in Berkeley and with close relationships to the State Department of Education, Clio is specifically concerned with problems of schools in California, a big and diverse state. But Clio's activities are appropriate for virtually all schools throughout the United States.

The first item on the Clio agenda is simply to gather data on the place of history in the schools. It is extraordinary that outside of general impressions so little is known about precisely what goes on in history classrooms in California. We have initiated survey research through which we will develop data based on representative samples of California social studies teachers, administrators, and others concerned with history education.

We have initiated a program to improve the quality of textbooks and thus to solve a problem about which there is widespread agreement. We are developing a method of analysis and evaluation, making systematic comparisons and defining criteria to aid in evaluating text-books for those who must select them. Our first step, actively underway, is to develop a consensus among historians, teachers, and curriculum specialists about what makes a good history textbook.

A related project concerns developing materials to supplement text-books, materials drawn from primary historical sources and chosen not only to appeal directly to children but also to be of real historical value. We are concentrating on materials produced by young people—diaries, for example—or about their interests—sports, popular culture, gender relations, and the like. Such materials are particularly needed by teachers in junior high schools and middle schools, whose students are still unready to understand or appreciate the abstract, conceptual schemes of formal history.[9] For a similar reason we are also attempting to rejuvenate an older style of history, no longer in fashion among academics but still appealing to the young. This style may, for example, present heroic figures acting against an exciting narrative background—a device that can turn history into a colorful, personal, and dramatic story. We want to develop materials of this sort, which engage the student fully and still maintain the standards and integrity of good history.

Our project is firmly committed to the proposition that curriculum reform must involve school teachers as equal partners in the curriculum development process. For example, we have initiated a number of seminars in which academic and school teachers together develop classroom materials. We have already successfully conducted such seminars and developed materials on American urbanization and on recent immigration into California. In the future we envision a curriculum development center with a small staff to facilitate the regular bringing together of scholars, teachers, and curriculum specialists in specified areas.[10] History teachers in the schools need to be brought into the general history community. Their concerns need to be acknowledged by academic historians, and they, in turn, should be in closer touch with the intellectual currents that move academics.

The Clio project also will deal with ways in which children representing California's many ethnic cultures can be educated together in common schools. We recognize public schools as a significant point of contact between immigrant children and American culture. Our efforts are directed according to the twin principles of teaching American citizenship to immigrants and of honoring and preserving the cultural diversity that immigrants bring us.

Finally, our greatest emphasis is on in-service training for history teachers. We differentiate among teachers and their various needs; advanced placement teachers, for example, are generally well prepared yet must be helped to keep up with current research. Other teachers, well trained in the scholarship of a generation ago, may have lost touch with academic history and have sometimes grown intellectually stale. For these teachers, in-service training in a university atmosphere brings them up to date on current research and revives their intellectual curiosity. Still other teachers are poorly prepared and may have had very little course work in history. These teachers obviously need in-service training in the basics. Teachers in junior high schools and middle schools also have special requirements. Many, though not trained in history, must nevertheless possess both a wealth of the sort of colorful details that appeal to the young and a firm grasp of basic historical fact and interpretation.

Like other Clio projects, our in-service institutes and workshops take a collegial approach. Our normal procedure is to have a morning lecture with a professor and a class of teachers and then an afternoon curriculum development session that turns the lecture into usable classroom material. Master teachers facilitate the translation of academic lectures into instructional materials.

Clio's first step was to convene a conference in August 1984 entitled "History in the Public Schools: What Shall We Teach?" The conference was a success in a number of ways but especially in the tremendous response and enthusiasm shown by the entire history community: school teachers, administrators, state officials, and professors of history and education. Over seven hundred attended, many of whom participated in the lively workshops and discussions. Since one of the primary objects—of Clio in general and the conference in particular—was to bring together the different layers of the history and education communities, we regarded the response to the conference as a magnificent beginning.

Many of the pieces included in this book were originally given at the conference and, we feel, deserve a wider audience. We begin with papers (part 1) that discuss the history of history teaching in America. From the late nineteenth century to today, history has struggled to maintain its independent identity in the curriculum. In the course of these struggles history has allied itself with (and asserted its independence from) patriotism, Americanization, progressivism, social efficiency, social science, and much else. Many of these alliances have been useful to history, yet they have all tended to turn history into a means rather than an end and have therefore threatened to undermine the integrity of the subject. Moreover, history has suffered from the flight of academic historians into their narrowly professional concerns and school administrators into theirs. These problems are still with us today, and so a history of history teaching is especially relevant.

Part 2 concerns two related areas: on one hand, the use of history to teach values and good citizenship and, on the other, the extent to which the nation's multicultural heritage ought to be represented in history courses. The problems are related because education in values and citizenship must inevitably be education in particular values and particular modes of citizenship. Some of our contributors feel that the school's essential mission is education in democratic values and that history ought to be taught with this mission in mind. Others want history to be taught for its intrinsic worth as an intellectual pursuit, not as a means to ends outside history itself. And still others express fear that when education stresses values it represents an enforced conformity to ideals and institutions connected to a melange of puritan, capitalist, white values that they feel have submerged and dominated other ethnic cultures in American history.

The key resource that university historians can bring to school teachers is a depth of scholarly understanding in the discipline and knowledge about current developments in academic research. It is difficult for teachers, given their many other commitments, to keep as up to date as they should with academic thought. In part 3, therefore, we present three essays by eminent historians who approach the topic "What Shall We Teach?" simply from the point of view of good history. They do not concern themselves (except incidentally) with citizenship, values, or the requirements of multicultural history, or with ways by which history can be taught to teenagers.

In part 4 we present papers that offer specific advice on classroom teaching. Here we have wide agreement: textbooks must be de-emphasized. Teachers need to be supplied with primary material that more directly appeals to young people. These essays discuss the use of such materials, including the American folk song and materials from local history, blending a concern for teaching methodology with a concern for good history.

Contributors to this volume disagree on many issues: history for history's sake or for the sake of something else; history of the powerful or of the powerless; a common culture or ethnic diversity. These are important disagreements, and we hope this volume at least frames these issues—which are sure to remain controversial. What is also controversial among many is the very existence of history in the school curriculum. On this matter, all of the contributors are in agreement— history is an essential part of education; we need more, not less, history in the schools; and we need to teach it better. We are also in agreement that the time is nigh for improvement in history in the schools. It is to this concept that this study and Clio are dedicated.

NOTES

1. National Commission on Excellence in Education, *A Nation at Risk: The Imperative for Educational Reform* (Washington, DC: U.S. Government Printing Office, April 1983).
2. Ibid., p. 5.
3. Ibid.

4. For a review of some of these activities, see Hazel Whitman Hertzberg, "The Teaching of History," in *The Past before Us: Contemporary Historical Writing in the United States*, edited by Michael Kammen (Ithaca: Cornell University Press, 1980), pp. 494–495.

5. Richard J. Merrill and David W. Ridgeway, *The CHEM Study Story: A Successful Curriculum Improvement Project* (San Francisco: W.H. Freemen and Company, 1969).

6. James Gray, "University of California, Berkeley: The Bay Area Writing Project and the National Writing Project," in *School-College Collaborative Programs in English*, edited by Ronald Fortune (New York: Modern Language Association, 1986), pp. 35–45.

7. James R. Vivian, "Issues in Establishing and Developing an Educational Collaboration: The Yale-New Haven Experience," in *Education and Urban Society*, Vol. 19, No. 1 (November 1986), pp. 59–76.

8. Bernard R. Gifford, *The Good School of Education: Linking Knowledge, Teaching and Learning* (Berkeley: Graduate School of Education, University of California at Berkeley, 1984). Also see Bernard R. Gifford, "Prestige and Education: The Missing Link in School Reform," *The Review of Education*, Vol. 10, No. 3 (Summer 1984), pp. 186–198.

9. For more on Clio's efforts to introduce the study of the lives of children into the study of history, see the following articles by Matthew T. Downey, former professor of American history at the University of Colorado, who is currently visiting professor of history education, Graduate School of Education, University of California at Berkeley and Clio project director: "The Children of Yesterday," *Social Education*, Vol. 50, No. 4 (April/May, 1986), pp. 260–261, "Teaching the History of Childhood," op. cit., pp. 262–267. and "The History of Childhood: An Annotated Bibliography," op. cit., pp. 292–293. Also see the following articles by Clio project collaborating teachers: Suzie McLean-Balderston, "Being Young in Early California, *Social Education*, Vol. 50, No. 4 (April/May, 1986), pp. 268–270; Lillian Valle-Condell and Karen Gordon, "Teaching with Ada Millington's Diary," op. cit., pp. 276–279; Carole Chin, "The Berkeley Children's History Trunk," op. cit., pp. 280–282; and Karen Jorgensen-Esmaili and Rosalind Sarah, "Intergenerational Interviews," op. cit., pp. 288–290.

10. Paula Gillett, "Reuniting a Divided Profession: The Search for Excellence in History Education," *Perspectives, American Historical Association Newsletter*, Vol. 25, No. 8 (November 1987), pp. 17–19.

Part I
TEACHING HISTORY IN AMERICA

Hazel Hertzberg and Diane Ravitch lead off with essays on the history of history education in America. Hertzberg explains how and why school administrators and university departments of education began to concentrate on teaching methodology, paying little attention to the actual content of history, while academic historians moved in the opposite direction, abandoning concern for methodology and focusing narrowly on historical content. This unfortunate division of labor, so familiar now, had its origins in the 1920s, though it was not until the 1960s that it became complete. Before World War I, Hertzberg explains, both historians and educators were vigorous participants in the formulation of curriculum and educational policy and in the joint problems of method and content. Many leading academic historians of the late nineteenth century spent the early years of their career as school teachers. The American Historical Association and the regional history associations were not yet narrowly professional; members included school teachers, university professors, and patrician amateurs. It was largely professional historians who wrote the series of great reports prior to World War I that for the first time established history as an important part of the curriculum. Naturally, these historians were concerned with historical content: they recommended four years of history, one each of ancient European, medieval and modern European, English, and American. Interestingly, they were also concerned with teaching methodology and the aims of citizenship and social reform, all of which they believed to be complementary to good history.

After World War I, university historians increasingly lost their interest in the schools. For historians, professionalization meant intensive research on narrow, closely defined topics that were of interest only to other professionals. The generalist history taught in the schools and the problem of teaching methodology, though vital to the classroom teacher, were scorned by university historians. History retained a strong position in the curriculum during the interwar period. But when a variety of forces combined to weaken history in the schools after World War II, historians made little effort to defend it.

By and large the schools—or at least those who ran the schools—did not miss the historians. Hertzberg explains that school administrators were on a professional path of their own that defined the educator as a person expert in teaching methodology but indifferent to the content and integrity of subject matter, except to the extent that content served classroom purposes. Their schools taught students, not subjects.

Prior to World War I, history was regarded as a modern, practical subject, essential for the understanding of current social problems. Progressives and social scientists supported a strong history program, trying to use history to forward their aim of social reform. While this alliance was beneficial in the sense that history was supported as an eminently practical subject, it was dangerous. In the 1920s a narrow vision of social reform, embodied in the movements for "social efficiency" and for "social control," captured the imagination of school administrators. The wider society and economy, it was believed, needed people who possessed certain clearly specifiable competencies, and it was the role of the schools to deploy their resources efficiently in order to turn out student-products with the requisite skills. The so-called "content" of education, having been limited to mere "skills," fell away, leaving educators to discover the most efficient methods for teaching the necessary skills. History was neither utilitarian enough nor concrete enough to satisfy scientific administrators. Professional historians concerned with content and professional educators concerned with methodology went their separate ways. Both would have become lost.

Ravitch, author of the well-known *Great School Wars*, takes up many of Hertzberg's themes but from a different point of view. Hertzberg focuses on the growth of a narrow professionalism among historians and educators that had the effect of separating historical content from teaching method. Ravitch's main concern is with the use—or abuse—of history in service of nonhistorical ends. Ravitch argues strongly for the study of history as an end in itself, but she also agrees with one of the main beliefs of the more broad-minded advocates of social usefulness: a knowledge of history is an essential means for the understanding of the present. Yet history can only provide that sort of understanding when it maintains its integrity as an intellectual discipline. Ravitch chronicles the myriad of social causes that since the late nineteenth century have sought to take bits and pieces from history in order to support particular goals. Social efficiency and Americanization are, for Ravitch as for Hertzberg, the most egregious of the social objectives that have distorted the teaching of history. Subordinated to social usefulness, history became background to a subject, not a subject in its own right. For the more narrowly vocational, history was worthless even as background.

For those of us who wish to support history in the schools, Ravitch's position is difficult but important. The fact is that public schools—and Ravitch notes that it is the public schools, with their social objectives, not private schools, that have largely eliminated history—will inevitably be used to subserve social objectives. Virtually the entire curriculum, not just history, faces a struggle to maintain its integrity. It is futile, perhaps even undesirable, to resist society's wish to have students educated in citizenship or in the technical competences needed to serve a complex economy. And yet, in the midst of all this, history has a place. As Ravitch insists, history as an intellectual discipline subserves an end that is—or should be—meaningful to all.

Chapter 1

Are Method and Content Enemies?

HAZEL WHITMAN HERTZBERG

The question, Are method and content enemies? has been answered differently by different groups at different times in the history of the social studies. It is a significant question because it goes to the heart of the relationships among at least three parties involved in the secondary school curriculum: classroom teachers, school administrators, and college and university historians.

Most classroom teachers are quite clear on the matter: their answer is an emphatic No. They realize that serious problems arise when either content or method (in which I include the scope and sequence of the curriculum, the organization of the course and the lesson, the materials of instruction, and the style and procedure of teaching) is downgraded or ignored. The chief offenders are content exclusivists and mad methodists. To the former, content is all, method anathema; to the latter, method is all, content irrelevant. But real teachers in real classrooms with real students have to integrate all the elements of method and content in a way appropriate to the age, interest, and capacity of their students and to the concerns of society for an effective and educated citizenry.

Most people today simply assume that history and the other social sciences were always mainstays of the high school and college curriculum. But it is not so. A century ago "history and allied subjects," as the social subjects were then called, barely existed in either the high schools or colleges. Their entry into both institutions and their development into major subjects are among the most significant aspects of the transformation of American society that took place in the late nineteenth and early twentieth century.

I am going to focus on the role of college and university historians in this great curriculum shift for several reasons directly related to the situation of the social studies today. First, these historians played a critical part in the shift; second, they constituted for well over half a century the chief friend and defender outside the schools of the whole field of the social studies, not just history, a role none of the other social sciences has been able or willing to assume; third, their retreat from this role has had serious consequences for both the social studies and the historical profession; and fourth, these two groups have common problems that cannot be solved by either one alone. An understanding of how the present came to be is, I believe, a necessary basis for the rapprochement we so badly need.

The alliance of method and content was one of the guiding principles for the generation of historians who founded the historical profession in the 1880s. As Albert Bushnell Hart put it in 1887, "Whatever the aim of a school, it is of little importance unless it is aided by adequate methods."[1] Lest you think that Hart was simply an early mad methodist, let me point out that he was not only a founder of the historical profession but also one of the most important historians of his generation. In 1887 he was at the beginning of a brilliant career, one characterized by his continued commitment to problems of teaching. Hart was author with Edward Channing of what became *The Harvard Guide*; editor of the pathbreaking Epochs of American History series and the American Nation series; editor of the *American Historical Review*; president of both the American Historical Association and the American Political Science Association; and the author of numerous books and textbooks, source books, and readers. He was also a great teacher (one of whose pupils was Franklin Delano Roosevelt). Hart described the situation of history teaching in 1887:

> It is not many years since the question, how is history taught in the United States? could be answered in only one of two brief ways; it was not taught at all; or it was taught perfunctorily from single text-books. A certain quantum of knowledge of affairs in the ancient world was imbibed by students of the classics; some people old and young, read history for the love of it; an acquaintance with the past was thought desirable for the statesman; only here and there a choice spirit taught his pupils, in school or college, what history actually meant.[2]

Hart summed up his survey of secondary schools thus: "In many schools little or no history is taught; where taught, the best methods are not always employed; where good methods prevail, there is often a lack of books and apparatus; where there are the best facilities, pupils sometimes neglect them."[3]

From such modest beginnings in a shadowy half-life in schools and colleges, history moved to the sunny center of the curriculum of both by 1920. To what may we attribute this extraordinary change? One factor was educational expansion—especially the growth of the public high school, on the one hand, and the university, on the other. These two institutions symbolized and helped to bring about the transformation of American society a century ago. By the end of the 1880s there were for the first time more public high schools than private academies, even though only a small number of the eligible boys and girls actually went to high school and a much smaller number graduated. The university movement was well underway, challenging the dominance of the old-time college.

Expansion alone would no doubt have given rise to a serious national consideration of the high school curriculum. But there were other factors as well. One was the curricular war raging between the "classics" (Latin, Greek, and mathematics) and the "moderns" (English, history, science, and modern languages). In general, colleges upheld the former and the universities the latter. In secondary education the lines were less sharply drawn. Many schools offered both a classical and an English (moderns) program or variations thereof. History, be it noted, had a foot in both camps: it was allied with the classics through ancient languages, with the moderns through the new "scientific" history.

The immediate occasion for the attempt to bring a semblance of order out of curricular chaos was the perilous passage from secondary school to higher education, for which no reliable charts—or rather, far too many charts—were available. Each college or university set its own admission requirements in such particularistic terms that it was literally impossible for a student to prepare for more than a very few. Although not many young people actually went to college, in fairness to those preparing for college and to the vast majority for whom the high school was "the people's college," some solution had to be found that would not place impossible demands on schools and students.

It was the newly rejuvenated National Education Association (NEA)—which in the 1880s had a considerable infusion of new members and new energy—that took the lead. An NEA Committee of Ten (with subcommittees representing all the classics and modern subjects) was formed in 1892 to consider the problem. The future social studies were well represented by the Conference on History, Civil Government, and Political Economy (economics), with the president of the University of Wisconsin, Charles Kendall Adams, as chairman, Albert Bushnell Hart as secretary, and Woodrow Wilson as a guiding spirit. The work of the ten represented the first national consideration of what the high school curriculum should be.[4]

Like the other subcommittees, the history ten moved quickly to broad recommendations that went far beyond the original charge. The aim of secondary schools, the committee believed, was not to prepare boys and girls for college but for life; thus, the high school course should be the same for both groups. The virtue and advantages of history and allied subjects were that

> they serve to broaden and cultivate the mind; that they counteract a narrow and provincial spirit; that they prepare the pupil in an eminent

degree for enlightenment and intellectual enjoyment in after years; and that they assist him to exercise a salutary influence upon the affairs of his country.[5]

Working from these purposes, the committee made strong recommendations on a broad and continuous course of study: biography and mythology in grades 5 and 6; American history and civil government in 7; Greek and Roman history in 8; French and English history in 9 and 10, both taught so as to elucidate medieval and modern history; American in 11; civil government and a special period to be studied intensively in 12. The resulting curriculum established the history/civil government (or civics) nexus that dominated the social studies until the 1960s.

The committee urged that the study of civil government avoid theoretical questions and focus on practical matters and that it be closely intertwined with history. (In fact, political science then was actually a part of history.) Economics should be taught in connection with U.S. history, civil government, and geography, and not as a separate subject. In this way the Committee of Ten sought to bring the incipient social sciences into the curriculum.

The report of the committee contained an extended discussion of methods in line with its view that the chief object of teaching was not the imparting of facts but rather

> the training of the judgment, in selecting the grounds of an opinion, in accumulating materials for an opinion, in putting things together, in generalizing upon facts, in estimating character, in applying the lessons of history to current events, and in accustoming children to state their conclusions in their own words.[6]

The report recommended frequent use of comparison and cross-reference; such activities as debates and mock legislatures; independent student inquiry; brief informal talks rather than lectures; student-led classes; discussion; collateral reading; the judicious use of primary sources; written compositions; and the use of at least two textbooks as well as other reference works. The ten sternly opposed rote memorization and other such passive methods. Teachers, they asserted, not only should love their subject but must be well versed in both content and methods of teaching. For the Committee of Ten method and content were allies, not enemies.

Perhaps the most important accomplishment of the history ten was to define history/civil government as the backbone of the social studies curriculum. What the ten began became firmly established in the next two decades. The reasons for this are complex, and I can indicate them only briefly.

The dominance of history and, to a lesser extent, civics or civil government was based on an alliance between school administrators sympathetic to history and historians sympathetic to schools. These attitudes were grounded in beliefs about the nature of their professions and about the function of schools in society, and they were nourished by a sympathetic public opinion.

Nineteenth- and early twentieth-century school administrators were, in David Tyack's phrase, "managers of virtue" to whom education was a secular religion. They saw in the study of history and civil government a way of expressing their deepest beliefs: they conceived of the United States as a redeemer nation, and they committed their efforts to ensuring the educated and dedicated citizenry they believed necessary to build it. (I hasten to add that this did not imply that they believed that only American history should be taught or that U.S. history should be chauvinistic.) In addition to the value of history/civil government in educating citizens, administrators welcomed history's alliance with the moderns and the fact that the history offered to the schools by the new professionals was "scientific." History was also flexible: it had the convenient capacity to include materials from the incipient social sciences, thus offering considerable curricular latitude. In this formative period so critical for the future of the curriculum, history carried the promise of a better-educated citizenry, the stamp of science, and the cachet of modernity.

If there were strong reasons for school administrators to favor history, there were strong reasons also for historians to involve themselves with the schools, particularly with methods. History as a profession was created by men who went to Germany for the advanced work not available here and returned with new ideas for a new age. They thought of themselves as scientific historians, by which they meant primarily followers of the "scientific" or historical method of the German seminar, the scientific laboratory of history. This method was at the heart of professionalized history. It involved using original sources, painstaking testing and sober weighing of evidence, and the development of a critical and well-informed mind. Scientific history required new ways of teaching and learning to which the rote recitation then prevalent (in American colleges as well as in the schools) was utterly antithetical. The seminar method, which these historians saw as essential for graduate training and suitable for some undergraduate education, could be used only in modified form and in moderation in the schools. For secondary education, therefore, scientific historians advocated teaching methods that were believed to develop qualities they prized, such as systematic inquiry and well-based judgment. This concern with method was thus an integral aspect of the history they espoused.

Another reason had to do with the commitment of scientific history to the importance of the state in history and of history in the state.

Scientific historians saw the state as the chief arena in which the historical process took place and saw knowledge of state history as an essential element in the consciousness of its people. To establish history in American schools and colleges was not only a practical matter of educating citizens but also part and parcel of their conception of the role of history as the conscience of the state. Scientific historians Americanized this conception; if in Germany history created subjects, in America history created citizens. Another reason was prudential. The new generation of historians knew that to prosper in higher education, history needed a solid base in the schools. Those who went forth to teach would first have been students. The profession of history had its economic base in the elementary and secondary classrooms of America.

Another factor connecting historians with the schools was the fact that so many new professionals had been schoolteachers themselves. In the nineteenth century numbers of young men taught school for a few years before entering the professions (including academia or business), a pattern followed by a few young women as well. Teaching school gave insights into the real world of the classroom that were based in personal experience. The good common sense of historians' recommendations for the schools was thus partly a product of the personal connections between the profession and the schools.

Finally, historians were the first on the scene and could thus speak with an official voice; they belonged to the first of the social disciplines to form a professional organization. Moreover, the new German-trained professionals who founded the American Historical Association (AHA) in 1884 were wise enough to include older, patrician, nonacademic historians in the new association. The AHA thus united two groups who might conceivably have become enemies. The AHA thus kept contact with popular history.

This policy was in marked contrast to that of the economists. The American Economic Association, founded in 1885, was limited in practice to the institutional or historical school, virtually excluding laissez-faire economists and exacerbating animosity between the two groups. This bitter division in their ranks made it difficult for economists to influence the school curriculum, even had they wished to do so. The other social sciences did not acquire clear and separate identities and disciplinary associations until after the turn of the century. At a critical time in curriculum development, therefore, historians had the field virtually to themselves, and it was quite natural for school administrators to look to them for assistance.

In 1896, just when the committee's recommended curriculum began to make its way in the schools, the AHA, at the request of the National Education Association (NEA), appointed a new curriculum committee to consider the still unsettled question of college entrance requirements. Members of this group, the famous AHA Committee of Seven—six men and one woman—were leaders of the profession and had extensive contact with the schools. Its chairman, eminent constitutional historian Andrew C. McLaughlin, had been a high school principal in the Middle West. Three of its members had been secondary school teachers; one was a school board member; one had taught in a normal school; two had fathers who were school superintendents. Even though only one member concurrently was a secondary school teacher, the group represented a rich fund of secondary school experience and a powerful group in the profession. Herbert Baxter Adams, a founder of the AHA and its secretary since its inception, was a former secondary school teacher whose famous graduate seminar at Johns Hopkins turned out many of the period's major historians and social scientists. Adams was an indefatigable advocate of educational reform and, like other committee members, had written extensively on methods of teaching history. Ties with the earlier Committee of Ten were strong: Albert Bushnell Hart had been its secretary, and Charles Homer Haskins had sat in on its meetings.

The 1899 report of the Committee of Seven, *The Study of History in Schools*, built on the work of the ten but greatly expanded and enriched it. The purposes of teaching—the cultivation of judgment in students and the education of citizens in society—were set forth more extensively and perhaps more eloquently. The Committee of Seven concluded:

> One does not need to say in these latter days that secondary education ought to fit boys and girls to become, not scholastics, but men and women who know their surroundings and have come to a sympathetic knowledge of their environment; and it does not seem necessary now to argue that the most essential result of secondary education is acquaintance with political and social environment, some sense of the duties and responsibilities of citizenship, some capacity in dealing with political and governmental questions, something of the broad and tolerant spirit which is bred by the study of past times and conditions.[7]

The curriculum proposed by the seven modified that of the ten but kept the history/civil government nexus: ancient history and the early middle ages in grade 9, medieval and modern European history in 10, English history in 11, and American history and civil government in 12. To implement this curriculum, the committee suggested that every class needed a good textbook to provide a "main current" for the year's work. This should be supplemented by extensive collateral reading in works of genuine literary value, particularly in order to expose students to differing interpretations, which should comprise authentic, interesting, and comprehensible primary sources carefully selected to help pupils understand the historical process as well as to bring to life people and events from the past. The text should be supplemented also by audiovisual aids such as artifacts, maps, pictures, and models. A good library was, of course, essential. Such was the practical advice on methods offered by the seven, in whose opinion content and method were allies.

Teachers, the Committee of Seven believed, needed good training in content and methods:

> In teaching a vital subject like history, much depends upon the personality of the teacher, upon his force, insight, tact, sympathy, upon qualities that cannot be imparted by the university courses or by prolonged research. Though all this be true, every teacher should have had some instruction in methods of teaching and should have learned from precept what are the essentials of historical study and historical thinking; and—what is of much greater importance—he should have so worked that he knows himself what historical facts are and how they are to be interpreted and arranged. The highly successful teacher in any field of work needs to be a student as well as a teacher, to be in touch with the subject as a growing, developing, and enlarging field of human knowledge.[8]

The report of the Committee of Seven and its reception solidified the connection between schools and the historical profession. The recommended curriculum spread quickly throughout the high schools, becoming virtually universal by 1916. This process was greatly strengthened by the group's activities. Some members provided instructional materials; for example, Hart and McLaughlin wrote popular textbooks and edited books of sources. But far more important was the fact that the seven helped to start influential regional associations of teachers of history and allied subjects. These organizations in New England, the Middle Atlantic states, and the Middle West were composed of teachers from universities, colleges, normal schools, secondary schools, and elementary schools. They published proceedings, bibliographies, pamphlets, and aids to instruction. They made recommendations on such matters as teacher certification and training. In 1909 the regional associations acquired an unofficial national voice in *The History Teachers Magazine*. Rescued in 1911 by the American Historical Association from its initial financial difficulties, the periodical soon became a forum for articles on content and methods in social education as well as for information about regional groups and learned societies. It is entirely appropriate that these regional associations created a new curricular consensus that eventually modified the curriculum of the Committee of Seven.

The new consensus was embodied in the third major committee report on history and allied subjects, published in 1916. Like the Committee of Ten, the reporting body was a subcommittee of the NEA that developed from a need to reconsider the familiar but unsettled question of college entrance requirements, and that became part of a larger attempt to redefine the entire secondary school curriculum. Known as the Committee on Social Studies of the NEA Commission on the Reorganization of Secondary Education (CRSE), it bestowed the new and more convenient name "social studies" on the field still called "history and allied subjects," its earliest name. The new committee's recommended curriculum, a modification of earlier curricula, gradually supplanted that of the Committee of Seven and set a pattern that was not seriously challenged until after World War II.

Recommendations of the 1916 Committee on Social Studies reflected on four major factors, which were the stuff of familiar experience to the teachers in the regional associations and which helped to shape the consensus on what the curriculum should be.

The first was the rise of the school of "new" or "progressive" history, whose leaders, especially James Harvey Robinson and Charles A. Beard, were also teachers' association leaders. The new historians challenged the scientific history of the founding generation. Their kind of history was "history that speaks to the present," that would explain how the present came to be. They believed historical-mindedness was necessary for social progress and that recent history (by which they meant the previous few hundred years, not the previous decade) was more valuable to the present than ancient history. The new historians sought to ally themselves with the rising social sciences and to use the insights thus gained to enrich historical analysis and interpretation. Because of their belief in the potency of ideas in society, intellectual history was for them a major concern. They wanted a history broadened far beyond "past politics" to include the history of ordinary people and everyday life, of industry and technology, and of social and economic change. These historians constituted the historical wing of progressivism.

Yet the new history was not so far from the older scientific history as either side supposed. Both believed in progress; both were committed to a vision of history's contribution to public life; both stressed that understanding the past was a key to understanding the present; both attempted some degree of objectivity while recognizing the difficulty of achieving it; neither considered history a science in the manner of the social sciences. In at least one significant respect, however, the experience of the two sides was quite different. Few of the progressive historians had been school teachers: this nineteenth-century pattern was rapidly disappearing and with it some of the empathy with teachers that had accompanied it. In the teachers' associations, however, progressive and scientific historians worked together with only occasional disagreements. That many scientific historians supported a shift in emphasis to more modern history is evident in a review of the work of the

Committee of Seven by an AHA committee that recommended greater attention to the modern period.[9] Thus, at a crucial moment in curriculum development, a new history appeared that seemed as well suited to the needs of the modern school as scientific history had been in its time.

A second factor was the growth of the separate social sciences. Each in turn broke away from history; in the first decade of the twentieth century, each declared independence, and separate professional associations were formed. Except for the political scientists, those in the newly professionalized social sciences were rather indifferent to the schools. Economists and sociologists tended to regard their disciplines as too difficult for school children. Sociologists, who had considerable difficulty in defining their field, were interested in the social role of the schools but not in the school curriculum and, therefore, directed their energies more toward teacher training in the normal schools. Anthropology, with its focus on salvaging disappearing data about small nonliterate societies, had little concern with the schools. In spite of this massive lack of interest by the professional associations, economics and sociology grew modestly as school subjects.

Political scientists had a different view. Many, after all, also were historians; the head of the Committee of Seven was both. Their subject, in the guise of civics or civil government, was the junior partner in the history/civics-or-civil-government combination. Soon after the American Political Science Association (APSA) was formed in 1903, it began to issue reports on the teaching of various versions of political science in the schools. In spite of—or really because of—close ties to history, which they were trying to break, political scientists wanted their subject taught separately. This position was agreed to by the AHA committee set up to review the work of the Committee of Seven and by the teachers' associations.[10]

The new or progressive history was paralleled by the new or progressive political science, which took a functional rather than formal approach to government and which engaged many political scientists in firsthand contact with government and social agencies through research and/or consultation on public administration problems. If the new history represented the historical wing of progressivism, the new political science constituted its political base in the university. A major APSA study of teaching government in schools, colleges, and universities published in 1916 strongly recommended an active and functional civics.[11] Men who were themselves grappling with problems of contemporary public administration were quite naturally sympathetic to the idea that students should investigate the functions of government—especially of municipal government with which political scientists were most concerned. As with history, political science's central thrust made the subject, suitably garbed as civics, welcome in the schools. The APSA committee report of 1916, which dealt extensively with teaching methods, was almost identical in many sections with the report of the NEA Committee on Social Studies of 1916. In fact, one of the leading spirits of the latter, J. Lynn Barnard, was also a member of the former. The composition of the APSA committee shows the close connections between history and political science. Three members were professors of both history and political science or had written in both fields. In addition, two were political scientists only (including the chairman), one a historian only, another a school administrator.

The third factor considered by the committee was a deep and ultimately decisive shift taking place in the attitudes of many school administrators toward history and often toward all subject matter that was not immediately utilitarian. We have seen that in the late nineteenth and early twentieth centuries these "managers of virtue" had been decidedly sympathetic to history and government, their interest helping to promote rapid adoption of the AHA Committee of Seven curriculum. But by the end of the first decade of the twentieth century, the tide had begun to turn. Though the new history and the new political science reinforced the position of the social subjects—because they were attuned to contemporary needs and because they undergirded the historic role of the school in educating citizens—trends in administration tended to be hostile, at least to history. The most important factor in this shift was the rise of scientific management—what Raymond E. Callahan calls "the cult of efficiency." Here, modern (supposedly scientific) management ideas and techniques that stressed efficiency, cost effectiveness, and accountability were applied to this rapidly expanding field of school administration.

Closely allied to this development was the beginning of curriculum-making as a separate specialty. Both marched confidently under the banner of science, which in the eyes of many school administrators had fallen from the faltering hands of historians into the confident grasp of scientific ideologues such as Franklin Bobbitt, W. W. Charters, and the educational sociologist David A. Snedden. The "social efficiency" favored by these men valued not school subjects but rather the contribution these subjects made to the achievement of precisely engineered objectives, which in turn were based on "scientific" studies of activities performed in various occupations or social roles. Scientific administration and scientific curriculum-making sought to study the world as it was (or as they thought it was) and to turn out students who would fit neatly into the model they had thus created. Selection of subject matter was held to be strictly accountable to these purposes. As administration became more complex and more imbued with "scientific" management, many administrators lost sympathy with such subjects as history that did not seem to be properly utilitarian or sufficiently concrete and manageable.

In addition to ideas of scientific management, many administrators were increasingly drawn to "social control," a term introduced by the sociologist Edward A. Ross, whose book *Social Control* was published in 1901. While "social control" has a variety of shades of meanings, its core meaning posits the profound and overwhelming influence of social groups in shaping and controlling the beliefs, attitudes, and behavior of their members. The term may be used to refer to an ongoing process of which people are barely conscious or not conscious at all, or it may refer to a conscious effort to shape the process toward particular ends. The concept was amplified in its application to education by Snedden, who was Ross's student and who took the reform school as his educational ideal. Snedden advocated separate schools and different education for "consumers," who would occupy the higher echelons of society, and "producers" (also known as "the rank and file"), who were the children of laborers and persons of modest means. A liberal education, although somewhat revamped, would produce efficient consumers, Snedden conceded, but he did not pay much attention to this group or this type of education. He was more interested in the rank and file; what the "producers" needed was vocational education, well tailored to their station in life. Such an education would supposedly provide the state with good citizens, an outcome that Snedden valued highly. Snedden spent most of his career training generations of administrators at Teachers College, Columbia University, an institution from which arose also the most cogent criticisms of his doctrine.

Snedden represented an extreme version of "social efficiency," one that united scientific management with a steely social control. Many others who sought scientifically determined and implemented objectives rejected Snedden's rigidly differentiated system as undemocratic. Nevertheless, the introduction of a hawkish version of social efficiency as a standard for evaluating educational purposes and results drove a wedge between content and method. To the question—Are content and method enemies?—the answer of the scientific managers/social controllers was often Yes.

The final factor to be considered is the evolving philosophy of John Dewey. Although it had more impact in the elementary than in secondary schools, Dewey's work drew attention to the need for coordinating teaching with the growth processes of students and for active student engagement with content. He had his own version of social efficiency.

Dewey's meanings have to be understood within the context of his view of education as "that reconstruction or reorganization of experience which adds to the meaning of experience, and which increases ability to direct the course of subsequent experience."[12] His conception of social efficiency differed radically from that of the proponents of scientific management/social control. Dewey specifically warned against trying "to fit individuals in advance for definite industrial callings, selected not on the basis of trained individual capacities, but on that of the wealth or social status of parents" and against the implication that "we must adopt measures of subordination rather than utilization to secure efficiency."[13] His own definition was as follows:

> In the broadest sense, social efficiency is nothing less than that socialization of *mind* which is actively concerned in making experience more communicable; in breaking down the barriers of social stratification which make individuals impervious to the interests of others. . . . Social efficiency, even social service, are hard and metallic things when severed from an active acknowledgement of the diversity of goods which life may afford to different persons, and from faith in the social utility of encouraging every individual to make his own choice intelligent.[14]

Dewey's *Democracy and Education*—published in the same year (1916) as the NEA Committee on Social Studies report—devoted a chapter to history and geography, which he called "the information studies *par excellence* of the schools" and "the two great school resources for bringing about the enlargement of the significance of a direct personal experience."[15] If the past "were wholly gone and done with, there would be only one reasonable attitude toward it. Let the dead bury their dead," Dewey wrote. "But knowledge of the past is the key to understanding the present. History deals with the past, but this past is the history of the present. Past events cannot be separated from the living present and retain meaning. The true starting point of history is always some present situation with its problems."[16] He advocated intellectual history and industrial history (the history of inventions and of work) as the most important kinds of history for students. The new, progressive history was so well attuned to Dewey's own ideas that for him it represented the ideal history for the schools.

Democracy and Education called for "the unity of subject matter and method." Dewey wrote:

> The idea that mind and the world of things and persons are two separate and independent realms—a theory which philosophically is known as dualism—carries with it the conclusion that method and subject matter of instruction are separate affairs. Subject matter then becomes a ready-made systematized classification of the facts and principles of the world of nature and man. Method then has for its province a consideration of the ways in which this antecedent subject matter may be best presented to and impressed upon the mind; or, a consideration of the ways in which the mind may be externally brought to bear upon the matter so as to facilitate its acquisition and possession. . . . But since thinking is a directed

movement of subject matter to a completing issue, and since mind is the deliberate and intentional phase of the process, the notion of any such split is radically false. . . . Method means that arrangement *of* subject matter which makes it most effective in use. Never is method something outside the material. . . . Method is not antithetical to subject matter; it is the effective direction of subject matter to desired results."[17]

For Dewey, method and content were inseparable.

The four factors we have considered—the new or progressive history, the new political science or civics, the new scientific management and social control, and the new Deweyan educational philosophy—were powerful forces that inevitably would affect any new formulation of the curriculum. They are usually considered aspects of progressivism, demonstrating once again its numerous facets as well as its many contradictions. What they had in common was an emphasis on the social, in spite of the different meanings they gave the term.

When the NEA Committee on Social Studies was first formed it was called "Committee on Social Science in Secondary Schools." But social science, once looked on as a unified field containing differing tendencies, was not becoming "the social sciences." The committee name shifted from the singular to the plural and from science to "studies."

So powerful and ubiquitous was the term "social" in this period that it is not surprising that the term "the social studies" began to replace the earlier and rather awkward "history and allied subjects." Beyond mere convenience, the words "the social studies" expressed the spirit of an age in which "social" was a favorite designation. The name also helped define the field by stating what, broadly speaking, its constituent elements dealt with in common. Then, too, "social" had a dual meaning—of socializing students and of designating basic subject matter. It was also conveniently flexible. One or more of the social sciences could be included or not, and the name begged the question of whether history was a social science. Courses could be based on the separate disciplines or "fused" in some fashion. It served better than "history and allied subjects" to characterize the work in elementary and junior high school where the boundaries between disciplines were more fluid than in the high school. It also had an introductory air about it; "social studies" often was applied to introductory college courses.

The committee got its new name from the chairman, Thomas Jesse Jones, a Welsh immigrant who was a sociologist and a minister (the links among religion, reform, and sociology were very strong in those early days) as well as an official of the U.S. Bureau of Education. Jones had taught at Hampton Institute (for blacks and Indians) where from 1902 to 1909 he was head of research and of the program in "social studies." In 1912, while working for the education bureau, he became education director of the Phelps Stokes Fund. From this position, which Jones held for the rest of his professional career, he exerted an important influence on the education of blacks and Indians in the United States and on the education of black Africans in Africa. Jones was the very model of a foundation executive. He was also a deeply committed man, and the tone of the report, at once businesslike and fervent, was probably due to him.

Composition of the NEA Committee on Social Studies was quite different from that of the earlier committees of ten and seven—both of which were long on college and university teachers and short on secondary school teachers or administrators. Most NEA committee members were secondary school teachers or administrators, including several superintendents. The solid core of the committee had been active in regional associations, chiefly the Association of History Teachers of the Middle States and Maryland. A number had written textbooks, teachers' guides, or other educational materials. The group included only two university historians—James Harvey Robinson of Columbia University, who had served on the original NEA Committee of Ten, and William H. Mace of Syracuse University, whose well-known text on methods of teaching history was an interesting and somewhat quirky book based on scientific history (though in later editions influenced by the new history).[18] There can be little doubt that one of the major intellectual influences on the committee was Professor Robinson, who was quoted extensively in the section on history. John Dewey also influenced the committee, but in a rather curious way, as will be explained later on in this chapter.

The watchword of the 1916 report was "social efficiency" of a moderate sort. The report began by defining the social studies as "those whose subject matter relates directly to the organization and development of human society, and to man as a member of social groups." The "keynote of modern education," the committee asserted, was "social efficiency," to which all subjects should contribute, adding that the social studies were particularly well suited to this purpose. They "should have for their conscious and constant purpose the cultivation of good citizenship," among whose characteristics were "a loyalty and sense of obligation to his [the pupil's] city, State and Nation as political units." The social studies should also cultivate a sense of membership in the "world community," with all the "sympathies and sense of justice that this involves as among the different divisions of human society.... High national ideals and an intelligent and genuine loyalty to them should thus be a specific aim of the social studies in American high schools," the report declared.[19]

The recommended curriculum consisted of two cycles: in grades 7–9, geography, European history, American history, and civics; in grades 10–12, European history, American history, and problems of democracy (social, economic, political). While the plan coincided roughly with the physiological periods of adolescence, the committee reported, the main reason for these cycles was that many students ended their schooling in grade 6 and another large contingent in 7 and 8. The course would offer a comprehensive program for each period, to be repeated in more depth and breadth. A number of possible variations on the major plan were discussed, offering considerable flexibility, including three years of high school history.

The grade 9 civics course clearly was the one most beloved by the Committee on Social Studies. It was conceived of as "community civics," which meant a functional rather than formal and descriptive approach and applied not only to the local community but to the state and nation as well. In an extended discussion of various ways to organize the course, the report devoted attention to "the civic relations of vocational life" and called for "development of an appreciation of the social significance of all work." The course should emphasize the broader social and civic implications of vocations and of the services they rendered rather than "renumeration." Instruction from the viewpoint of "individual success should be made not the end but the means to a more fundamental social education," the committee believed.[20]

The report emphasized the role of history, no doubt because of history's importance as a school subject as well as the committee's desire to reform it. The history supported by the committee was clearly the new history. The old history had its problems. Of this the committee was convinced. Citing Professor Robinson, the report asserted that "one of the chief troubles in teaching history comes from the old idea that history is a record of past events: whereas our real purpose nowadays is to present past conditions, explain them so far as we can, and compare them with our own."[21] Robinson recommended that history be treated both chronologically and topically (a view universally held by history educators in that period). He raised the question as to "*what conditions and institutions should be given the preference, considering the capacity of the student on the one hand and the limitations of time in the other*" and suggested that the committee not "pronounce" on this matter but urge its importance on teachers and textbook writers.[22] However, the report did state "a partial answer" in the form of a principle for selecting "what is worthwhile":

> The selection of a topic in history and the amount of attention given to it should depend not merely on its relative proximity in time, nor yet upon its relative importance from the adult or from a sociological point of view, but also and chiefly upon the degree to which such topic can be related to the present life interests of the pupil, or can be used by him in his present processes of growth.[23]

The Committee on Social Studies pointed out that this new principle raised new questions: "What history does meet the needs of the child's growth?" and "How may a given topic be related to the child's interest?"

This principle, asserted the committee, throws the problem back to the teacher, the person who knows her own students.[24]

These questions were not easy for even the best teacher to answer. Realizing this, the committee offered examples of lessons, or what we would today call units: one on the War of 1812, one on Greek cities, one on medieval craft guilds and the development of crafts and commerce. The first linked the problem of neutrality in the current World War to neutrality in 1812; the second looked at ancient Greek architecture and the Greek organization of urban space with reference to contemporary city planning; the third compared medieval craft guilds and the history of occupations with current occupations of the fathers of students in a class in a girls' high school "representing the working classes" (all seem to have been artisans). "These three-type lessons illustrate the application to particular cases of the principle that history to function properly in the present must meet the needs of present growth in the pupils," the committee explained.[25] To the experienced eye, the lessons given as examples held the possibility of being either very good or disastrous in terms of both pupil interest and/or growth processes, on the one hand, and historical content, on the other. As examples, they did not do much to clarify what was meant by the basic principle.

The principle is still elusive some seventy years later. We know that "present life interests" of the student may actually be imposed, manip ulated, or imagined by the teacher or may be so transient as to be educationally valueless. It seems reasonably clear that the committee had no such shallow interpretation in mind. "Present processes of growth," which obviously meant something more substantial than "present life interests," is yet even harder to figure out. Most good teachers then and now would agree that material should be presented in such a way as to build on student interest and on the pupil's stage of development and to further intellectual growth. Thus expressed, these sentiments seem much like those in earlier reports. But members of the 1916 committee obviously thought these principles constituted a sharp break with the past or, to be more precise, with "traditional" practice: the recommendations of earlier committees were not mentioned.

Despite such breaks with the past, however, the committee had no intention of disregarding chronology in teaching history, saying, "No substitute for the chronological organization of history has been found that adequately meets the conditions and needs of secondary education." The report stated firmly:

> The gradual and orderly evolution, step by step, of institutions and conditions is of the very essence of history. It would be impossible, were it thought desirable, to eliminate this element from historical study. But the principle of organization is antiquated which results in what someone has called the 'what came next' plan of treatment, a mere succession of events:

in the building of United States history on the framework of "administrations"; and of English or Roman history on that of "reigns"; and in the
organization of entire history course in such a way that the pupil studies "ancient" history this year, "medieval" history next year, and "modern"
history the year following—provided, indeed, that he happens to begin his
history this year and continue it consecutively next year and the year following, which is by no means invariably true.[26]

The report seems to have been calling for chronological history with
a system of periodization based on the social and industrial history of
the progressive historians rather than on political or dynastic history.
This new history would at the same time mesh with and further the
interests and growth processes of students. To effectuate this was a
very difficult task, even more difficult than its advocates then realized.

The Committee on Social Studies was at some pains to defend the
recommendations against possible charges that they were downplaying
history. "Under the present four-unit plan a premium is placed upon ancient and American history, all that goes between being left largely to
chance," the committee argued. "Under the plan proposed by the committee a much larger proportion of the pupils will secure the benefits
of a study of the essentials of European history."[27] For the last three
years of high school the recommended course was a year of European
history to the end of the seventeenth century (including ancient and ori-
ental civilization, English history to the period mentioned, and American
exploration); a year or a half-year of European history since the seventeenth century; a half-year of American history since the seventeenth
century; and one year or a half-year of a course entitled Problems of
Democracy. This was hardly a curriculum that dethroned history, as
is sometimes charged. In fact, despite all the talk about "present processes of growth," history in its new-history manifestation was the only
one of the social sciences that kept any strong connections with the
parent discipline.

Community civics was the capstone of the junior high cycle, one of
its major functions being to convince students to remain in school. For
senior high, the capstone was Problems of Democracy, an ingenious
answer to the demands of the various social sciences for curricular
inclusion as well as one that provided "a more definite, comprehensive,
and deeper knowledge of some of the vital problems of social life, and
thus of securing a more intelligent and active citizenship."[28] None of
the social sciences "as developed and organized by the specialists, is
adapted to the requirement of secondary education," the committee
asserted, "and all attempts to adapt them have been obstructed by
tradition, as in the case of history." Therefore, the committee proposed
a course built around "actual problems, or issues, or conditions, as
they occur in life, and in their several aspects, political, economic,

and sociological." The course should be "adapted directly to the needs of secondary education" and the problems selected on the basis of "immediate interest to the class" and "their vital importance to society." While the report asserted that "the principle here suggested is the same as that applied to the organization of civics and history," in reality there was a difference.[29] Gone was the intense concern with "present processes of growth" or "the present life interests of the pupil" in favor of simple, immediate student interest.

One of the most interesting aspects of the 1916 recommendations was the use made of John Dewey's work. I said earlier that he influenced the committee in a rather curious way. The report included two quotations from Dewey, one on "attending to the needs of present growth," one on the uses of history in understanding the present. The committee expounded on these ideas:

> The high-school course has heretofore been determined too largely by supposed future needs and too little by present needs and past experience. The important fact is not that the pupil is getting ready to live, but that he is living, and in immediate need of such mental and social nourishment and training as will enable him to adjust himself to his present social environment and conditions. By the very process of present growth he will make the best possible provision for the future. This does not mean that educational processes should have no reference to the future. It does not mean, to use a concrete illustration, that a boy should be taught nothing about voting until he is 21 and about to cast his first ballot. It means merely that such instruction should be given at the psychological and social moment when a boy's interests are such as to make the instruction function effectively in his processes of growth. A distinction should be made between the "needs of present growth" and immediate, objective utility. As a boy's mental and social horizon broadens with the processes of education, he will become inquisitive about facts and relations perhaps long before he has direct use for them in the affairs of life. The best question that can be asked in class is the question that the pupil himself asks because he wants to know and not the question the teacher asks because he thinks the pupil sometime in the future ought to know.[30]

Aside from the use of "boy" to mean "boy and girl," this sounds rather Deweyan. What is most interesting, however, is that the report made no reference to Dewey's *Democracy and Education*, with its powerful discussion of the significance of geography and history in the curriculum and with an approach so compatible with that of the new history. It is difficult to believe that the committee was unaware of Dewey's book, since *Democracy and Education* had been widely reviewed in the spring and summer of 1916 just prior to the publication of the NEA report in November. The book was particularly important because it was far more explicit about school subjects than anything Dewey had written before and was far more applicable to secondary education.

If Dewey's thinking on history and geography (he does not, of course, use the term social studies) had been incorporated into the report, it would have been clearer, richer, and more useful to teachers. The report also would have benefited from his discussion of vocational education. *Democracy and Education* explicitly attacked narrow vocational training that "would give to the masses a narrow technical trade education for specialized callings, carried on under the control of others." Dewey advocated an education that "would give those who engage in industrial callings desire and ability to share in social control, and ability to become masters of their industrial fate. It would enable them to saturate with meaning the technical and mechanical features which are so marked a feature of our machine system of production and distribution." For those "more privileged," it "would increase sympathy for labor, create a disposition of mind which can discover the culturing elements in useful activity and increase a sense of social responsibility."[31] Such views—a direct attack on hardline social efficiency—were hinted at but not expressed very forthrightly in the report. Perhaps the authors were too cautious to do so. Whatever the reason, Dewey's influence on the report did not represent his most important contributions to consideration of the actual classroom curriculum.

The report of the NEA Committee on Social Studies had much in common with the two reports that preceded it and from which it had developed. All three treated method and content as allies, not as enemies. This was one of the chief sources of their strength. In fact, it would probably not have occurred to any of these committees that it was possible to make recommendations on content without making recommendations on method. Like its predecessors, the 1916 committee tried to bring history teaching into line with modern trends in the discipline and to include social sciences in the curriculum. Students were cast as active inquirers rather than passive absorbers of predigested knowledge. While all spoke in the name of educating citizens of a democratic society, the 1916 report stressed social efficiency, albeit in a soft rather than hardline version. The Committee on Social Studies gave a more central and controlling place to student interest and growth than did the two earlier committees, but while the language differed, there were many similarities in ideas. It is important to note also that all three were based on models that had been tried in schools.

With the publication of the report of the NEA Committee on Social Studies, the era of great national reports that so decisively shaped the curriculum came to an end. There were other reports in the decades that followed, but none had the enormous impact of the original three. We still live with the effects and the intricate web of relationships they created.

I have discussed this era in some detail because it is so significant and so little known. I can indicate only briefly some trends in the succeeding decades that directly affected the relationship of content to method. The separation between them—rooted in the professionalization of history, the social sciences, and school administration—widened sometimes rapidly, sometimes gradually, but seemingly inexorably.

A harbinger of conflicts that were to arise was the publication in 1918 of the recommendations of the parent body of the 1916 committee: the Commission on the Reorganization of Secondary Education (CRSE).[32] Like its predecessor, the NEA Committee of Ten, CRSE began by discussing the familiar problem of the relationship between the secondary schools and the colleges and went on to develop into a full-fledged reconsideration of the whole curriculum. But where the recommendations of the Committee of Ten were quite consistent with those of its full committee, there was considerable divergence between those of the commission and its social studies subcommittee. According to CRSE, the main objectives of education—known as the Seven Cardinal Principles—were: health, command of fundamental processes (reading, writing, and arithmetic), worthy home membership, vocation, citizenship, worthy use of leisure, and ethical character. These aims should control the selection of content, asserted the commission. CRSE's views on social efficiency and social control went considerably beyond those of its 1916 subcommittee, yet its versions of these doctrines were moderate rather than extreme. In any event, it was not the Seven Cardinal Principles but the 1916 Report of the Committee on School Studies that most influenced the curriculum of the high schools.

Historians continued to be the social studies' chief ally over the next quarter-century. Although increasing historical specialization helped to weaken the ties between schools and the historical profession, a major countervailing force was the growth after World War I of synthetic western civilization courses in the colleges. These courses, the meat and potatoes of history departments all over the country, helped to keep college historians reasonably close to general education and problems of method and thus kept alive their ties to the high schools. In the late twenties, the creation of the AHA Commission on the Social Studies (whose major intellectual influence was Charles A. Beard) signified the continued importance historians attached to school history and to cooperation with social scientists and school administrators, who were well represented on this commission. In addition to its own recommendations, the group published a number of important books on teaching methods, administration, the history of education, and the role of the various social sciences in the schools. The AHA also helped to subsidize *Social Education*, the National Council for the Social Studies (NCSS) magazine, with commission royalties. The work of CRSE interrupted but did not halt the slow unraveling of the bonds between secondary schools and the historians.

The other party to the alliance, school administrators, followed a somewhat different course. During and immediately after World War I, the enthusiasm of many school administrators for social efficiency and social control reached new heights. By 1920, Charles H. Judd—chairman of the Committee on Social Science of the National Association of Secondary-School Principals and a well-known educational psychologist—was urging historians to give up chronology in organizing the school curriculum. Judd went so far as to define the social studies by specifically excluding history. For him, the favored social subjects were sociology, economics, ethics, vocational guidance, and civics.[33] The rise of curriculum-making in the 1920s, closely allied with scientific administration, at times exacerbated this division. But Judd's view was by no means universal and came at a time of extreme postwar tension in the social studies. In the 1930s, the Fourteenth Yearbook of the Department of Superintendence of the NEA, *The Social Studies Curriculum*, essentially accepted the 1916 curriculum and took a friendly and relaxed view of history and the other social studies subjects in a volume containing many practical suggestions for the organization and teaching of social studies courses. Historian Charles A. Beard was a member of the commission that issued the report. Clearly the administrators were much influenced by the work of the AHA Commission on the Social Studies, of which Beard was so influential a member.

A third influence on the social studies curriculum in the postwar period was the National Council for the Social Studies, organized in 1921. Initially NCSS represented largely university and college teacher educators, most of whom were veterans of regional teachers' associations. This council continued the tradition of support for history and civics/civil government as the backbone of the curriculum and attempted to work closely with historians as well as with representatives of the other social sciences. From its inception, NCSS encountered suspicions among some historians that "the social studies" were antihistorical, suspicions at least temporarily laid to rest by the work of the historians' own Commission on the Social Studies, with which NCSS was closely associated. From other quarters there came attacks that the social sciences were so heavily weighted with history that the development of more modern and relevant curriculum and methods of teaching was prevented. The concern of NCSS with improved teaching of the social studies, including history, and with the social studies as prime subjects in the education of citizens thus involved an exasperating battle with suspicious historians and suspicious antihistorians.

The end of World War I brought a widespread interest in general education in the schools and colleges, an interest that generally helped the relation between school and college history. At the close of World War II it seemed as if a similar development would take place. But this brief resurgence of interest in general education was soon submerged by intensified specialization in history and the social sciences, accompanied by the neglect of general education and broad synthetic courses in the colleges, to say nothing of the schools. The rise of consensus history after the war, with its indifference and even hostility to reform and its renunciation of progressive history, offered little support for continued relations between schools and colleges. The historical profession rapidly distanced itself from school history while the other social sciences glanced in the schools' direction only occasionally. Anything smacking of "method" was deemed to be the ramshackle province of "educationists," who were regarded as mad methodists.

The old union of method and content that characterized the creative, formative period of the field of history and the social studies finally disintegrated. Even in the new social studies movement of the 1960s, based largely in the universities, historians played an insignificant role; momentarily leadership was assumed by the social science learned societies, following the lead of mathematics and the physical sciences. One result was the production of some excellent curricular materials in the several social science disciplines. These, however, were not very much used. Another result was the failure to consider how all the various social studies could fit together in a coherent curriculum—a problem that had been a major concern of the three great national reports I have described and to which each had offered a solution. Historians, who might have been expected to raise the question, abandoned their historic concern with the whole social studies curriculum along with school history itself, while university social scientists from the other social studies disciplines involved themselves only with the fate of their own school subject. It is understandable why the new social studies movement did not choose to address the problem. The curricular projects that constituted the heart of the movement, busy producing their own materials, were remote from the schools and oblivious of the connections between past and present. For the new social studies movement, the history of the social studies began in the 1950s. The traditional dominance of history as a school subject seemed inconvenient or outmoded. Most leaders in the movement did not seem to regard scope and sequence as any of their business, if indeed it occurred to them as a problem at all. To confront it would have required development of new perspectives on the entire curriculum, including ways to resolve difficult territorial disputes.

When the new social studies movement was rather abruptly superseded in the late sixties by the passion for social reform combined with individual self-realization, the process of curricular fragmentation was further intensified. In many high schools, the social studies curriculum, including its historical component, was slivered into discrete minicourses. Unlike the scientific history that helped establish history in the schools and the progressive history that sustained it, the new trends in historiography were antithetical both to cooperation between school and college historians and to the kind of broad, synthetic history the schools needed. Most New Left historians were as indifferent to the fate of their discipline in the schools as their consensus-history predecessors; moreover, the widespread New Left conception of schools as oppressive institutions only reinforced this attitude. Bits and pieces of specialized histories of ethnicities, race, and gender were awkwardly jammed into the curriculum. By the mid 1970s, as a reaction began to set in, the social studies curriculum began to be reassembled; but now its traditional spine was weakened. While history survived, the other component, civics, did not.

Civics and Problems of Democracy, not history, were the chief social studies casualties of the sixties and seventies.[34] Both the new social studies movement of the sixties and the social problems/self-realization movement of the seventies were either indifferent or hostile to the traditional purpose of social studies as the education most appropriate for people's public role as citizens. Each movement tended to fragment or ignore this role—the new social studies by substituting disciplinary attachment, the self-realization movement by substituting particular causes or private self-interest.

In the 1970s, resurgence of a rather tough version of social efficiency—with a renewed commitment to social control, accountability, cost effectiveness, and other elements of scientific management— gained a good deal of backing among school administrators as well as considerable public support. The curricular expression of the new wave of social efficiency was the back-to-basics principle. The social studies were not considered basic. They were in serious jeopardy in elementary schools, from many of which they disappeared. No longer was the historical profession ready, able, or willing to be the chief friend in court of the social studies or even of school history. Despite some modest revival of interest in the schools among some historians and political scientists and a much greater resurgence of interest in popular history, the abyss between the historical profession on the one side and the schools on the other was spanned only occasionally by bridges that seemed like those fragile and perilous structures connecting precipitous mountains in remote areas of the world. It is an unhappy fact that even these connections and contacts were excessively narrow. Because method and content had become enemies rather than allies in the consciousness of university and college historians and many public and private funding agencies, historians were cast in the role of content experts for whom problems of method lacked intellectual interest or challenge and were irrelevant to their professional concerns.

In this discussion I have focused on the relationship of content and method as they have appeared to professional historians, with only passing attention to school administrators and even less attention to classroom teachers. The consciousness of the latter has changed radically during the past century. I have tried to demonstrate that in the period when the social subjects were becoming established in the high school, a significant group of college and secondary school teachers remained reasonably close to each other and—especially through regional teachers' associations—worked together on common problems. As schools and colleges became more numerous and more bureaucratized and as specialization cut away their former common ground, the distance between them widened. So invisible had teachers become to university academics by the 1960s that the new social studies movement regarded them as necessary nuisances or docile direction followers. Today teachers are unwilling to accept placidly and without demur that inferior position in the educational hierarchy to which most college academics have assigned them.

A century after the historical profession was founded, the attitude of college historians toward the relationship of method and content has almost completely reversed. I have tried to show that there are historical explanations for this reversal as well as for the changing views of school administrators. My hope is that if we understand how the present came to be, a beginning will be made in developing a new relationship between college historians and high school social studies teachers. There are major problems concerning method in history and the social studies that link both groups. Three examples related to courses, instructional materials, and students will illustrate the nature of some of these problems.

One is the problem of historical synthesis. This is a perpetual problem for teachers in both high school and in introductory college courses because they necessarily teach nonspecialized courses that are, or should be, based on a synthetic treatment. It appears in particularly acute form in world history (or "global studies"), which is being revived in many high schools and colleges and for which almost no conceptual models exist. It is not surprising that synthesis is exceedingly difficult. The focus of graduate work in history since the inauguration of Herbert Baxter Adams's seminar at Johns Hopkins has become narrower. The profession is becoming increasingly specialized in what seems to be an almost inexorable process—a process that is not confined to history, of course. Doctoral candidates, becoming adept at the use of primary sources in the seminar method we inherited from Germany, are bringing these sources to bear on historical problems that are increasingly narrowly defined. When knowing more and more about less and less becomes the norm of graduate study, the ability to generate and manipulate that kind of knowledge becomes highly valued. The ability to use knowledge to produce the kind of sweeping historical synthesis that is routinely expected of teachers is not.

The assumption underlying narrowing specialization is that it is the only valid way to produce new knowledge—an assumption that should be examined rather than accepted. It is worth considering whether the effort at synthesis, because it involves putting things together in new ways, would raise new, powerful questions for historical inquiry. The effort at synthesis is worth making not only for school history but for all history.

A second problem in which historians in schools and colleges have a mutual interest is closely related to synthesis: the textbook. For coherence, textbooks depend on some kind of synthesis. It is no coincidence that, lacking a vital synthesis, many texts now are bland, boring, plodding, and untrue to good history. Their literary qualities often reflect their intellectual poverty. We need a way of incorporating or rejecting information in a text other than through the demands or pleas of special interest groups. But we do not have to wait for syntheses to create a way to improve those history books read most widely (although not necessarily most willingly) by the public—our students. It should not be beyond the power of imagination to find appropriate ways of reviewing textbooks in the historical journals, thus holding them as accountable as other historical work. To the reviewer textbooks present problems more complex than those of a standard monograph, but such problems are by no means insuperable.

A third is the problem of making history intelligible to students and significant and useful in their intellectual and humane development. We need to know much more than we do now about what characteristics of history itself—such as its profound relation to time and change—constitute both avenues and barriers to learning. If we knew what perceptions of the past and of history are held at different ages and stages of life, we might teach, as well as learn, more effectively. Such information would help us to examine what I believe is—or can be—the unique role that history, with its essential temporal dimension, can play in the development of the individual.

Last, I want to mention the need to reunite method and content by using a language that illuminates rather than obscures, that opens up vistas rather than closing them down. To define method as merely a species of classroom gimmickry or as a set of tips for teaching makes it impossible to explore seriously the relationship of method and content. Such a definition often appeals to teachers because they are always looking for ways to make classes more interesting. But if this is the only or major way that method is discussed, it is a terrible disservice to teaching. It is the classroom equivalent of mindless specialization. A further concept that blocks effective and productive discussion is the notion that because some teaching procedures (such as the discussion, lecture, or independent investigation) are used in a number of different subjects or disciplines, no specific, organic, and appropriate relations exist among a particular method, a particular content, and particular students. One approach might be to look at method partly as we might view a performing art, partly as we might review a book. Another place to begin is with the work of John Dewey. By the time Dewey wrote *Democracy and Education* the separation of content and method had sufficiently advanced that he could address it as a problem. His approach represents only one possible direction to take, but it offers productive possibilities.

The problems mentioned briefly above are significant in the work of both secondary school and college historians. Reunification of method and content cannot be resolved through imposing the dominant mode of the delivery of content by college historians on school historians. Valuable and even inspirational as the delivery may be, such efforts unfortunately become a diversion from or a substitute for addressing those problems that persist precisely because they are both fundamental and neglected. If, as our society, our students, and our subjects deserve, we are to improve the teaching of history and the other social studies, we will have to rediscover our common territory, of which each is a piece of the continent, a part of the main.

NOTES

1. Albert Bushnell Hart, *Studies in American Education* (New York: Longmans, Green and Co., 1895), p. 97.
2. Ibid., p. 91.
3. Ibid., p. 104.
4. National Education Association of the US, Committee of Ten on Secondary School Studies, *Report of the Committee on Secondary School Studies* (Washington, DC: Government Printing Office, 1893).
5. Ibid., p. 167.
6. Ibid., p. 170.
7. American Historical Association, Committee of Seven, *The Study of History in Schools* (New York: Macmillan Co., 1899), p. 17.
8. Ibid., pp. 117–118.
9. American Historical Association, Committee of Five, *The Study of History in Secondary Schools* (New York: Macmillan Co., 1911).
10. Andrew C. McLaughlin was also chairman of the Committee of Five, which included Robinson in its membership.
11. Charles Grove Haines, *The Teaching of Government* (New York: Macmillan Co., 1916).
12. John Dewey, *Democracy and Education* (1916; reprint, New York: The Free Press, Macmillan Co., 1944), p. 76.
13. Ibid., pp. 118–119.
14. Ibid., pp. 120–121.

15. Ibid., pp. 210, 217–218.
16. Ibid., p. 214.
17. Ibid., pp. 164–165.
18. William H. Mace, *Method in History* (Chicago: Rand McNally, 1914).
19. US Bureau of Education, Report of the Committee on Social Studies of the Commission on the Reorganization of Secondary Education of the National Education Association, *The Social Studies in Secondary Education* (Washington, DC: Government Printing Office, 1916), Bulletin no. 28, pp. 9–10.
20. Ibid., pp. 26–27, 29.
21. Ibid., p. 42.
22. Ibid., p. 43. (Italics in original)
23. Ibid., p. 44. (Italics in original)
24. Ibid., p. 44.
25. Ibid., p. 47.
26. Ibid., p. 48.
27. Ibid., p. 36.
28. Ibid., p. 52.
29. Ibid., p. 53.
30. Ibid., pp. 11, 21.
31. Dewey, *Democracy*, pp. 319–320.
32. US Bureau of Education, Report of the Commission on the Reorganization of Secondary Education, Appointed by the National Education Association, *Cardinal Principles of Secondary Education* (Washington, DC: Government Printing Office, 1918), Bulletin no. 35.
33. Charles H. Judd, "Report of the Committee on Social Studies in the High School," *Fourth Yearbook, National Association of Secondary School Principals* (The Association, 1920).
34. For a further discussion of this point, see Matthew T. Downey, ed., *History in the Schools* (NCSS, 1985), Bulletin no. 74, pp. 9–10.

Chapter 2

From History to Social Studies: Dilemmas and Problems

DIANE RAVITCH

When I attended public school in Texas in the 1950s, I took the standard three-year social studies sequence, which included a year of World History in grade 9, a year of American History in grade 11, and senior-year civics. I had a superb ninth-grade teacher, but the course was impossible; it covered too much material. Students hastily picked up a smattering of events, dates, and cultures in a forced march across thousands of years and all continents. The grade 11 American History course was worse: the teacher used every incident in American history to support her own cranky political bias. When I reached college, I realized just how poorly educated I was in history; I felt hopelessly inadequate compared to fellow students who had attended private schools. Many of them seemed to have a wide-ranging knowledge of ancient, medieval, and modern European history that was utterly beyond my grasp. What was more, their knowledge of history was enhanced by an exposure to art and literature that my school had never even attempted.

My strength, I mistakenly believed, derived from a keen interest in current events. So, in college, I majored in political science, a decision that I now believe to have been a grievous error because I simply compounded the flaws of my high school education. The issues that seemed so urgent in the late 1950s are today of merely antiquarian interest. Why should anyone care about Quemoy and Matsu anymore except as a footnote to contemporary Asian history? Does Sputnik really matter now except as a milestone in the history of technology? Why should anyone recall the confrontation between Governor Faubus of Arkansas and President Eisenhower in 1958 except as one incident in the history of racial relations in America? Almost everything that once seemed important has now faded, remembered only by those who are interested in history.

Eventually I turned to the full-time study of history, when I realized that I could not understand the present without studying the past. My continued interest in contemporary issues made me a historian; there was simply no other intelligent way to understand the origins of our present institutions, problems, and ideas. As a latecomer to the field, I am—like all converts—a zealous advocate. I believe in the importance and value of the study of history, and would like to see it strengthened as a subject in the schools.

From this perspective I began to inquire into the condition of history in the schools and how it got that way. As of mid-1984, when this essay was written, however, it was nearly impossible to determine the current state of history in secondary schools. Educational data-collection today is so inadequate that no one can say accurately how history is taught, how well it is taught, what is taught, or what is learned. Most states have tabulated course enrollments, and some national surveys have totaled up the percentage of children enrolled in courses titled "history," but these figures are highly suspect. Because of the enormous variety of practices extant, there is not necessarily any identity of content among courses bearing the same label.

Furthermore, we have no reliable measures of achievement. The makers of standardized tests long ago abandoned the attempt to assess historical or literary mastery and instead devoted their entire attention to abstract verbal and mathematical skills. We cannot say with certainty whether high school graduates today know more or less than their counterparts of ten, twenty, or thirty years ago; we have no good measures of historical knowledge at present, nor did we have any in the past. The possibility of agreeing on such a measure today seems remote. Because we live in a time of cultural fragmentation, the idea of testing large numbers of students for their knowledge of history seems outrageous. It was not surprising, for example, that the many national reports of 1983 cited test scores in mathematics, science, and verbal skills but omitted any mention of humanities. We have no objective data to tell us how we are doing because we lack consensus on the minimum knowledge that should be expected of all students. We do not agree on what literature is important, nor do we agree on what history should be taught to all American youngsters.*

We know that many states require high school students to study

*Editor's note: However, by 1987 the first national assessment of 17-year-old students was released: See, Diane Ravitch and Chester E. Finn, Jr., *What Do Our 17-year Olds Know?* (New York: Harper & Row, 1987). This survey had not begun when this essay was written in mid-1984.

at least one year of U.S. history, but we do not know what lurks behind the course label. National data tell us that 65 percent of high school graduates in 1982 took at least three years of social studies, but it is almost certain that few of these credits came from history.[1] A survey published by the Organization of American Historians (OAH) in 1975 revealed that in at least five states—New York, Indiana, Iowa, Oklahoma, and Oregon—virtually no training in history was required for high school history teachers.[2] In New York City, the history teacher's license was abolished in 1946, and at present no study of history is required in order to obtain a license as a high school social studies teacher.[3]

If one were to judge by the accumulation of anecdotal reports—a notoriously unreliable source of evidence—many college professors hold that freshmen know little about American history, European history, or any other history. One frequently hears complaints about students who know next to nothing about events that occurred before the twentieth century or who are ignorant of the Bible, Shakespeare, the Greek myths, and other material that was once common knowledge. Or, as one Berkeley professor put it to me a few years ago, "They have no furniture in their minds. You can assume nothing in the way of prior knowledge. Skills, yes; but not knowledge."

While it is not possible to know definitively how history is faring in the schools today, there is increasing reason to fear that history is losing its integrity and identity as a field of study within the umbrella called the social studies. The field of social studies, in the view of a number of its leaders, is in deep trouble. Bob L. Taylor and John D. Haas claimed in 1973 that "secondary school social studies curricula are in a state of 'curriculum anarchy'; which is to say that local curriculum patterns are more varied than at any other time in this century. No longer is it possible to describe a typical state, regional, or national pattern of social studies curriculum. Furthermore, it appears [that] each junior or senior high school in a given school district is 'doing its own thing.'"[4] A 1977 study by Richard E. Gross of Stanford University found the field characterized by increased fragmentation and dilution of programs, by a growth of electives and minicourses, by a rapid proliferation of social science courses, by a drop in required courses, and by a tendency toward curricular anarchy. In keeping with these trends, other reviews of the field noted a singular absence of agreement about the content of the field.[5]

While the field of the social studies was having an identity crisis, history as a subject was struggling for survival. The 1975 OAH study reported a significant dilution and fragmentation in secondary-school history teaching. In New Mexico, the trend was toward ethnocultural courses; in Hawaii, history was integrated into a social science framework focused on problem-solving, decision-making, and social action; in Minnesota, teachers were encouraged to shift away from historical study towards an emphasis on concepts that transcend "any given historical situation"; the OAH representative in California predicted that history would lose time to such "relevant" topics as multicultural studies, ethnic studies, consumer affairs, and ecology. Similar reports about the deteriorating position of history within the social studies curriculum came from Vermont, Rhode Island, Connecticut, New York, Maryland, Wisconsin, Missouri, Nebraska, North Carolina, Oklahoma, West Virginia, Illinois, and Iowa. The OAH report confirmed what many had long feared: the study of history in public high schools has been seriously eroded, absorbed within the increasingly vague and amorphous field of the social studies.[6]

Like the Gross survey, the OAH survey was conducted in the mid-1970s and reflected the curricular fragmentation of that time. A survey conducted a decade later would doubtless show that many states, cities, and school districts had raised their graduation requirements substantially. Yet even a cursory review of actions taken in the early 1980s would show that history continues to be left out in the cold and that social studies requirements have been increased without reference to history. Even the tough-minded National Commission on Excellence in Education failed to mention history as a necessary subject of study for all American students. In view of the currently unfocused nature of social studies, students may meet the higher requirements by taking courses in current events, drug education, sex education, environmental education, citizenship education, values education, law studies, economics, psychology, or other nonhistorical subjects.

How did history fall to this sorry state? A review of the "history of history teaching" suggests that certain ideological and political trends caused history to lose its rightful place in the public high school curriculum. Any historical investigation begins with questions, and the questions that I posed for my inquiry were: How did history become part of the social studies? What are the social studies? Why do most private schools continue to have history departments, while almost every public high school has a social studies department?

History as a regular subject of study entered the public school curriculum before the Civil War but did not become well established until the end of the nineteenth century, as secondary school enrollments grew. History, English, modern foreign languages, and science entered the curriculum as modern subjects in contrast to the classical curriculum of mathematics and ancient languages.[7] Most public schools offered one or more history courses, such as ancient history, medieval history, English history, modern European history, and U.S. history. Nineteenth-century schools also offered courses that foreshadowed the

social sciences: courses, for example, in civil government, political economy, and moral philosophy. By 1895, 70 percent of the nation's universities and colleges required a course in U.S. history for admission and
more than a quarter required the study of Greece and/or Rome.[8]

In order to understand the fate of history over the years, it is necessary to follow the rationale for its inclusion in the curriculum. Why
study history? It was argued, first, that history offered valuable lessons
in morals by demonstrating the kind of personal and national behavior that should be admired or abhorred; second, that history enhanced
personal culture by revealing great achievements and ideas of the past;
third, that history inspired patriotism; fourth, that by defining civic
virtue history trained good citizens; fifth, that history reinforced religious ideals; and sixth, that history strengthened and disciplined the
mind.

Some of these rationales were profoundly damaging to the integrity
of the subject. Using history as an instrument for teaching morals,
religion, and patriotism undermined respect for history by turning it
into propaganda. It distorted the most essential value in history, which
is the search for truth. The subject of history was even more severely
injured by proponents of mental discipline, who believed that rote
memorization of the textbook strengthened the mind; this method must
have destroyed student interest in the content of history, and it certainly
reared up legions of people who hated history as a subject rather than,
properly, hating the tyrannical method by which it was taught.

Between 1892 and 1916 three major reports on the public school
curriculum appeared that bore directly on teaching history; these reports were important not only because they influenced practice, in
some instances quite substantially, but also because they vividly portrayed ideas that were dominant or gaining ascendancy among leaders
of the education profession. Everyone interested in history as a secondary school subject should study these reports because, by reading
between the lines, it is possible to discover the answer to the question:
What happened to history?

The first major report on the curriculum appeared in 1893, the
product of a group called the Committee of Ten.[9] The specific influence
of this report is hard to estimate, but it did encourage good relations between professional historians and the school establishment and helped
undermine the legitimacy of rote memory methods. A few years later,
the National Education Association invited the American Historical Association to create yet another committee, this time devoted entirely
to the history curriculum and to college entrance requirements. This
group, called the Committee of Seven, wrote a document that affected
the teaching of history for many years. Like the Committee of Ten's history conference, the Committee of Seven was deeply critical of the rote

system of history teaching.[10] The Committee of Seven believed that the best way to understand the problems of the present was through study of the past; that students would best understand their duties as citizens by studying the origins and evolution of political institutions, not only in their own society but also in other societies and in other times; that the ability to change society for the better depended on knowledge of our institutions and our ideals in their historical setting. Further, the committee believed that historical study taught students to think, cultivated their judgment, and encouraged accuracy of thought.

In viewing this curricular history, one must bear in mind the Committee of Seven's rationale—that history honestly taught yielded valuable benefits. Study of the past, Committee members believed, would create intelligent, thinking, responsible citizens, men and women who had "acquaintance with political and social environment, some appreciation of the nature of the state and society, some sense of the duties and responsibilities of citizenship, some capacity in dealing with political and governmental questions, something of the broad and tolerant spirit which is bred by the study of past times and conditions."[11] They were convinced that such study was valuable both intrinsically and extrinsically. They saw history as a synthesizing subject that belonged at the center of the curriculum because it gave meaning and coherence to everything else that was studied.

The report of the Committee of Seven in 1899 set a national pattern for the history curriculum. By 1915 the overwhelming majority of high schools offered courses in ancient history, medieval and modern European history, English history, and American history. Furthermore, in most high schools American and ancient history became required subjects. An historical survey of history teaching in 1935 held that history departments of the nation's high schools "attempted to swallow the report of the Committee of Seven 'hook, line, and sinker.'" The so-called "four-block" plan was widely adopted, and there was an increase in both history courses offered and history courses required of all students. Further strengthening the influence of the Committee of Seven Report, textbook publishers used the Report as a model for their history series.[12] This situation, following the Committee's Report, was a far cry from 1893, when history was still struggling to gain legitimacy as a proper subject of study in the high school.

If the story had ended in 1915, there would now be good news about the status of the history curriculum. Most high schools would be offering at least three years of history, including ancient history, European history, and American history; and nearly half would offer English history.[13] It would be necessary to recall the reports of several other numerically-named committees—the Committee of Eight, the Committee of Fifteen, and the Committee of Five, among others—and to note the emphasis on biography, mythology, legends, and hero tales in the elementary grades. The same approach, brought up to date in the 1980s, would certainly include histories of non-Western societies. But 1915, alas, was the high-water mark for traditional, narrative, chronological history in the schools.

Nascent social and political trends made their mark on the public school curriculum, deeply affecting the teaching of history. In the 1890s, history was considered a "modern" subject, but only a few years later, during the first decade of the twentieth century, educational progressives began to treat it as part of the "traditional" curriculum. The traditional curriculum became a target for progressives, who sought to modernize the schools and make them responsive to contemporary needs and problems. In the opening decades of the twentieth century, progressivism emerged as a dynamic movement in American life, committed to social progress, social betterment, and social reform. Many of the ills of the nation were associated with the vast hordes of poor immigrants who crowded into the cities. Schools inherited the primary responsibility for Americanizing immigrant children. Not only were schools to function as academic institutions, teaching English to their charges, but also they were to assume a custodial role, preparing the newcomers to be good citizens, training them for the job market, and introducing them to such ordinary necessities of daily life as nutrition and hygiene.

To meet some of these needs, new courses entered the high school curriculum, such as training for specific trades, sewing, cooking, and commercial studies. As high schools added practical courses, curricular differentiation became common. Many schools offered a manual training course of study, a vocational course, a commercial course—and, for the academic elite, a college preparatory course. A "course of study" was a carefully sequenced series of individual courses, lasting two, three, or four years; in schools with fully developed curricular differentiation, in keeping with the latest pedagogical thinking, the students' selection of a course of study was often tantamount to choosing a vocation. The admonitions of the Committee of Ten and the Committee of Seven on behalf of liberal education for all children were scorned by progressives as an attempt to force everyone into a narrow academic curriculum. Reformers insisted that an academic curriculum was inappropriate for children who intended to go to work and that the small minority who were college-bound should have programs different from those open to the vast majority who were work-bound.

Vocational education became popular in the early decades of the twentieth century as part of a broad reform movement designed to make the work of the schools more practical. Since the nation's economy was shifting from an agricultural to an industrial base, progressive educators believed that the schools had to readjust their programs and goals in order to keep in step with the demands of the new era. Furthermore, vocational education seemed an appropriate response to the problems of educating slow learners in the school population, many of whom came from illiterate immigrant families. American industry needed skilled workers, and the schools accepted the responsibility to prepare adolescents for the world of work. Vocational education seemed the logical solution. Reformers could find little of value in the traditional academic curriculum for working-class or poor children. They insisted that academic studies such as history, literature, science, and mathematics failed to meet the needs of modern society or of most students. Except for the small minority that was college-bound, most children needed more specific job training. Those not intending to go to college, said the reformers, had no need for academic studies; rather, they needed the skills to participate in the new industrial age as efficient workers, farmers, and homemakers.

This new educational ideology was strongly influenced by the reformist spirit of the times. Educational thinkers began to look to the school not merely as an instrument for making intelligent citizens but also as an instrument for social improvement. Sociologists, such as David Snedden of Teachers College, saw the schools as splendid agencies of social control, which should be used to direct the population into socially useful occupations. Educators started speaking of the role of the schools in sociological terms, demonstrating a growing belief that the fundamental purpose of schools in a democracy was not to empower individuals but to meet the needs of society.

Progressive educators became accustomed to thinking of schools in terms of their social function and to asserting that the work of the schools must meet the test of social efficiency. In education, social efficiency meant that every subject, every program, every study must be judged by its social usefulness. Did it meet the needs of society? To the new profession of curriculum makers and policymakers, no doubt, the prospect of shaping society was far more exciting than merely teaching literature or history or science. In contrast, the traditional curriculum, based on particular subjects, seemed anachronistic. Why teach history, science, literature, mathematics, and foreign language to children who would never go to college? How was society served by wasting their time in such manifestly "useless" and impractical studies? Although not all school officials or teachers went along (and many strongly disagreed), educational leaders in national organizations and in major schools of education repeatedly asserted that the traditional curriculum was intended only for children of the elite and was inappropriate for schools in a democracy. Teaching children to think and imparting to them knowledge about science and culture clearly did not belong on the table for those who made social utility their touchstone.

By the time of World War I, social efficiency was widely accepted as the chief goal of education, and this consensus emerged full-blown in the third major report on the secondary curriculum, prepared by the National Education Association's Commission on the Reorganization of Secondary Education. Published in 1918, the Report of this group—known as the "Cardinal Principles of Secondary Education"—is generally considered the single most important document in the history of American education. It proclaimed a utilitarian credo that deeply influenced the nation's schools for decades to come. The main objectives of a high school education, according to the Commission, were these: "1. Health. 2. Command of fundamental processes. 3. Worthy home-membership. 4. Vocation. 5. Citizenship. 6. Worthy use of leisure. 7. Ethical character."[14] In contrast to the Committee of Ten and the Committee of Seven, the "Cardinal Principles" strongly endorsed differentiated curricula, based on future vocational interests such as agricultural, business, clerical, industrial, fine arts, and household arts. The Report gave a powerful boost to proponents of vocational education, curricular tracking, and useful subjects; it disappointed those who wanted all children to have a liberal education and reinforced the belief that academic studies were only for the college-bound elite.*

Acceptance of social efficiency as the touchstone of the high school curriculum proved disastrous to the study of history. What claim could be advanced for the utility of history? Knowing history did not make anyone a better worker; it didn't improve anyone's health; it was much less useful for citizenship training than a course in civics. When judged by the stern measure of direct utility, history had no measurable claim except meeting college entrance requirements. Professional historians—who might have argued that the study of history taught children how to think, how to reach judgments, how to see their own lives and contemporary issues in context—seemed content to abandon curricular decisions to the pedagogues, who scorned such claims. Nor could history meet the immediate needs of young people, in the sense that it could not tell adolescents how to behave on a date, how to be popular with the crowd, or how to get a job. In the new era of social efficiency and pupil interests, the one-year course in ancient history began to disappear from American schools; and before long the four-year history sequence was telescoped to three, then two, and, in many places, to only a single year of American history.

In the decades after the 1916 Report of the Committee on the Social Studies, the social studies curriculum shifted its emphasis towards current events, relevant issues, and pupil-centered programs. Introduction of such courses was not, in itself, a bad thing. A modern, dynamic soci-

*Editor's note: For a more detailed discussion, see Hazel Hertzberg's chapter in this volume.

ety needs schools in which students study the vital problems of the day and learn how to participate in the democratic process. But the time for the new subjects was subtracted from history classes. Except for American history, thought to be useful as preparation for citizenship, the place of historical studies shrank in the schools. Even in the elementary schools, where earlier generations had studied biography and mythology as basic historical materials, the emphasis shifted to studying the neighborhood, the community, and preliterate peoples—a trend encouraged by the Report's recommendation of courses in "community civics."

Of course, the Report of the Committee on Social Studies in 1916 was not in itself responsible for this erosion of the position of history; the Report merely reflected the ideas, values, and attitudes of the newly-emerging education profession. These principles were not—unfortunately—congenial to studying history for its own sake, nor even to studying history as a means to the improvement of children's intelligence. The ideology expressed in the 1916 Report was hostile to a field of study that had no practical value and that offered so little promise of immediate social betterment.

Subsequent efforts to reexamine the social-studies curriculum did little to resuscitate the position of history because the ideology of social efficiency continued to prevail. When the American Historical Association created a commission to analyze the social studies in the midst of the Great Depression, the commission declared that the most important purpose of the social studies was to produce "rich and many-sided personalities."[15] Whatever the other courses in the social studies may have been capable of doing to promote personal development, it is hard to imagine anyone claiming that the study of history produces "rich and many-sided personalities."

Even the innovative curricula produced after Sputnik (known collectively as "the new social studies") failed to restore history in the secondary schools. This was not because the case for history was weak but because the position that should have been taken was never taken at all. The "new history" of the 1960s proceeded on the assumption that children should be taught to think like historians and to learn the historical method, just as students of science were learning to think like scientists and learning the scientific method. The problems with this approach were many: first, few children then or now actually know enough history, enough context, to make it worthwhile or possible for them to conduct a genuine historical investigation; second, historians themselves do not agree on the definition of a single "historical method"; third, learning the process of how to *write* history is appropriate to graduate students but not to school children, and it is certainly far less interesting than learning the actual stuff of history.

At this point, I would like to recapitulate the question with which I began. I have tried to show how changes in our educational ideology placed history within the social studies. I have tried to explain why this development was deleterious to the position of history in the curriculum: history could not meet the criterion of social utility applied to the rest of the field. In trying to answer the question, "What are the social studies?" I found that the definitions were legion, and that they changed from decade to decade, from report to report, almost from one educator to the next. At some times the social studies were plural, at other times a single, integrated subject. From the point of view of history, the salient fact is that situating history within the social studies moved history towards the social sciences and away from such humanistic studies as philosophy, the arts, and literature. Textbooks reflected the shift by becoming more analytical, more superficial, and less literary in their approach to historical material. Why do most private schools have history departments while most public high schools have social studies departments? The answer, I believe, is that public schools inherited the ideology of social efficiency; they have been expected to shape children, to use the social studies to teach good citizenship and socially correct values; private schools rarely saw themselves as instruments of social control; they aimed to educate children, not to prepare them to meet the needs of society.

History will regain its rightful place in the schools only if educators accord value to the study of history both for its own sake and for its value as a generator of individual and social intelligence. History has a right to exist as an independent study; it should be taught by people who have studied history, just as is true in science and mathematics. The other social studies also have unique contributions to make, but these should not be made by stealing time from history or by burying the study of history in non-historical approaches.

In 1932, Henry Johnson of Teachers College, Columbia University, wrote a delightful review of the teaching of history throughout the ages, somewhat misleadingly titled *An Introduction to the History of the Social Sciences*.[16] Johnson quoted a sixteenth-century Spanish scholar, Juan Luis Vives, to explain why it is valuable to study history. "Where there is history," wrote Vives, "children have transferred to them the advantages of old men; where history is absent, old men are as children." Without history, according to Vives, "no one would know anything about his father or ancestors; no one could know his own rights or those of another or how to maintain them; no one would know how his ancestors came to the country he inhabits." Vives pointed out that everything "has changed and is changing every day," except "the essential nature of human beings." Johnson referred to seventeenth-century French Oratorians, who believed that the study of history cultivated judgment and stimulated right conduct. He cited their view that "History is a grand mirror in which we see ourselves. . . . The secret of knowing and judging ourselves rightly is to see ourselves in others, and history can make us the contemporaries of all centuries in all countries."[17]

History will never be restored as a subject of value unless it is detached from the vulgar utilitarianism that originally swamped it. History should not be expected to teach patriotism, morals, values clarification, or decision-making. Properly taught, history portrays the great achievements and the terrible disasters of the human race; it awakens youngsters to the universality of the human experience as well as to the magnificence and the brutality of which humans are capable. Properly taught, history encourages the development of intelligence, civility, and a sense of perspective. It endows students with a broad knowledge of other times, other cultures, other places; it presents cultural resources on which students may draw for the rest of their lives. These are the values and virtues gained through the study of history. Beyond these, history needs no further justification.

NOTES

1. National Center for Education Statistics, Bulletin 83-223, "How Well Do High School Graduates of Today Meet the Curriculum Standards of the National Commission on Excellence?" (Washington, DC: U.S. Department of Education, September 1983).
2. Richard S. Kirkendall, "The Status of History in the Schools," *The Journal of American History* 62 (1975): 557–570.
3. Telephone conversation, Office of Social Studies Director (New York City Board of Education, June 1984).
4. Bob L. Taylor and John D. Haas, *New Directions: Social Studies Curriculum for the 70's* (Boulder, CO: Center for Education in the Social Sciences, University of Colorado, and Social Science Education Consortium, 1973).
5. Richard E. Gross, "The Status of the Social Studies in the Public Schools of the United States: Facts and Impressions of a National Survey," *Social Education* 41 (March 1977): 194–200, 205.
6. Kirkendall, *History in the Schools*, pp. 563–564.
7. Edward A. Krug, *The Shaping of the American High School 1880–1920* (Madison: University of Wisconsin Press, 1964), pp. 4, 29; and Rolla M. Tryon, *The Social Sciences as School Subjects* (New York: Charles Scribner's Sons, 1935), pp. 100–117.
8. Tryon, *Social Sciences*, p. 142.
9. National Education Association of the U.S., Committee of Ten on Secondary School Studies, *Report of the Committee on Secondary Schools Studies* (Washington, DC: Government Printing Office, 1893).
10. American Historical Association, Committee of Seven, *The Study of History in Schools* (New York: Macmillan, 1899), pp. 120, 122.
11. Ibid., p. 17.
12. Tryon, *Social Sciences*, pp. 177, 187–189.
13. Ibid., p. 182.

14. U.S. Bureau of Education, Commission on the Reorganization of Secondary Education, *Cardinal Principles of Secondary Education* (Washington, DC: Government Printing Office, 1918), Bulletin 35.
15. American Historical Association, *A Charter for the Social Sciences in the Schools* (New York: Charles Scribner's Sons, 1932).
16. Henry Johnson, *An Introduction to the History of the Social Sciences* (New York: Charles Scribner's Sons, 1932), pp. 3, 21, 29, 30.
17. Ibid.

Part II
TEACHING VALUES

Our next section focuses on the crucial problem of teaching values, especially American values. For centuries history has been allied to nationalism; and this was a prime reason for including history in the public school curricula of the late nineteenth and early twentieth century. Schools were expected to turn out good Americans—in particular, to erase the culture of southern and eastern European immigrants and replace it by an American version of English culture. In the last twenty years the increasing self-consciousness and militancy of non–northern European Americans has led to a thorough revaluation of immigration, Americanization, and, of course, the role of schools and of history teaching. Simply put, a radical, direct attack on ethnic cultures in the name of conformity with an "all-American" norm is no longer acceptable. Ethnic groups change but the overall problem remains.

America is now experiencing a new tidal wave of immigration, largely from Mexico, Latin America, and Asia. How will our schools handle these new Americans? Not surprisingly, many of the contributors are acutely concerned with this problem. Ethnic conflict, therefore, is bound to be a major theme of American education, especially education in history which, as we have seen, is a subject traditionally bound to nationalistic themes. While there is general agreement that narrow-minded Americanization must be avoided, there are many who do want the schools to teach values central to democratic citizenship; we are a democracy, and schools should teach democratic participation. A knowledge of American history is important for all Americans of whatever origin. But we must be sure to give full recognition to the conflict and diversity of American life.

California's recently proposed Model Curriculum Standards hold that experiencing—as well as learning about—a diversity of languages, family patterns, religions, cuisines, dress, and leisure positively benefits the overall culture. On the other hand, "cultural pluralism is balanced by common values uniting us socially and politically. We all desire a society in which justice, freedom, due process, equality of opportunity, and access to education are available to us all."*

*From *Model Curriculum Standards Grades Nine through Twelve: History—Social Science* (Sacramento: California State Department of Education, 1985), p. 5.

To teach "old" Americans to accept cultural diversity while "new" Americans learn about democratic participation are important and controversial educational aims. Freeman Butts, a distinguished historian and educator, argues strongly in his contribution to Part II of this study that history in the schools should be taught primarily to enhance American citizenship. Butts is careful to disassociate himself from the coercive Americanization campaigns of the early twentieth century; nevertheless, he does think a successful democracy requires an active citizenry that adheres to a set of common values. Butts notes that political theory going back to Aristotle and the Founding Fathers has always assumed that the success of a democracy depended on the quality of its citizens and that the quality of citizens, in turn, depended heavily on public schools. Citizenship was considered an important part of social studies education in the United States until the 1960s, when the attempt of the social sciences to teach a value-free, scientific view of history and society drove out all values, including citizenship, from the schools. Since the mid-1970s, however, Butts has been detecting a growing chorus of voices calling for values training in the schools. True, some of this has come from religious groups oriented toward "traditional moral values," but Butts is at pains to stress that pressure for education in values comes also from groups broadly ranged along the political scale. Butts himself wants students to be educated to participate in and find a sense of purpose in their participation in society rather than to be educated for the sake of refining their private pleasures.

Although Butts is concerned with more than the teaching of history, he does give history great prominence as a subject in a civics-oriented education. History teaches students the relationship between current civic concerns and the past. Thus, he suggests that students would benefit from a historical treatment of the relations between church and state or of the civil rights movement and affirmative action.

Butts goes beyond a general call for civics by providing a list of values that ought to be taught and debated. The major dichotomy in his scheme is between Unum and Pluribus (the one and the many, as inscribed on the Great Seal of the United States). For example, there is a valid, continuing tension between the Unum of justice and the Pluribus of freedom. Schools should teach both justice and freedom, focusing especially on their tensions and interrelations and on how these positive values may be corrupted into extreme forms, justice turning into "law and order," freedom into anarchy. A virtue of Butts's scheme is that it does not intend to indoctrinate students into a hard and narrow form of Americanism.

William Sullivan, another contributor to Part II, shares many of Butt's conclusions, though he arrives at their common destination by a different route. Following Whitehead, Sullivan sees narrow specialization as the dilemma of modern society. Individuals are educated to master a particular, limited body of fact and theory and then to deploy this knowledge skillfully. What is lacking, Sullivan believes, is the failure of education to develop the ability to make judgments outside the area of expertise, to understand interrelations between one specialty and another, and to make moral judgments that can come only from a broad view of human life. The economic system and the government bureaucracy—which demand and reward well-trained, if narrow, specialists—represent a massive weight driving the individual to specialize and the educational system to provide the necessary training. However, workers in large organizations find that their motivation remains entirely individualistic and utilitarian. Partly in reaction to this, "expressive individualism" has influenced many. The expressive individualist wants personal growth, directness, and authenticity and is unwilling to give up the desires of his heart for generalized "good," that is, the ambivalence of the goal of common values. According to Sullivan both versions of individualism—utilitarian and expressive—leave the individual bereft of values, purpose, and direction, which must, of their very nature, come from the identification of the individual with a larger whole.

Sullivan explains that the existence of a common culture throughout the nineteenth century greatly influenced the public schools, the natural purveyor of common culture. This culture, a compound of *Poor Richard's Almanac*, the Federalist Papers, Protestantism, and the New Testament gave meaning and purpose to many Americans. And yet this culture failed. Industrialization destroyed the rural and small-town society in which this culture best flourished, and it promoted in its place the utilitarian individualism that, while well adapted to industrialization, left the individual alone and purposeless.

How does Sullivan propose to ameliorate this situation? A curriculum seeking to promote a common culture must, first, present the student with a critical version of individualism. History, in particular, will be essential for such a program in that it forces the individual to locate himself within the drama of human striving. This culture, though common, must also be pluralistic. Again, history, "a living conversation, an argument in the best sense of the word, among our several traditions concerning the meaning and direction of our common life," is particularly important to the understanding and appreciation of this mix of common and plural cultures.

Finally, schools must teach the sort of civic participation that Butts also advocates. Sullivan's stress is different from that of Butts, however. For Sullivan, civic participation, while essential to democracy, is also essential to the individual who, by participation, transcends the naked and narrow individualism that leaves him so unsatisfied.

As a professional educator with a background in natural science, an amateur historian, and one who has participated in many debates and curriculum battles between humanists and scientists, I take up in one of the essays that follow the theme of the contribution of the humanities to education. Humanists feel that, whatever the outcome of a particular debate or curriculum decision, their position remains under long-term siege and that the practical appeal of scientific, technical, and vocational training inevitably will undermine the position of the humanities in education. I suggest that the humanities should insist that they offer the means to a sort of knowledge that science cannot emulate—that there are questions that simply cannot be answered by scientific modes of inquiry. What constitutes a good and worthy life is a question that is not amenable to scientific methodology, as valid as that methodology is in areas of knowledge appropriate to it. Scientific methodology cannot deal with questions of value.

Immigration and the schools is the theme of Charles Wollenberg's essay. Wollenberg (member of the Clio Project and a California community college teacher) notes that by the 1981–1982 academic year minorities already comprised the majority of students in kindergarten and the first grade in California public schools and that early in the twenty-first century California will become the first state that has no ethnic majority. Immigrants are flooding into California, and it will be our task to educate them. Wollenberg suggests that a good way to do this is to focus our history courses on immigration itself. Although he states his position in terms of the history of the state of California—and thus his essay is particularly useful for teachers of California history—Wollenberg suggests that immigration may be usefully made the central theme of all American history.

Wollenberg deems such history "a usable past for a multi-cultural state" because it links past and present, tries to understand the historical roots of current conditions, and respects the racial and ethnic variety of California and the nation. We may contrast Wollenberg's approach to that of Butts and Sullivan. Wollenberg's "usable past" is justified first on the basis of being good history: immigration, it is argued, is a key theme of California history. It is also justified in terms of the values of pluralism; Wollenberg is very concerned that respect be paid to the cultural diversity of American life. He is not worried about the inculcation of citizenship or common values that so concern Butts and Sullivan. Wollenberg wants to give students a certain minimum knowledge about American history, culture, and politics, but wants (especially) to avoid another Americanization campaign, which he believes would only denigrate the heritage of immigrants.

Nathan Huggins, a leading American historian and author of a recent life of Frederick Douglass, states explicitly and radically in his essay what is implicit in Wollenberg's argument. For Huggins, the concern with common values and common culture masks a fear of ethnic diversity experienced by native Americans who are afraid that their majority culture will be overwhelmed by immigrants or by others who do not share the majority's position. What Huggins fears is not the disintegration of the nation into a variety of cultures that have no common basis for cooperation but rather an enforced conformity to the culture of the historical majority.

This view of pluralism extends to Huggins's idea of history. History has no single historical point of view but is a mélange of viewpoints, usually stemming from the contemporary interest of the historians who "create" it. Huggins wants no single version of "truth" or "culture" to impose itself on the rest. The history taught in schools should not flatter ethnic pride—whether native American or minority pride. It should be good history—history giving cogent expression to a variety of points of view. A chief virtue of history as an intellectual discipline, Huggins contends, is that it forces us to see things in perspective.

Huggins's radically relativistic position has been for some time the prevailing approach among professional historians, who now only rarely claim to write "scientific" truth. But radical relativism is easier to sustain in the world of scholarship than in the world of schools, funding, and political process. Thus, it might be argued (though Huggins does not) that a strictly private school system is the only answer for such diverse society. If there are no common values, what is the point of forcing cultures together in the public schools? Butts and Sullivan might say that the public schools will be able to weld these disparate elements into a common whole, but this justification Huggins explicitly rejects. His position thus contains serious practical problems. Its strength is that the historical record—and contemporary society—show the great burden that narrow Americanism can place on the schools and on minorities.

Chapter 3

History and Civic Education

R. FREEMAN BUTTS

To the query posed by the Clio Conference—What history shall we teach?—we could give two kinds of answers about the topic of history and civic education. One deals with the specific role of history in the overall educational effort to prepare the young for citizenship. The other looks at the relative importance of the study of history, in comparison with the other social studies, as an instrument for civic education. Both topics are important today, but neither was in the forefront of thinking about education in the early days of the American republic. As Hazel Hertzberg points out, history as a widespread, separate, and distinct subject of instruction in schools and colleges is only about a hundred years old in the United States.[1]

Nevertheless, it is worth noting that the founders of the republic were virtually unanimous in their belief that the welfare of the republic rested upon an *educated* citizenry capable of achieving civic virtue, that is, possessing a willingness to put obligation for the public good above private interest.

Because the founders viewed their revolution primarily in political rather than economic or social terms, they talked about education as a bulwark for liberty, equality, popular consent, and devotion to the public good—goals that took precedence over using knowledge for individual self-fulfillment or preparation for a job. Over and over, those revolutionaries, both liberal and conservative, believed not only that the welfare of the republic rested upon an educated citizenry but also that republican schools—especially free, common public schools—would be the best way to educate the citizenry in the cohesive civic values, knowledge, and obligations required for a democratic republican society.

The principal ingredients, most agreed, were literacy and inculcation of patriotic and moral virtues. Only a few stressed studying history along with the principles of republican government itself. The founders and almost all their successors were long on exhortation of the value of civic education but left it to the textbook writers to distill the essence of those values for school children. And since most of the textbook writers turned out to be of a conservative persuasion (more likely Federalist in outlook than Jeffersonian), they almost universally agreed that political virtue must rest upon moral and religious precepts. Since most textbook writers also were New Englanders, the early texts were infused with Protestant and, above all, Puritan principles.

Noah Webster's spellers, readers, and grammars exemplified the combination of faith in literacy (Americanized), didactic moral instruction, patriotism, and Protestant devotion to duty. Immediately following the Revolution, schoolbooks began to celebrate the values of national cohesion, love of country, and love of liberty. All things American began to be glorified. Even the staid *New England Primer*, which taught generations of Puritan children to learn the alphabet through Biblical injunctions, changed its couplet for "W" from "Whales in the Sea, GOD's Voice Obey" to "Great Washington brave, His Country did Save." Indeed, Washington became the object not only of extravagant praise but of virtually religious devotion. Ruth Elson quotes a 1797 textbook which said of Washington: "The most unexceptionally, the most finished, the most Godlike human character that ever acted a part on the theatre of the world."[2]

In the first half-century of the Republic, spellers and readers were the most influential carriers of civic education in the schools. Their paramount theme was to "attach the child's loyalty to the state and nation. The sentiment of patriotism, love of country, vies with the love of God as the cornerstone of virtue: 'Patriotism . . . must be considered as the noblest of the social virtues.' "[3]

One of the few founders of the new Republic who put real faith in the study of history, rather than religion, as preparation for the duties of citizenship, was Jefferson. In reviewing the reasons for his proposal in 1779 of a Virginia law to establish public schools, Jefferson stated a classic view of the importance of history in forming the political judgment of citizens. His words are peculiarly resonant at this tenth anniversary of the resignation of Richard Nixon:

> Of the views of this law none is more important, none more legitimate, than that of rendering the people the safe, as they are the ultimate, guardians of their own liberty. For this purpose the reading in the first stage, where *they* will receive their whole education, is proposed, as has been said, to be chiefly historical. *History* by apprising them of the past will enable them to judge of the future; it will avail them of the experience of other times and other nations; it will qualify them as judges of the actions and designs of men; it will enable them to know ambition under every disguise it may assume; and knowing it, to defeat its views. In every government of earth is some trace of human weakness, some germ of corruption, and degeneracy, which cunning will discover, and wickedness insensibly open, cultivate and

improve. Every government degenerates when trusted to the rulers of the people alone. The people themselves therefore are its only safe depositories. And to render even them safe their minds must be improved to a certain degree. This, indeed, is not all that is necessary, though it be essentially necessary. An amendment of our constitution must here come in aid of the public education. The influence over government must be shared among all the people.[4]

In addition to history, the study of civil government was advocated as a basic element in civic education. In this early period, however, government was generally reserved for college students; such young men, expected to be the rational citizen-leaders devoted to public service, were generally assumed to be those who most needed to study government. Washington put it this way in his final message to Congress in 1796:

The common education of a portion of our Youth from every quarter, well deserves attention. The more homogeneous our Citizens can be made in these particulars, the greater will be our prospect of permanent union; and a primary object of such a national Institution should be, the education of our Youth in the science of *Government*. In a Republic, what species of knowledge can be equally important? And what duty, more pressing on its legislature, than to patronize a plan for communicating it to those, who are to be the future guardians of the liberties of the country?[5]

While Washington was never to see his dream of a national university realized, a similar emphasis upon the study of government motivated Jefferson in his successful efforts to establish the University of Virginia. As stated in 1818, his first two purposes were:

To form the statesmen, legislators and judges, on whom public prosperity and individual happiness are so much to depend;

To expound the principles and structure of government, the laws which regulate the intercourse of nations, those formed municipally for our own government, and a sound spirit of legislation, which, banishing all arbitrary and unnecessary restraint on individual action, shall leave us free to do whatever does not violate the equal rights of another.[6]

Thus, Jefferson urged that two of his ten proposed schools for the new university be primarily devoted to civic education: a school of government and a school of law.

It is also worth noting that Jefferson's stress upon history, rather than religion, as a means to wise political judgments, reflected a long and influential stream of Western political thought that viewed citizenship as a high, if not the highest, moral and political role for human beings. A classic statement of this high ideal of citizenship was expressed by Pericles in his funeral oration during the first year of the Peloponnesian War in 43 B.C. Though it was indeed an idealized version, it did make claims upon the loyalties and commitments of Athenians similar to those that Lincoln's address on the battlefield of Gettysburg made upon Americans. Pericles said:

> Our constitution . . . favors the many instead of the few; this is why it is called a democracy. If we look to the laws, they afford equal justice to all in their private differences; if to social standing, advancement in public life falls to reputation for capacity, class considerations not being allowed to interfere with merit; nor again does poverty bar the way, if a man is able to serve the state, he is not hindered by the obscurity of his condition. The freedom which we enjoy in our government extends also to our ordinary life. There, far from exercising a jealous surveillance over each other, we do not feel called upon to be angry with our neighbor for doing what he likes. But all this ease in our private relations does not make us lawless as citizens.
>
> Our public men have, besides politics, their private affairs to attend to, and our ordinary citizens, though occupied with the pursuits of industry, are still fair judges of public matters; for, unlike any other nation, regarding him who takes no part in these duties not as unambitious but as useless, we Athenians are able to judge at all events if we cannot originate, and instead of looking on discussion as a stumbling block in the way of action, we think it an indispensable preliminary to any action at all.[7]

Here, then, was the ideal that all citizens could become "fair judges of public matters."

But the most influential voice to define the classic Greek view of citizenship was that of Aristotle. He described three major forms of government—a classification that proved to be a starting point for political philosophers for some two thousand years. The government, supreme authority of the state, may be in the hands of one, few, or many. Each type has a true form which, unhappily, may take a perverted or corrupted form. In the true forms, the rulers act on behalf of the common good, while in the perversion, they act on behalf of the private interest of the ruler. So, the paradigm became:

True Form (serves the public good)	*Corrupted Form* (serves the private interest of)
One: Monarchy	Tyranny: The King
Few: Aristocracy	Oligarchy: Wealthy Property
Many: Republic or Commonwealth (Constitutionalism)	Owners Democracy: The Needy, the Poor

Aristotle thus did not unequivocally favor any one form of government, but his biases generally came down on the side of aristocracy or constitutionalism. His aristocratic leanings showed when he confined citizenship to the "free man," thereby ruling out not only women, children, and slaves but also mechanics, traders, and farmers who, forced to work for a living, did not therefore have the education, ability, or leisure to engage fully in the task of ruling. But when he spoke about the citizen class itself, Aristotle sounded very much like a constitutionalist or a republican. All citizens were equal in their political rights and responsibilities, and all citizens had the capacity to act as rulers and judges in the legislative assemblies and courts of the commonwealth.

Two further points from Aristotle: he viewed the *political* community as the most important means for human fulfillment and justice, and he argued that education should be a public function of the polity rather than a private preserve for family, kinship, or religious groups. On the first point, Aristotle put it this way: "Every state is a community of some kind, and every community is established with a view to some good. . . . But if all communities aim at some good, the state or political community, which is the highest of all, and which embraces all the rest, aims at good in a higher degree than any other, and at the highest good."[8]

Since the ultimate object of the state is the virtuous life, citizens must be inculcated with good habits and rational principles: "A city [state] can be virtuous only when the citizens who have a share in the government are virtuous, and in our state all the citizens share in the government."[9] And how is this to be done? Aristotle advocated a common public education conducted for all citizens by the state. The ideas concerning citizenship contained in the preceding quotation and in the following one were expressed over and over in the late eighteenth century by the framers of the American Republic. Aristotle again:

> No one will doubt that the legislator should direct his attention above all to the education of youth; for the neglect of education does harm to the constitution. The citizen should be molded to suit the form of government under which he lives. For each government has a peculiar character which originally formed and which continues to preserve it. The character of democracy creates democracy and the character of oligarchy creates oligarchy: and always the better the character, the better the government.
> . . . since the whole city [state] has one end [virtue], it is manifest that education should be one and the same for all, and that it should be public, and not private—not as at present, when every one looks after his own children separately, and gives them separate instruction of the sort which he thinks best; the training in things which are of common interest should be the same for all. Neither must we suppose that any one of the citizens belongs to himself, for they all belong to the state, and are each of them a part of the state, and the care of each part is inseparable from the care of the whole.[10]

That education should be regulated by law and should be an affair of the state is not to be denied, but what should be the character of this public education, and how the young should be educated, are questions which remain to be considered.[11]

Unfortunately, Aristotle in his *Politics* did not get around to telling us what should be the proper political education for citizens, beyond mentioning the usual elementary subjects taught in most city-state schools: reading and writing, gymnastics, music, and possibly drawing. It would have been interesting to see how he would have prescribed differently for education in each of his types of government: monarchy, aristocracy, and constitutional republic.

In somewhat the same manner, the American founders were convinced that education was important for the welfare of the republic, but there was little agreement concerning just *what kind of history teaching* would best prepare citizens to make better political judgments and thus become better citizens. Similarly, there was little agreement concerning *what kind of study or government* would best contribute to civic virtue and civic judgments. If textbooks prevailing in the nineteenth century can be trusted as guides, it was widely assumed that the teaching of history ought to be a handmaiden to Protestant Christianity and that the teaching of government ought to be a handmaiden to Federalist orthodoxy.[12]

I believe that it is extremely important for all social studies teachers today to become more aware of the history of the teaching of history and government. Here I will mention only a few generalizations, drawn principally from the excellent and detailed research being conducted by Hazel Hertzberg and also from some secondary studies of my own.[13]

The point is that when history became a separate, identifiable, and important subject in the secondary school curriculum toward the end of the nineteenth century, it was promoted by the new professional historians as a disciplinary subject equal in value to the classics and mathematics. Its value for honing political judgment was scarcely mentioned. Later, progressive historians and social scientists of the early twentieth century who urged the reform of secondary education did indeed move cultivation of good citizenship again to the forefront of the goals of the social studies. But this was accompanied (a) by a stress on a kind of history that would primarily "speak to the present" and be seen as related to the present life interests of students and (b) by a vigorous espousal of the alliance between the new social sciences and history as a means to the study of contemporary problems and as the key to the civic mission of education.

Then, in the 1960s and early 1970s, a strange combination of influences served to dilute the civic purposes of the school curriculum in general and social studies in particular. The growth of specialized research in history and in the social sciences diverted the attention of teachers away from history as a molder of political judgment. On top of this, the wave of protests and campus unrest attendant upon Vietnam and Watergate led to a distaste for an allegedly irrelevant study of the past as well as a rejection of the role of education in developing anything that sounded so chauvinistic as "civic virtue." The "New Social Studies" of the 1960s and 1970s were largely ahistorical, if not antihistorical, and indifferent to the civic mission of education. Hazel Hertzberg summed up the new social studies view as follows:

> Citizenship education—as represented by the traditional civics, government and "problems of democracy" courses—was ignored, or assumed to take care of itself when intellectually able and inquiring citizens were produced. The new social studies were unified by a shared approach and shared methodologies, not by a conception of shared content or shared civic purposes. Clearly something had to give. History, it was agreed, had to move over.[14]

So, we come to the mid-1970s It is clear that in the past decade the educational profession in general and the social studies profession in particular have begun to reassert, more forcefully than in nearly half a century, the argument that education for citizenship is *the* fundamental purpose of universal education in American society. I call to your attention several signs of this revival of the civic mission of education, but I urge you to keep raising the question: will *history teaching* become a significant element in this revival, or will the revival be left to civics, government, law-related education, moral education, and other offshoots of the social sciences and humanities?

For the past dozen years the chorus of voices on the citizenship theme has been rising, and the consensus among professional educators has been widening, both outside and inside the social studies. I can mention only a few. In 1975 the National Council for the Social Studies (NCSS) board of directors resolved that citizenship education once again should become the main focus of social studies. In 1977 Barr, Barth, and Shermis asserted: "After decades of disagreement, there is now general agreement that the primary, overriding purpose of the social studies is citizenship education."[15] In 1979 the governing boards of twelve professional education associations (including NCSS) endorsed a statement on *The Essentials of Education* that claimed flatly: "Educators agree that the overarching goal of education is to develop informed, thinking citizens capable of participating in both domestic and world affairs."[16] The 1979 revision of the NCSS *Social Studies Curriculum Guidelines* stated: "The basic goal of social studies education is to prepare young people to be humane, rational, participating citizens in a world that is becoming increasingly interdependent."[17]

In 1980 the NCSS *Essentials of Social Studies* went so far as to list the democratic beliefs that should permeate exemplary social studies programs under the explicit heading "Democratic Beliefs":

> Fundamental beliefs drawn from the Declaration of Independence and the United States Constitution with its Bill of Rights form the basic principles of our democratic constitutional order. Exemplary school programs do not

indoctrinate students to accept these ideas blindly, but present knowledge about their historical derivation and contemporary application essential to understanding our society and its institutions. Not only should such ideas be discussed as they relate to the curriculum and to current affairs, they should also be mirrored by teachers in their classrooms and embodied in the school's daily operations.

These democratic beliefs depend upon such practices as due process, equal protection and civic participation, and are rooted in the concepts of:

- Justice
- Equality
- Responsibility
- Freedom
- Diversity
- Privacy[18]

In 1983 the Task Force on Scope and Sequence of the National Council for the Social Studies (NCSS) echoed the *Essentials* statement almost word for word, expanding the heading to "Democratic *Values and Beliefs*" and adding to the list of concepts two items:

- Rule of Law
- International Human Rights[19]

In both statements the history of the United States and of the world leads the lists of areas of knowledge that should be taught. Both history and social studies should be taught so as to embrace the goals of knowledge and democratic values and the skills of thinking and participation.

I mention these statements emanating from national organizations and from NCSS in order to highlight movements in California that have paralleled and in some respects have led the national movement. The California *History/Social Science Framework* of 1981, the California State Board of Education's *Raising Expectations* of 1983, and the California State Department of Education's development of *Model Curriculum Standards* in 1984 have all agreed to the general goal stated in the *Framework:* "The central purpose of history/social science education is to prepare students to be humane, rational, understanding, and participating citizens in a diverse society and in an increasingly interdependent world—students who will preserve and continue to advance progress toward a just society."[20]

Let me underline the key words of consensus in these national and California statements:

- the *primary, overriding* purpose
- the *overarching* goal
- the *basic* goal
- the *central* purpose

These are strong and important adjectives with which to describe the priority of citizenship education in American schools in general and in the social studies in particular. I believe that it is both timely and extremely important for us to take these statements more seriously than ever and to apply them to history as well as to the social sciences. And I believe that the section on democratic *Values* in the 1981 *Framework* points to the direction we ought to take. But for many reasons the task will not be easy.

We all know that the academic profession has long been uneasy about the whole question of "values" in teaching the social and political sciences. This has sprung from a genuine belief in value-free or value-neutral behavioral science and in empirical scientific methods as well as a fear of indoctrination, censorship, and partisan interference in the educative process. The experiences of the late 1960s and early 1970s with Vietnam, Watergate, and campus unrest made many, if not most, teachers wary or even hostile toward espousing anything that approached flag-waving patriotism. The very phrase "Be a good citizen" often brought forth ironic laughter or jeers.

Thus, social studies teachers felt more comfortable with a "New Social Studies" that stressed the structure and methods of the social science disciplines or with an "inquiry method" that skirted questions of indoctrination or inculcation of values. Competency-based behavioral objectives were transferred to citizenship competencies with little or no mention of values. And even when values *were* directly confronted, it was often with a stress upon the *process of valuing* rather than upon substantive study of the value concepts basic to a democratic society.

In this connection I need only mention one article addressed to social studies teachers in which Sidney Simon said: "In place of indoctrination, my associates and I are substituting a *process* approach to the entire area of dealing with values in the schools, which focuses on the process of valuing, not on the transmission of the 'right' set of values. We call this approach values-clarification, and it is based on the premise that none of us has the 'right' set of values to pass on to other people's children."[21]

Elements of this point of view on "valuing" are clearly present in the NCSS Curriculum Guidelines of 1971, again in 1979, and in the *California Framework for Social Sciences* of 1975, which this present *Framework* now replaces. But my point is that an important momentum in the profession, in the academic world, and in the public is now stressing that *mere* process in "valuing" is no longer adequate in an increasingly fragmented and fractionated society.

Within the social studies profession itself, as I have said, the call for greater and closer attention to democratic values has been growing rapidly during the past decade. I cannot begin to mention the roster of individuals by name, but many of them have been associated not only with the NSSC and CCSS (California Council for the Social Studies) but also with the law-related education movement represented nationally by the American Bar Association's Special Committee on Youth Education for Citizenship and in California by the Constitutional Rights Foundation and by Law in a Free Society, a project of the Center for Civic Education established by and affiliated with the State Bar of California.

In addition, this trend is noticeable within the academic disciplines themselves. I will mention only a few of the recent voices that call for schools to deal more directly with the substantive core of civic values that serve to strengthen the basic principles of the democratic society. These include powerful representatives from the mainstream of humanities and social science scholarship: the Carnegie Foundation for the Advancement of Teaching, *Daedalus* of the American Academy of Arts and Sciences, the Rockefeller Commission on the Humanities, the Association of American Colleges, and the National Endowment for the Humanities.

Individual scholars in history, philosophy, political science, and sociology have become more concerned with the normative, moral, and civic role of their disciplines in order to counteract the heavily empirical and value-free emphasis that has dominated teaching as well as research in these fields. This trend could profitably become a most valuable resource for teachers of history and social studies in the schools, as they seek to give vitality to the statements on essentials I have mentioned.

In history, teachers need what William H. McNeill, chairman of the history department of the University of Chicago, calls a generalized picture of the past "that speaks to the general concerns of ordinary citizens. . . . Specialized 'post-hole' courses in subjects of arcane professional debate will not do. . . . Better than any other discipline, history can define shared, public identities—national, civilizational, human, as well as local, ethnic, sectarian."[22]

Paul L. Murphy, professor of American constitutional history and American studies at the University of Minnesota, focuses the normative argument explicitly upon U.S. history:

> Students must again be exposed to the constitutional basics of why we ratain a two hundred year old document, the principles and values it incorporates, where it has worked and when and how it has failed. Above all they should understand what they can do generally and concretely to see that it continues to function to restrain human frailty and channel human creativity toward the positive ends of a society dedicated to "liberty and justice for all."[23]

This normative view of history, however, runs up against the predilection of historians not only to dig deeper into specialized interests but also to try simply to describe narratively what happens in the past, presumably with no ideological biases. This view ranges, interestingly enough, across a fairly wide spectrum of social and political points of view: from Frances FitzGerald, who has argued that history should be taught simply as the story of the past; to such revisionist historians of education as Henry Perkinson, Clarence Karier, and Michael S. Katz, who have argued that history in the public schools should not try to teach any lessons or civic values because it would necessarily indoctrinate an exploitative capitalist ideology.[24]

In the social sciences over the past few decades an empirical, scientific, and behavioral view of citizenship has dominated much of the thinking of political scientists, sociologists, and psychologists. They have withdrawn from the classical "high" ideal of citizenship, finding it irrelevant and unattainable in modern society. They have abandoned the normative objectives and commitments of the classical ideal in favor of realistic descriptions of political behavior. This "withdrawalism" is summarized by Richard Flathman in his article "Citizenship and Authority" prepared for a project entitled "Ethical Issues: Citizenship and Political Education" and supported by a grant from the National Endowment for the Humanities to the American Political Science Association.[25]

In the field of political theory, teachers of social studies could well listen to Flathman, who finds value in the normative questions raised by the classical theories of "high citizenship" and recently revitalized by such diverse writers as Hannah Arendt, Benjamin Barber, Carole Pateman, Dennis J. Thompson, John Rawls, and Michael Walzer.[26] One could add others in political and economic theory, including Michael J. Sandel, Ronald Beiner, and A. O. Hirschman.[27] In sociology, the normative values of civic education are touched upon from a variety of ideological positions by Amitai Etzioni, Robert Bellah, Morris Janowitz, and Manfred Stanley.[28]

These recent movements within the academic and educational professions reflect the timeliness of the renewed interest in civic values; and recent political trends in the broader society underline the urgency. We all hear a rising clamor from the public for greater attention to "teaching values" in the schools—from voices representing a fairly broad spectrum of political and social views that range from reactionary to conservative to liberal.

An increasing number of groups are asking or demanding that schools should indeed teach the "right values," very often summed up in the phrase "traditional values." For example, in 1981 the *California Monitor of Education* announced the formation of LITE (Let's Improve Today's Education); the group's goal is to clarify and implement the purposes of public education, which are not only to teach the basic skills and ordered discipline but also "to teach an appreciation of the principles upon which our heritage, history and culture are founded—

freedom, personal and family responsibility, private enterprise, limited constitutional government, and one nation under God."[29]

When social studies teachers come up against movements like these—or those of the Moral Majority, or Biblical fundamentalists, or new right Christians, or scientific creationists—their tendency is often to be defensive, or to plead academic freedom, or to try to ignore them. But the call for attention to *civic* value is now coming from liberal elements in the public as well as from conservative. An excellent example is the article by Jack Beatty, an editor of *The New Republic*, entitled "The Patriotism of Values." He argues that patriotism should not be given away to conservatives:

> For America's patriotism is unusual among the patriotisms of the world. It is a patriotism not of blood and soil but of values, and those values are liberal and humane. . . . Without the Constitution and Bill of Rights, America's very nationhood would vanish. . . . American patriotism is in the service of, indeed is identical with, the political purpose of the American republic. . . . It is exactly here that liberals can make their fresh appeal to patriotic feeling. They must become the sponsors of a revived ideal of citizenship. They have long been the champions of rights; . . . now, it is time to speak up for obligations. . . . It is now for liberals to urge a revival of the public realm and the public virtures.[30]

An important point here is that both conservatives and liberals are urging the schools to deal with the civic values and principles of the *constitutional order*, though they may not agree as to how these values should be interpreted. This is exactly the time for the social studies profession not to be defensive or indifferent or timid but rather to argue that its designated public purpose is to apply the best scholarship the academic world can produce in political and social science, law and jurisprudence, history, and the humanities to the citizenship function that the California *Framework* of 1981 calls for:

> The history-social science curriculum, K-12, should be most particularly and most explicitly concerned with those substantive values which form the common core of American citizenship. At all grade levels and subjects, and in accordance with the developmental capabilities of students, the curriculum should focus on the basic civic values and principles which undergird our democratic constitutional order. (p. 8)

At this point, the *Framework* refers to my formulation of a "decalogue of civic values" in my recent book, *The Revival of Civic Learning*.[31] Naturally, I am pleased by this and hope that the social studies teachers of California will find it useful. When the *Model Curriculum Standards* for grades 9 through 12 were adopted in 1985 many of the basic ideas were maintained, especially in the sections on responsibilities for educators and recommendations for implementation.

But there is still a monumental task ahead to give life and substance to these ideas. For more than two hundred years the basic values of political democracy have been set forth and debated. Assertions range from the most eloquent and persuasive statements in the English language to endless pedantic and trite mouthings. Yet, when crises arise or fundamental decisions are made, certain key concepts emerge that lay claim to the beliefs, commitments, loyalties, and actions of American citizens. In my book I selected ten basic ideas or value-oriented claims that I thought could be used as an intellectual framework for designing civic education programs for the schools. I make no claim for their originality. Too much has been thought and said over too long a period of time to make any such claim. And each value often elicits wide differences of interpretation. My indebtedness to many others is obvious. In fact, I have modified my "decalogue" in response to the *Framework* committee's adaptation of my original proposal.

In any event, let me now suggest a table of twelve value concepts classified into two general types: the *obligations* of citizenship that primarily promote desirable cohesive and unifying elements in a democratic political community; and the *rights* of citizenship that primarily promote desirable pluralistic and individualistic elements in a democratic political community. There is a continuing tension, sometimes overt conflict, between these values, which I have named respectively *Unum* and *Pluribus*, but I believe that programs of civic education must, just as American democracy must, try to balance, honor, and promote both. (See table 1.)

As a whole, these concepts represent the kinds of civic values that I believe schools should seek to exemplify in their whole operation as well as in their teaching and curriculum. As "values," they are not lists of competencies or specific goals of behavior. They are, rather, conceptions of the desirable elements in our political system that could be used as criteria by which particular competencies or specific goals of behavior may be selected and practiced. To put it another way, I believe that those in charge of designing curricula in history and social studies should reexamine the elements of their programs to determine to what extent they incorporate these values in their instructional materials, learning activities, and governance practices.

It will be obvious that these are normative concepts, each based on extensive histories of scholarly analysis and controversial interpretation in the humanities, law, and social sciences. But because they are also the very stuff of practical political life and public affairs, I believe that schools should confront these concepts directly, explicitly, and critically in ways appropriate to the age and capacity of students. They are not the "new" social science concepts of "role," "status," "stratification," "socialization," "political culture," "decision-making," and the like, as

TABLE 3.1.   "Twelve Tables" of Civism for the Modern American Republic*
(with apologies to the "Laws of the Twelve Tables" of the early Roman Republic
and to Aristotle's paradigm of the later Greek Republics)

| UNUM | | PLURIBUS | |
| The Obligations of Citizenship | | The Rights of Citizenship | |
Corrupted Forms of Unum	True Forms of Unum	True Forms of Pluribus	Corrupted Forms of Pluribus
"Law and order"	Justice	Freedom	Anarchy
Enforced sameness; conformity	Equality	Diversity	"Unstable pluralism"
Authoritarianism; totalitarianism	Authority	Privacy	Privatism
"Majoritarianism"	Participation	Due process	"Soft on criminals" policy
"Beguiling half-truth"; plausible falsehood	Significant truth	Property rights	"Property rights superior to human rights" policy
Chauvinism; xenophobia	Civic virtue; patriotism	International human rights	"Cultural imperialism"
	Democratic civism		

*Adapted from the "Decalogue of Democratic Civic Values," in R. Freeman Butts, *The Revival of Civic Learning* (Bloomington, Indiana: Phi Delta Kappa Foundation, 1980), p. 128.

behavioral political scientists might prefer. Nor are they couched in the terms of the personal moral qualities of character (such as persistence, tact, self-reliance, generosity, or hard work) that some parents might prefer. But they do appear in the highest reaches of political discourse and jurisprudence as well as in the ordinary language of governance in schools and communities, in political discussions and campaigns, and in the proceedings of courts, hearings, grievance committees, and policy councils. These concepts require nothing less than a lifetime of consideration if they are to become more than sunshine symbols or crisis crutches.

Such ideas and values are not discrete or mutually exclusive; some often conflict with others; and all are subject to many different interpretations, as really important ideas always are. What I view as corruptions, others may view as true forms. But I believe they exemplify the *kinds of ideas* that should be uppermost in an efficacious program of civic education. I would not argue for any particular order of priority in pedagogical treatment. Some teachers, some schools, some systems may well start at different points or even with different words for the concepts, depending upon their sense of fitness for the local situation, but it seems to me that a full-fledged acknowledgment of the civic role of education will lead to consideration of them all—at major points in the school's program, and in relation to each other.

I have no illusions that such a formulation will have universal appeal, but I would argue that these concepts more nearly define a revitalized civic education than do the laundry lists of "traits" or "competencies" so often listed by professional educators in curriculum guides. And I believe the proper civic mission of public education is to stress *civic* values that bind us together in a democratic political community rather than those "traditional moral values" that are defined in the public statements of advocates of particular personal life-styles or religious persuasions. The "traditional values" that *schools* should promote are the common *civic* values that underlie our democratic constitutional order.

From the founding of the Republic, civic education has been a mandate for public education. Civic education is our business. The social sciences and the humanities are essential to that business. Charles Frankel once described it this way: "In every generation in which the humanities have shown vitality, they . . . have performed an essential public, civic, educational function: the criticism and reintegration of the ideas and values of cultures dislocated from their traditions and needing a new sense of meaning."[32]

I believe that Frankel's statement about the humanities applies also to the task that lies before the social studies profession—namely, to engage in thoroughgoing study of the traditional values that underlie our common *civic* life; to reintegrate those ideas and values into a new, defensible, normative vision of American citizenship for the present decade—a decade that culminates in the bicentennials of the framing and adoption of the Constitution and Bill of Rights.

This requires not only the most exhaustive and continuing kind of self-study through our own professional meetings, commissions, and academic courses but also a concerted series of discussions, seminars, and national commissions that will enlist the support of public groups and voluntary organizations with the welfare of public schools at heart. The educational profession should not undertake this task in isolation from the public; rather the profession and the academic community should take the lead. Many public interest associations already exist for such collaboration. Two newly formed coalitions of national organizations seem particularly appropriate: the Council for the Advancement of Citizenship and the Domestic Policy Association.

The time is ripe for renewed efforts along these lines. What is called for is a frankly normative analysis of moral and philosophical assumptions that should be the basis of a common framework of civic ideals and that bind together the nation's diverse racial, ethnic, religious, po-

litical, and economic interests. This formulation of a defensible normative vision of American citizenship could be the basis of a variety of
programs of civic education in the coming decade. This is *not* an appropriate task to leave to agencies of government, for fear of political
or partisan indoctrination. It is *not* an appropriate task to leave to
voluntary groups organized to promote special economic or political
interests, nor to research think tanks that favor "value free" empirical
research or that push monolithic ideological views. It should not be left
to sectarian religious, ethnic, or social groups; nor to the press, other
media, or influential commentators.

Such groups, of course, will go on making special claims for particular social, civic, or moral values—and should be free to do so. But more
necessary is a sustained effort by outstanding public leaders, scholars,
and teachers in the humanities, in the social sciences, and in the law
to state explicitly and persuasively what the meaning of American citizenship should come to be during the final decades of the twentieth
century, and what schools, colleges, and teacher training institutions
can and should be doing about it. This would involve not only the most
fundamental consideration concerning the kind of society and world
we face in fact but also the kind of society and world we would like to
bring about as the United States enters its third century. Thus far, no
major group in the present educational reform movement has undertaken this task.

What does all this say about teaching history in the public schools
of California? It calls for a greater attention to two kinds of linkages:
(1) making more explicit the connection of the past with the present by
stressing, even requiring, sustained study of the historical origins and
present meaning of the civic ideas that have been named in the 1981
Framework and in the 1985 *Model Curriculum Standards* in history and
in government; and (2) making more explicit the connection between
the study of such civic values in history and government courses and
the present realities of student concerns. Both kinds of linkages could
be strengthened and enlivened by illustrations from those basic constitutional ideas and principles involved in recent Supreme Court cases
and from legislative proposals that apply directly to educational policies
and activities of students and teachers.

Take, for example, the several controversies over religion and education. This, one of the oldest and most complex issues, was involved
in the very founding of the American colonies and states, in framing
the federal Constitution, in establishing a common public school system, and in the continuing viability of a pluralist democratic society.
Students, teachers, administrators, and politicians are woefully weak in
their historical understanding of what civic principles and values are
at stake in organized prayers, Bible reading, or Christmas pageants in

public schools and other public places. We have had recurring political and educational battles over these issues ever since the debates over framing the First Amendment nearly two hundred years ago.[33]

And, now, after long congressional wrangling, we have the equal access act. This requires local public schools to let student groups hold discussions (outside regular classroom hours) on "religious, political, philosophical or other matters." Since such discussions are not to be under the guidance of teachers or public authorities, who will undertake serious study of the historical origins of the relevant constitutional principles? Will classroom history teaching deal with such issues or avoid them and become even more bland or remote from the practical arenas where civic virtues or civic vices are being molded? Will teachers of history take seriously Jefferson's hope that history can qualify citizens as "judges of the actions and designs" of their rulers?

The converse of conflicts over religious instruction in public schools is the recent battle over use of public funds for private and religious schools. This issue goes back at least fifty years, to the *Cochran* case of 1930, and especially to the *Everson* case of 1947. It involves the original meaning of the "establishment" clause of the First Amendment, which itself goes back more than two hundred years. The contemporary versions concern tuition tax credits or vouchers to help parents send children to religious schools. By and large, the Supreme Court has tended to hold a wavering line against myriad efforts to channel tax funds into private schools. In 1983, however, the Court upheld state tax credits in Minnesota on the grounds that applying them to public as well as private school expenses would avoid violating the establishment clause.

At almost the same time, the Supreme Court held that tax exemption was not appropriate for religious educational institutions that discriminated against black students, even though these schools argued that religious convictions required such discrimination. Here was a fascinating complex of constitutional issues involving questions of justice, freedom, equality, diversity, and due process, and involving both the First and Fourteenth Amendments.

And, of course, interpretation of the Fourteenth Amendment's equal protection clause has had a tortured history from the early 1950s through the *Brown* case in 1954, the civil rights acts of the 1960s, and right down to the Civil Rights Act of 1984. Even though desegregation mandates requiring busing did not directly affect most American students, affirmative action mandates for equality in women's sports, more flexible admission standards for minorities, and competency tests that allegedly discriminate against minority students and teachers did come close to home for many millions of students. Again, nearly all the civic values and democratic beliefs listed in the California *Framework* are at stake here; these issues call for much greater historical treatment if wise political judgment is to surmount special interest advocacy.

The range of contemporary controversies that affect education in one way or another and that should be viewed with greater historical perspective includes the efforts of certain groups to censor textbooks; the rights of children of illegal aliens to public education; creationism versus evolution in science teaching; the constitutionality of the draft registration act and compulsory attendance laws; state certification of private school teachers; and state regulation of curriculum requirements in private schools. And, even if none of these issues sparks the interest of students, the question of the privacy of student lockers and purses (suspected by teachers or principals of containing illegal drugs) certainly should lead some students to an interest in their constitutional rights, if not their civic obligations.

And, finally, if the issues of religion and politics as they touch upon such matters as abortion and homosexuality are too explosive for the serious, scholarly, classroom study of their legal and constitutional implications, then teachers and students might ponder together the ruling of a federal judge in Springfield, Illinois, in 1983 that Brown County High School officials violated the civil rights of a pregnant student by expelling her from the school's chapter of the National Honor Society. What a web of "traditional values" and "educational excellence" this situation reveals.

I am not, of course, arguing that U.S. history courses be given over to discussion of the whole range of contemporary issues or current events. Rather, I would argue that there are plenty of current issues that need to be approached through fundamental historical study of our constitutional principles, especially as revealed in the First, Fifth, and Fourteenth Amendments. And these cannot be understood in isolation from political, social, and cultural history in general.

I am arguing for greater attention to the role of history in developing an intellectual frame of reference whereby students will be better prepared to make the political judgments necessary for preserving and strengthening the civic values set forth in the *Framework* and the *Model Curriculum Standards*. The teacher of grade 10 World History, for example, could anticipate the U.S. History and Government studies lying ahead; the teacher of grade 11 U.S. History could build upon the World History and anticipate the Government/Civics to come; and the grade 12 teacher of Government/Civics could draw upon and deepen the concepts and values studied in earlier courses.

The basic idea is to find a way to connect and integrate social studies as a whole. Such a framework of common civic concepts or themes could provide a coherent bridge between grade levels and among the subject matters of history, humanities, and social sciences, which together make up the scholarly foundations for the social studies. Such a frame of reference could not only provide useful criteria for selecting topics and subject matter to be studied, in accord with the *Framework* and the *Model Curriculum Standards,* but also the stress on *civic* values would reaffirm the overall civic mission of public education. History and the social studies should concentrate on the effort to form the political judgment of the citizenry through serious study of the common civic values of the democratic constitutional order. This is the modern educational road to civic virtue envisaged by the founders.

But this goal will not be achieved unless students are required throughout the high school years to encounter the basic civic values upon which our democratic, constitutional system rests. Sustained study of the idea of citizenship, based upon scholarly knowledge and searching criticism, could provide a perspective and frame of reference by which teachers and curriculum-makers could select pertinent material from the almost limitless resources of the humanities and social sciences. From Graeco-Roman times through the modern revolutions in Europe and America to the present-day aspirations and struggles of the Third World, the theme of citizenship—revealing the varying ideas, values, and practices of the past and present—could give coherence and integration to the history/social science curriculum for grades 9–12. I hope that the new *Framework* drawn up for 1987 will culminate the process begun in 1981. There could be no better way to begin the commemoration of the bicentennials of the Constitution and Bill of Rights.

NOTES

1. Hazel Hertzberg, "The Teaching of History," in *The Past before Us*, edited by Michael Kammen (Ithaca, NY: Cornell University Press, 1980), p. 474.
2. Ruth Miller Elson, *Guardians of Tradition: American Schoolbooks of the Nineteenth Century* (Lincoln: University of Nebraska Press, 1964), p. 195.
3. Ibid., p. 282.
4. Thomas Jefferson, *Notes on the State of Virginia*, 2nd American ed. (Philadelphia: Samuel H. Smith, 1974), pp. 215–216.
5. *The Writings of George Washington, from the Original Manuscript Sources, 1745–1799*, edited by John C. Fitzpatrick (Washington, DC: Government Printing Office, 1940), vol. 35, pp. 316–317.
6. Saul K. Padover, *The Complete Jefferson* (New York: Duell, Sloan & Pierce, 1943), p. 1098.
7. Thucydides, *History of the Peloponnesian War,* translated by Richard Crawley (London: J. M. Dent, 1910), pp. 121–124.
8. Aristotle, *Politics and Poetics,* translated by Benjamin Jowett and S. H. Butcher (New York: Heritage Press, 1964), p. 5.
9. Ibid., p. 251.
10. Ibid., p. 267.
11. Ibid., p. 268.
12. Elson, *Guardians of Tradition,* p. 338.

13. Hazel Hertzberg, "The Teaching of History"; *Social Studies Reform (1880–1980),* ED 211429 (Boulder, CO: Social Science Education Consortium, Inc., 1981); R. Freeman Butts, "Society's Expectations for School Instruction about the Constitution: An Historical Overview," in *Teaching about the Constitution in American Secondary Schools,* edited by Howard D. Mehlinger (Washington, DC: Project 87, 1981).
14. Hertzberg, "The Teaching of History," p. 481.
15. Robert D. Barr, James L. Barth, and S. Samuel Shermis, *Defining the Social Studies,* Bulletin no. 51 (Washington, DC: National Council for the Social Studies, 1977), pp. 67–68.
16. *Organizations for the Essentials of Education,* a statement of the governing boards of twelve professional education associations including the National Council for the Social Studies, 1979.
17. *Social Education* 43 (April 1979): 262.
18. *Essentials of the Social Studies* (Washington, DC: National Council for the Social Studies, 1980).
19. "Report of the NCSS Task Force on Scope and Sequence in Social Studies," *Social Education* 48 (April 1984): 251–252.
20. *History–Social Science Framework for California Public Schools Kindergarten through Grade Twelve* (Sacramento: California State Department of Education, 1981), p. 3.
21. Sidney Simon, "Values Clarification vs. Indoctrination," *Social Education* 35 (December 1971): 902.
22. William H. McNeill, "History for Citizens," *AHA Newsletter* 14 (March 1976): 4–6. See also Thomas Bender, "Making History Whole Again," *New York Times Book Review,* October 6, 1985.
23. Paul L. Murphy, "The Obligations of American Citizenship: A Historical Perspective," *The Journal of Teacher Education* 34 (November–December 1983): 10.
24. Frances FitzGerald, "Rewriting American History," *The New Yorker,* 26 February, 5 March, and 12 March 1979; Henry Perkinson, review of "Historical Inquiry in Education," in *Educational Studies* 14 (Winter 1983), pp. 321–326; *History of Citizen Education Colloquium* (Philadelphia: Research for Better Schools, Inc., Winter 1978).
25. A publication of the American Political Science Association, *News for Teachers of Political Science* (Washington, DC: Summer 1981).
26. Hannah Arendt, *Between Past and Future,* new enl. ed. (New York: Viking Press, 1968); *The Origins of Totalitarianism,* 2nd enl. ed. (New York: Meridian Books, 1963); Benjamin R. Barber, *Strong Democracy: Politics in the Participatory Mode* (Berkeley: University of California Press, 1984); Carole Pateman, *The Problem of Political Obligation* (Chichester, NY: Wiley, 1979); Dennis F. Thompson, *The Democratic Citizen* (London: Cambridge University Press, 1970); John Rawls, *A Theory of Justice* (Cambridge: Harvard University Press, 1971); Michael Walzer, *Spheres of Justice: A Defense of Pluralism and Equality* (New York: Basic Books, 1983).
27. Michael J. Sandel, *Liberalism and the Limits of Justice* (New York: Cambridge University Press, 1982); Ronald Beiner, *Political Judgment* (Chicago: University of Chicago Press, 1984); A. O. Hirschman, *Essays in Trespassing* (Cambridge: Cambridge University Press, 1981); same author, *Shifting Involvement: Private Interest and Public Action* (Princeton, NJ: Princeton University Press, 1982).
28. Amitai Etzioni, *An Immodest Agenda: Rebuilding America before the Twenty-First Century* (New York: McGraw-Hill, 1983); Robert N. Bellah,

Varieties of Civil Religion (San Francisco: Harper & Row, 1980); Robert N. Bellah and others, *Habits of the Heart: Individualism and Commitment in American Life* (Berkeley: University of California Press, 1985); Morris Janowitz, *The Reconstruction of Patriotism: Education for Civic Consciousness* (Chicago: University of Chicago Press, 1984); Manfred Stanley, *The Ivory Commonwealth: A Case for Civic Higher Education* (in preparation for University of Chicago Press).

29. *The California Monitor of Education* 4 (January 1981); this periodical is published in Alamo by Betty Arras. The LITE Committee was formed through the efforts of the Pro-Family Coalition, Huntington Beach, CA.

30. Jack Beatty, "The Patriotism of Values," *New Republic* 4 July 1981, p. 18; 11 July 1981, p. 20.

31. R. Freeman Butts, *The Revival of Civic Learning* (Bloomington, IN: Phi Delta Kappa Educational Foundation, 1980).

32. Charles Frankel, "The Academy Enshrouded," *Change* 19 (December 1977): 64.

33. See R. Freeman Butts, *Religion, Education, and the First Amendment* (Washington, DC: People for the American Way, 1985).

Chapter 4

Educating toward the Public Good: Reconnecting the Humanities and the Social Sciences in a New Civic *Paideia*

WILLIAM M. SULLIVAN

THE RETURN TO THE HUMANITIES

American education is once again the locus of concern and controversy. Intense public scrutiny of educational institutions is not new in our national life; heated, sometimes violent, controversy over educational direction, purpose, and governance has been a relatively frequent accompaniment to periods of major social change or reevaluation in the wider society. Schools, even more than universities and colleges, are the institutions that by reason of their profound influence represent the nation's hopes for its future. So it is not surprising that "great school wars," in Diane Ravitch's phrase, from time to time sweep the American Scene.[1]

While the reforms of the early 1900s sought quality by placing schools in the charge of experts and those of the 1960s sought to bring in "the community" to control the experts, today's concern is as much over the content of education as with its governance. A rather diffuse and global worry seems to underlie the concern with basics and technical studies. Through a logical progression, this has generated

---

Paideia, a Greek word used in the title of this essay, refers to the upbringing of children. *Paideia* connotes a general humanistic education as opposed to a technical or professional training.

renewed attention toward humanities in the curriculum. Since the humanities have always been associated with educational efforts to provide a coherent sense of meaning and direction, a major turn of attention toward the humanities curriculum seems a sign of widespread concern with these basic cultural and social needs.

Consider the report issued in 1980 by the Rockefeller Commission on the Humanities. In diagnosing the problems of education in the humanities, the commission described an educational situation long on various kinds of process but short on substance. In response, the commissioners urged that subject areas designated as humanities—such as literature, the arts, history, philosophy, and aspects of the social sciences—should be more emphasized in school curricula and that instruction should be improved by, among other strategies, increased collaboration of schools with colleges and universities. That the commissioners intended thereby to augment the capacity of schools to give students a more coherent and integrated understanding of things seems evident from their exhortations: "We urge educators to view the humanities in terms of the links between skills, knowledge of cultural traditions, aesthetic judgment and enjoyment and moral values."[2] A tall order indeed! And yet despite its awkwardly vague formulation, the commissioners clearly intended the humanities to play a reflective and integrating role in influencing discourse among citizens of our diverse, complex democracy. The question is how such a thing might be achieved.

A DIAGNOSIS OF THE PREDICAMENT
OF MODERN CULTURE

Writing in the 1920s, the philosopher Alfred North Whitehead characterized the currents then becoming dominant in the organization of intellectual disciplines, universities, schools, and other major institutions of industrial society. Whitehead saw the crucial aspect of modern societies in the twentieth century as their capacity for ceaseless scientific and technological innovation, a capacity he traced to a new social and cultural formation, "the discovery of the method of training professionals who specialize in particular regions of thought and thereby progressively add to the sum of knowledge within their respective limitations of subject." The long-term effect would be an accelerating rate of technological change that would render "the fixed person, with fixed duties, who in older societies was such a god-send, in the future a public danger."

Whitehead drew attention to the costs of this social innovation for the individual and, even more seriously, for modern societies. The key to technical progress is thinking accurately, precisely, and methodically—a habit of mind Whitehead called thinking in a groove. "The groove prevents straying across country. . . . But there is no groove of abstractions which is adequate for the comprehension of human life." The danger to the individual is that the habits of mind developed by specialized training and the skills and qualities needed to succeed in a competitive world of work will distort and overwhelm awareness of the larger order of connections and balances, thereby narrowing attention and vision. Given a cultural climate of individualism, Whitehead feared that the new social forms of technological society would lead to the belief that there were "not merely private worlds of experience but also private worlds of morals" so that "the moral intuitions can be held to apply only to the strictly private world of psychological experience." Whitehead concluded from this possibility that, despite the increase of a certain kind of technical rationality, the social and political strength of reason in democratic society was actually being weakened.

> The leading intellects lack balance. They see this set of circumstances or that set; but not both sets together. The task of coordination is left to those who lack either the force or the character to succeed in some definite career. In short, the specialized functions of the community are performed better and more progressively, but the generalized direction lacks vision.[3]

Thus, for Whitehead, to find a "directive wisdom" appropriate to modern societies would be one of the "most useful discoveries for the immediate future."

The way modern American society has developed bears out the main outline of Whitehead's characterization. The United States has come to believe wholeheartedly in professional specialization. To a considerable extent, the value of education to society as a whole reflects belief—on the part of business, government, and the public at large—that continued progress depends on the flexible and efficient deployment of more and better trained specialists of all types, professionals and paraprofessionals: engineers, accountants, research scientists, "health care professionals," lawyers, managers, administrators, technicians, teachers, psychotherapists. There is a genuine fit between the modern scientific attitude—which regards valid knowledge as only that gained through expert deployment of method and apparatus—and the functional order of technological society. Corporations, like modern governments, seek to solve problems by the methodical employment of technique and have tended to reward those attitudes and skills that view all areas of life as potential fields for effective management—for the mobilization of personalities and ideas as well as of physical resources.

A generally uncritical belief in the social efficacy of technical advance has provided a spurious sense of order in this historical era and, at the same time, has contributed to undermining conceptions of humanistic culture that once strove to give coherent shape and vision to social life. For reasons similar to those Whitehead enumerated, the unparalleled technical advances of this century have been unable to awake in American society a new vision of any depth or coherence. The renewed interest in humanistic knowledge and curricula thus may be seen as an awareness that something is missing from the technical-managerial view of things. The ability of American society to respond effectively to the new economic, demographic, and geopolitical situation of our time depends upon reconstructing a more realistic and effective sense of ourselves as a diverse people united by an interwoven history and a convergent destiny.

THE "NATIONAL *PAIDEIA*" AND AMERICAN INDIVIDUALISM

The history of American education and of the humanistic disciplines turns out to manifest the same features as Whitehead's general characterization of the general developmental tendencies of the modern age. As will become clearer shortly, those same features connect the history of education with that of American work and public life.

At the beginning of this century, American education at all levels was still guided by what Lawrence Cremin called the nineteenth-century ideal of a "national *paideia*" expressed in a variety of regional forms of "vernacular education." The public or "common" schools were expected to provide a sense of cultural direction and moral purpose that could unify a diverse people becoming steadily more diverse, then as now, by massive immigration. The ideal was "the self-instructed person of virtuous character, abiding patriotism and prudent wisdom."[4]

This idea of a national *paideia* was in fact very unevenly realized. It was often withheld from immigrants, minorities, women, and the poor in exclusionary ways, and certainly not all embraced it. Nevertheless, it did represent a general belief in education, not just as a necessary support system for developing effective "human capital," but also as training in a broad cultural identity as citizens of a republic. It was a *paideia* "that united the symbols of Protestantism, the values of the New Testament, *Poor Richard's Almanac* and the *Federalist* papers, and the aspirations asserted on the Great Seal" (which referred to both the biblical notion of a people of special calling and the Virgilian motto of a republic of Roman stature).[5] Rather too readily this earlier American *paideia* assumed that its joining of cultural traditions—a mix of biblical, republican, and utilitarian traditions—represented a single, unified culture at once religious and civic; it was, however, neither so unified nor as inclusive as its proponents believed.

Yet for all its limitations, the ideal of a national *paideia* not only was explicit about the need to integrate the various fields of learning into an intelligible vision of the whole but also insisted on the need to draw the implications of this vision for living a good life both individually and socially. Beginning around 1900 the nation saw a variety of efforts to reform American education in a way appropriate to urban industrial life within an increasingly diverse nation. Probably the most persistent and important tendency of American education in the twentieth century has been that variegated movement known as progressivism. Its leaders conscientiously tried to continue and adapt the integrating spirit of the old national *paideia.* Educational theories of thinkers such as John Dewey complemented the desire of political progressives to update democratic culture by encompassing the emerging specialized, technical division of labor and a truly national economy and government. Progressives wished to continue and strengthen the unity and ethical meaning of education, but within the context of the developing professional specialization required by the new political economy.

Progressive intellectuals in education—like their colleagues in law, government, and business—fervently admired the possibilities of scientific intelligence for improving social life and thus often were impatient with the nontechnical outlook of the cultural "generalist" cultivated by traditional humanities disciplines. Yet, at the same time, intellectual progressives did acknowledge the moral obligation of scholars to speak to the major ethical questions of society as a whole. They were quite traditionally American in their eagerness to promote an "enlightened citizenry." At their most idealistic, progressives such as Dewey sought, through the reform of the schools, to generalize a common method of social progress and reform, which would develop "the responsible and enlightened citizen informed by the detached and selfless expert, the two in a manifold and lifelong relationship that would involve every institution in every realm of human affairs and ultimately transform all politics into education."[6]

The progressives, thus, hoped that the understanding of work demanded by the new industrial and technological division of labor would reinvigorate the traditional ideal of work as a calling, as contribution to the community of diverse but interconnected callings. However, under a combination of economic and technological pressures spurred by these very economic developments, the organization of work throughout society was developing in ways that rendered it harder for Americans to experience work (even professional work) as a calling in its traditional public sense. As a calling, work completes and validates the self by drawing the person into a disciplined practice that is perceived as not only valuable for what it does but as good in itself—both a contribution to others and a means of self-development.

But the institutional basis for this ideal, a reconstituted civic *paideia* for technological society, was much weaker than the progressives reckoned. Rather than integrating individual advancement and personal fulfillment with an enlightened public sense, the new industrial forms of work reinforced an older, nineteenth-century dream of purely individualistic success. The idealized civic environment of the new progressive schools thus proved less than fully successful against the educative power of the workplace and the job market.

The emerging industrial society strengthened an older American cultural tendency to see life as a struggle to master external nature and manipulate social institutions. This is utilitarian individualism, a cultural attitude that prefers thinking in an instrumental way, looking for effective means to fulfill desires. While, as a theory, utilitarian individualism can be traced back to the ideas of Thomas Hobbes in the seventeenth century and aspects of the Enlightenment in the eighteenth, it is in practice the characteristic style of the marketplace, of the traditionally masculine world of business. Individualism in America is subtle. It has been both the source of great moral courage and a cause of hardened isolation. Thus, although progressives looked to the new educational system and the development of professional codes of loyalty to temper and restrain this individualism much as religious morality and local civic participation had done in the nineteenth century,[7] reality turned out differently.

The new economic order broke individuals free of older community ties and pulled them not into an active civic order of meaningful participation, for which the progressive school tried to prepare them, but into the whirl of competitive striving. This situation seemed frighteningly anomic to many turn-of-the-century observers, one that neither the traditional American small-town civic culture nor the churches seemed able to handle.[8] Recent immigrants, along with the native-born, sensed the confusions, as did the middle classes entering the new professions.

But as the century wore on, a new pattern of culture began to develop—one markedly individualistic yet not so aggressive as the utilitarian strain, though its roots also go deep into American cultural soil. This second type of individualism has been called expressive or romantic. Conceiving the desires of the human heart as more than material acquisition and mastery of circumstances, expressive individualism seeks personal "growth" and "authentic expression," directness, simplicity, and warm mutuality with others. Ill-disposed toward both competition and involuntary communal bonds, expressive individualism promotes the notion that the real aim of life should be personal experience rather than achievement, and voluntary association with the like-minded rather than constricting ties of kinship and imposed identity.

The culture of expressive individualism has continued to gain strength in American life. While it can be seen in part as an effort to protect vulnerable individuals against the ravages of utilitarian aggression in a situation of weakened communal ties, it shares with utilitarian individualism a confidence that initiative and fulfillment of personal desires are the best guides to living. Thus, in fact, the expressive style complements the ontological individualism of the utilitarian type; for both it is the individual alone—not social relationships or cultural meanings—that is real. Ideally, for both forms of individualism, all social relationships should be voluntary, with ties and commitments binding only so long as they serve the individual pursuit of desires or the growth of an authentic self. Older understandings—of the family as a society of mutual trust and commitment, of work as a calling, or of the republic as a community of dedication to the common good (which had curbed, and to some degree, educated individualism in America)—have become hard to sustain within an individualistic ethos.[9] And the progressive generation was the first to confront the new situation in its full scope.

STRENGTHS AND LIMITATIONS OF PROGRESSIVISM IN EDUCATION

Leading progressive educational thinkers such as Dewey very much wanted to avoid having to choose among specialized competence, personal development, and civic vision as educational goals. However, the new industrial economy's irresistible demand for specialized expertise that required intensive professional training was strongly felt in American education, particularly in the emerging research universities, which soon came to set the standards for judging genuine intellectual competence. In the new context, learning not accredited by the community of expert competence was suspect, so that the loose world of the "educated public" as the tribunal of intellectual worth gradually lost ground to specialized organizations and forms. The effect of this transformation was to divide the curriculum into segregated specialties defined by reliance on various "methods."

In this cultural climate the young social sciences began to break off from history and moral philosophy. Progressives, who generally saw this process as an advance in social rationality, vigorously supported it. Given their enthusiasm for applications of expertise to solve problems, it is not surprising that progressives championed such new social sciences as economics, sociology, political science, and psychology—alongside, and sometimes in competition with, traditional subjects such as history.

John Dewey saw both history and the social sciences in a social studies curriculum as having moral and civic as well as intellectual value for "cultivating a socialized intelligence." By focusing on the whole "environment" of the school as a simplified cultural and moral version of society as a whole, Dewey sought to form in pupils an intelligence at once active and social, instrumental yet guided by shared norms of practice that were to be exemplified and developed in the actual operation of the institution. This progressive ideal of an activist, democratic community of learning rested on what Dewey termed an experimental and instrumental conception of knowledge and intelligence—developed, appropriately enough, at a "laboratory school." Dewey found its ideal type in the scientific community. For scientists ideas were tools and instruments by which to rearrange the environ-ment in the interest of a more fulfilled life. Moreover, science was morally exemplary, as a community governed by a shared search for common truth rather than by dogma or coercion.

The focus of this instrumental idea of knowledge was the "prob-lem situation," those circumstances that inhibited action. In Dewey's activistic, future-oriented epistemology precision and accuracy in anal-ysis were to be tested by their success in redescribing the problem so that it could be resolved by a rearrangement of its parts. This concep-tion of knowledge had the flavor of engineering, in which obstacles are conquered or removed by transforming a problematic environment, as in bridge-building or flood control. Dewey, like many Americans of his time, was impressed by modern science and technology; he saw that their power derived from attention to the meshing of tools, cognitive as well as mechanical, with the problems at hand. Not surprisingly, those favoring such an approach were impatient with mere custom and ac-cepted practice.

Thus, while Dewey could find a significant place for history, it was now precisely as a potential problem-solving tool. To apply this method to history is one-sided if it means only validating the truism that the present social state cannot be separated from its past. It means equally that past events cannot be separated from the living present and yet retain meaning. The true starting point of history is always some present situation with its problems.[10]

The purpose of history in the curriculum, then, was to provide fu-ture citizens with an understanding of how knowledge of the past could be used as an effective approach to social problems. But Dewey's fur-ther hope—that his experimental and instrumental method would en-courage the growth of a new integrating civic *paideia*—was not ulti-mately realized. Dewey's optimism was confounded by the utilitarian orientation of much of the progressive education movement as well as by the difficulties of institutionalizing his ideas in a social climate enamored of efficiency and eager to find simple formulas for making education contribute to "social efficiency."[11]

Exponents of progressivism failed to appreciate how deeply their

own assumptions and commitments were implicated in the very social trends that progressivism wanted to control. The core of Dewey's
theory was a generalization of his somewhat idealized version of the
community of scientific practice. In common with much of the American pragmatic tradition Dewey was presenting a more social and institutional version of the eighteenth-century Enlightenment ideal—that
science should displace religion and the old humanistic tradition as the
ordering principle of social life. And as heir to American republican
and liberal traditions, Dewey projected the ideal of an enlightened, experimental citizenry, at home with both technology and nature, constructing what he called the "Great Community." Progress would be
measured by "the extent to which the interests of a group are shared
by all its members," while an undesirable society (including all those of
the past) was one "which internally and externally sets up barriers to
free intercourse and communication of experience."[12]

But in practice, the way modern technological societies have developed confirms Whitehead's fears more closely than Dewey's hopes.
Something has gone wrong with the vision of scientific progress, even
in its most socially involved and democratic form of the Deweyan vision
of democracy. The roots of the difficulty lie in those aspects of human
cultural life that progressives denigrated or underestimated at the outset. In practice Dewey's enthusiasm for science as the cultural norm of
rationality meant that he minimized the significance of the older humanistic tradition as a means of orienting educational practice, while
his allegiance to the ideals of the liberal Enlightenment rendered his
appreciation of ethnic (especially religious) traditions minimal at best.[13]

Dewey, however, recognized quite clearly the dangers utilitarian
individualism posed for democratic culture. In his writings of the
1920s and 1930s, he continually called for a "new individualism" that
could provide a more secure public matrix through which individuals
could weave their restless search for personal growth and fulfillment.[14]
Dewey argued that satisfaction of expressive desires could come to rest
only in a secure sense of selfhood, which in turn required at least partial
identification of the self with a larger order of shared ideals and meanings. Indeed, Dewey's educational and social philosophy was a search
for just such a practical and theoretical understanding of the instrumental and expressive desires of the individual self within a larger civic
whole. But having eliminated so much of traditional American and European culture, particularly religion, as being irrelevant or positively
detrimental to modern needs, Dewey was left with too fragile a cultural platform on which to stand. In the end, he fell back on an idea
of pure communication—drawn from his idealized picture of science,
but also resonant with an expressive individualism—in which the self
finds its ground everywhere and nowhere, in uninterrupted but form-

less communication. "For democracy is a name for a life of free and enriching communion. It had its seer in Walt Whitman. It will have its consummation when free social inquiry is indissolubly wedded to the art of full and moving communication."[15]

WHAT SHALL WE TEACH?

HISTORY AND THE SOCIAL SCIENCES AS ASPECTS OF A PUBLIC PHILOSOPHY

The task confronting those who would promote an education that takes seriously both the context of history and the insights of the social sciences is indeed formidable. The spirit of the progressives' search for a new civic *paideia* must be reanimated if American education is not to succumb to the very limited visions bequeathed us by individualism. In contemporary America both the high culture of the universities and the mass culture of entertainment are heavily dominated by the two unstable visions of individualism. On the one hand, the public world of our economy and politics seems ruled by the utilitarian standards of calculation, bargaining, and unending competition, in which effective technique alone is valued. On the other hand, supported by the technological apparatus of modern society, we find a different set of traits such as sentiment, spontaneity, and, above all, individual fulfillment. But neither culture comprehends the other, nor the historical and social ties that connect them. This fragmentation is expressed in our disjoined curriculum of technical fields such as the physical and mathematical sciences, which have little organic relation to cultural and humane studies.

The approach to learning characteristic of the old humanistic *paideia* at its best offers a hope for cultural coherence that individualism, particularly expressive individualism, needs and seeks but cannot find by itself. The humanistic understanding of learning centers on a concern for the whole: the whole person in relation to others, to institutions, to cultural understandings, to the past and the future. But neither the self nor social relations can be understood coherently apart from a frame of reference and habits of thinking and acting that encompass and give shape to a conception of life as a whole. It is the business of the humanities at their full stature to provide the resources and the intellectual abilities to form such an encompassing conception.

And this is not a solitary nor a passive project but, as John Dewey intended, a public task, an effort to create a community of understanding capable of talking, thinking, and acting as a self-governing society. In this sense, humanistic learning is both reflective and public. Its *paideia* points toward what we could call a public philosophy concerned with developing mutual understanding and enduring connections among the disparate occupational, ethnic, and religious groups that are separated by the workings of economic competition and individualistic culture. To spur this development a viable humanistic resurgence must take place in the universities as well as the schools. It must move toward a new public philosophy, which can act as a common language for the dialogue of citizens throughout the society.

How can we develop this sense of the whole in our schools? What would such a renewed civic *paideia* have to say about the humanities curriculum? How does the perspective of public philosophy affect the old argument about the relation between history and the social sciences—the curricular battleground (and backwater) of social studies? First, a curriculum concerned to educate toward a vision of the whole of society and the world community would have to be, at every educational level, at once historical and informed by the social sciences. The social sciences have given us valuable information about many aspects of contemporary society but often with little or no sense of history. Yet what we need from history—and why the social scientist must also be, among other things, a historian—is not merely comparable information about the past but also some idea of how we have gotten from the past to the present—in short, a narrative. Narrative is a primary and powerful way in which we learn about a whole. What a society (or person) is, in an important sense, is its history. Yet this does not mean simply patriotic dogma, as it sometimes did in the past. In a reflective history, and in a reflective society, such stories can and must be contested, amended, and sometimes replaced. A key task of school curricula must be to see how the stories that scholars tell relate to stories current in society at large, and thus expose them to mutual discussion and criticism.

But this understanding of the role of history and the social sciences as contributing to a public philosophy carries an important implication for the practice of academic disciplines themselves. Since facts become relevant only when interpreted within a clear and comprehensive frame of reference, a recovery of the public vocation of history and social science means that the recent, and ultimately arbitrary, boundary between the humanities and the social sciences has to come down. The progressives too argued for eliminating the boundary, but they did so in order to press history into service as a tool for scientific problem-solving. The present proposal is in a sense the reverse. The prevailing view in the academy is that while history, philosophy, literature, and the other humanities are concerned with cultural traditions and their interpretation, the social sciences involve the scientific study of human action. The assumption is that the social sciences are not cultural traditions but rather occupy a privileged position of pure observation and, thus, that observations about human action derived from the humanities do not really become knowledge until "tested" by the methods of science, from which alone comes valid knowledge. But social science is not a rational procedure independent of history; in fact, it is a tradition (or set of traditions) deeply rooted in the philosophical, humanistic, and religious history of Western culture. Social scientists, becoming conscious of the cultural roots of this tradition of investigation, would be reminded that the choice of assumptions means becoming involved in controversies that lie deep in the history of Western thought. Thus social science would be brought into an explicitly historical and cultural discussion.[16]

Very likely, such an opening up of a new kind of collaboration between history and the social sciences would change the present forms of both—bringing professional discourse much closer to the search now going on in many areas of American life for a more adequate self-interpretation than currently available. Certainly, recognizing that scholarly research in the social sciences as well as the humanities takes place from within certain institutions and assumptions, which themselves are inescapably rooted in traditions and aspirations, ought to make scholars and teachers more aware of and sympathetic toward the diverse vernacular traditions that give meaning to the lives of most citizens. And being made aware that we are all at least partially formed by the ideals and hopes of the past is the essential first step toward taking up a critical yet loyal stance within our imperfect, fragmented, yet living heritage.

INSTITUTIONALIZING AN INTEGRATING *PAIDEIA*

All this is to say that history can be a way to understand American culture as a living conversation, an argument in the best sense of the word, among our several traditions concerning the meaning and direction of our common life. The very nature of American society, always unfinished and in process of formation, requires that understanding ourselves and our place in the world necessarily be a continuing and changing process. Thus, a modern curriculum cannot fail to understand and teach that our heritage as Americans is in fact one of various, sometimes conflicting, traditions. But neither can an adequate civic curriculum present the naive pluralist image of a vast array of "lifestyles" and "cultures" as though, in the language of expressive individualism, they were distinct "value systems" available to individual choice as to a spectator at a pageant. Instead, a new civic *paideia* must give students a point of orientation by bringing them into the complex, but not infinitely diverse, cultural understandings through which Americans have directed and reflected on their lives.

A curriculum aiming to develop this kind of reflective understanding has to be structured by at least three considerations. The first is that the real "first language" of most contemporary American culture is individualism in its two variants. Certainly the world of the economy and to a large extent that of politics—indeed the public world apart from home life, churches, synagogues, and neighborhoods—is dominated by the culture of utilitarian individualism. The guiding principal there is relentless achievement, in the sense of advancing one's relative position in the general competition and ending up better than one began. Without including critical reflection, a curriculum and an extracurriculum that seek to prepare students for "real life" run a major risk of helping to transmit this culture of individual mobility and success while providing little awareness that there is more to life as well as more to America. Without conscious counterweight, the mass video culture certainly educates to little more than versions of individualism, often massaging bruises received in utilitarian striving by nestling the feelings in intimate surroundings.

But what this "vernacular" education dispensed by the commercial media too often lacks is the sense of participation in a larger life. It is deficient in reverence for the lives and achievements of others and in joy beyond the sense of winning or possessing—such as joy in efforts at justice, in service well done, and in the legacy of past generations. These, the permanent goods of the humanistic tradition, are the essentials of a decent society and of a life worth living—not frills or archaic survivals, which we can postpone until the "practical" tasks of meeting needs are satisfied. Thus, the strong, central place of the humanities is the second essential in a curriculum designed for the critical self-reflection of active citizenship. The very practical contribution of the humanities could be to provide the discipline of a strong cultural frame within which teachers and students could learn to evaluate aspects of our way of life for providing purposes and ends worth devoting one's life to.

The task of humanistic culture is to name the important things in life so that we are able to form our lives around them. It has served us historically as a way to lift lives beyond what Erazim Kohak has described as "the lock-step of need and gratification," beyond the reference point of simple personal preference to an awareness of "the generically human vision of a moral sense of life." This moral sense of life, the awareness that others have an intrinsic value and that the good life is a common endeavor, is precisely the dimension that can fulfill and secure the individual's expressive strivings. As Kohak puts it: "The perspective focused on the sole question, 'How do I feel about it?' is the essence of barbarism."[17] The central importance of the humanities derives from their capacity to educate the moral sense, to lead toward a higher and more realized individuality by providing a strong cultural frame. The great texts and achievements of humankind presented in the humanities curriculum can enable students to locate and explore the main features of a developed humanity, relating their own desires to them and, hopefully, cultivating such traits in themselves.

The intellectual climate is perhaps more favorable to this endeavor today than for some time previous. Within the academy there is a growing recognition that the narrative and interpretive dimensions of human understanding cannot be subsumed into the project of technological mastery.[18] This awareness has made it possible to see more clearly the difference between scientific and technical knowledge, on the one hand, and the aim at deepened and clarified self understanding characteristic of the humanities, on the other. This recognition opens the possibility of a genuine reappropriation of the insights of tradition in a way that is neither nostalgic nor idiosyncratic, by allowing us to argue for the applicability of traditional meaning to present conditions. And, at the same time, in trying to "apply" tradition to our situation, we come to understand it by establishing communication between the present and the past.[19]

The third essential feature of an adequate curriculum is that it provide a reflective orientation toward the American project of a democratic civic order. Civic republicanism is a tradition of political vision that emphasizes the value of citizenship, defined as the moral cultivation of responsible selves. It asserts that the search for a meaningful life cannot succeed as a private quest, one that avoids the effort to achieve a just society. In contrast to utilitarian individualism, but somewhat like expressive individualism, civic republicanism addresses the desire for a life of inclusion in a community of mutual concern. Only, unlike the expressive culture that starts with an isolated, almost naked self, the republican understanding considers the self a unique individual because of its relations to others and its past, not in spite of them. For the awakening of self-consciousness always takes place within an unfolding life narrative already marked by common aims, even when the person consciously rejects or refashions those aims. In this way a civic curriculum must be rooted in a history—indeed in the variety of histories—of the school community from the start.

But civic republicanism as a curricular focus can also restrain and educate the individualistic strands of our culture by rooting them within the wider project of the search for the common good. For the United States, republican citizenship has always meant loyalty to those ideal goods which define the nation as a democratic republic; and its great figures have always united personal aspirations with concern for the common good. In recent history, Martin Luther King, Jr., demonstrated the strength and vitality still latent in the sense of the public good Americans have inherited. King's articulation of the biblical and republican strands of our national history enabled a large number of Americans, black and white, to recognize their real relatedness across difference. The powerful response King elicited, transcending simple utilitarian calculations, came from the reawakened recognition of many Americans that their own sense of self was rooted in companionship with others who, though not necessarily like themselves, nevertheless shared a common history, and whose appeals to justice and solidarity made powerful claims on personal loyalty.[20]

But institutionalizing a curriculum conceived with these things in mind has to take place within today's specialized, technologically advanced economy—that world of work to which schools are necessarily closely linked and that, for teachers, is, after all, the school itself. And this forces us to return to Whitehead's problem. In a real sense it is a misnomer to describe our dominant view of education as "vocational." The contemporary experience of work often bears scant relationship to the traditional sense of work as vocation. At its most purely utilitarian, work means holding a job that provides some measure of security and economic success. For others, professionals in particular, work is a career, a progress of advance in an occupation, which thereby provides an individual with a powerful source of identity and self-esteem that becomes an expression of self as well as an instrument for gain. Even this, however, is far less than the meaning of vocation.

Indeed, taking up a "vocation" has meant assuming a kind of public trust, a willingness to develop one's capacities for the benefit of all. This experience of work remains real for some—craftsmen, for example, and professionals such as physicians, teachers, and clergy—but it is increasingly compromised by the relentless demands of modern economic organization to respond to profit before all else. As the fusion of personality with work in the character of the dedicated craftsman or professional becomes less economically viable, relatively affluent Americans seek more and more to balance lives of unengaged work with such leisure activities as strenuous sports and demanding hobbies whose reward is the kind of self-realization accomplished in practicing an activity good in itself. But in leisure, unfortunately, realization of self takes place without establishing connection to any larger community save that of the like-minded. The public, integrating qualities of work are lost. The historical irony is that increased specialization of training and function has weakened the experience of work as a contribution to a common good at the very time that those same economic tendencies have made individuals more interdependent than ever before.

A renewed civic *paideia* must start with an effort to recover the sense of vocation as the desire to develop one's capacities for the benefit of all. For the measure of learning is how well it fits us to act as responsible persons, with both knowledge and character appropriate to make the best of our situation and involvements. While this is a task that confronts every institution in our society, and one that cannot possibly be left to educational institutions alone, it nonetheless is a project in which schools and universities have a naturally central role. If Whitehead was right, if development and application of "professional" knowledge and attitudes constitute the controlling dynamic of change in modern societies, then hopes for a more humane integration of professional expertise into a more genuinely democratic society necessarily must rest heavily on education. Yet this is not to overlook the fact that not all children will come to see their adult lives as professionals. Rather it is to stress that if a humanistic and civic education is to effect a more just social order, it will have to aim at infusing a genuinely public ethos into professional aspirations and training.

This effort must be grounded in the organization as well as in the curriculum of our educational institutions, especially the schools. In a word, education must become a profession in the full civic sense. At its best, a profession (like the traditional crafts) is a school of citizenship, a self-governing body that is also a community sharing certain moral as well as technical concerns. A profession continues a disciplined practice that gives individuals' lives a form because the work is good in itself as well as useful for what it does. Modern economic institutions—which demand monetary success at all costs, the tyranny of the bottom line—like the pressures of public bureaucracies, have often proven poor patrons of professional excellence. And certainly a key step toward a renewed *paideia* must be the active strengthening of the professional life of teachers in all its dimensions: as lovers of learning and participants in the cultural conversation as well as transmitters of knowledge and shapers of aspiration.

Finally, this great effort itself cannot hope to achieve the aims of humanistic culture unless it becomes a part of and a stimulus to reinvigoration of the common vocation—the project to renew a sense of genuine citizenship among all Americans in all aspects of public life, in the economy and government as well as in training a new kind of professional. It is a continuation of an effort deeply rooted in American tradition, indeed a project taking its direction from the hope that has defined the tradition. The American philosopher of community, the Californian Josiah Royce, spoke for its central insight when he observed that "you can love an individual. But you can be loyal only to a tie that binds you and others into some sort of unity, and loyal to individuals only through the tie."[21]

NOTES

1. The reference is to Diane Ravitch, *The Great School Wars: New York City, 1805–1973—A History of the Public Schools as Battlefield of Social Change* (New York: Basic Books, 1973).

2. *The Humanities in American Life,* Report of the Commission on the Humanities (Berkeley: University of California Press, 1980), p. 40.
3. Alfred North Whitehead, *Science and the Modern World* (New York: Macmillan, 1925), pp. 282–283.
4. Lawrence A. Cremin, *Traditions of American Education* (New York: Basic Books, 1977), p. 94.
5. Ibid., p. 87.
6. Ibid., p. 94.
7. For a fuller treatment of this issue, see William M. Sullivan, *Reconstructing Public Philosophy* (Berkeley: University of California Press, 1982).
8. See Paul Boyer, *Urban Masses and Moral Order in America* (Cambridge, MA: Harvard University Press, 1978).
9. For a fuller discussion of the forms of individualism in American culture, see Robert N. Bellah, Richard P. Madsen, William M. Sullivan, Ann Swidler, and Stephen M. Tipton, *Habits of the Heart: Individualism and Commitment in American Life* (Berkeley: University of California Press, 1985), especially chapters 2 and 6; also see Richard M. Merelman, *Making Something of Ourselves: On Culture and Politics in the United States* (Berkeley: University of California Press, 1984), especially chapters 1 and 2.
10. John Dewey, *Democracy and Education: An Introduction to the Philosophy of Education,* (New York: Macmillan, 1923), p. 251.
11. See Dewey, *Democracy and Education;* also see Martin S. Dworkin, *Dewey on Education* (New York: Teachers College Press, 1959). For contemporaneous trends in higher education, see Lawrence R. Veysey, *The Emergence of the American University* (Chicago: University of Chicago Press, 1965), especially pp. 342–380. The results of the progressive revolution in social studies has been criticized for lacking both rigor and comprehensive vision. See Arthur Bestor, *Educational Wastelands: The Retreat from Learning in our Public Schools* (Urbana: University of Illinois Press, 1953); also see Bestor, "History, Social Studies and Citizenship: The Responsibility of the Public Schools," *Proceedings of the American Philosophical Society* 104, no. 6 (December 1960): 549–551. More recently Frances FitzGerald has shown the intellectual weakness and civic irresponsibility of the textbook industry's history and social studies marketing in the 1960s and 1970s. See Frances FitzGerald, *America Revised: History Textbooks in the Twentieth Century* (Boston: Little, Brown and Co., 1979); also see Diane Ravitch, *The Troubled Crusade: American Education, 1945–80* (New York: Basic Books, 1983). On the history of the social sciences' divorce from history, see John Higham, "The Schism in American Scholarship," *The American Historical Review* 72, no. 1 (October 1966): 1–21.
12. Dewey, *Democracy and Education,* p. 115.
13. Modern postempiricist philosophy of science has in recent years seriously modified the general understanding of the sense in which scientific life is "rational." For an overview, see Richard J. Bernstein, *Beyond Objectivism and Relativism: Science, Hermeneutics and Praxis* (Philadelphia: University of Pennsylvania Press, 1984).
14. See John Dewey, *Individualism: Old and New* (New York: Capricorn, 1962), especially pp. 146–171.
15. John Dewey, *The Public and Its Problems* (New York: Henry Holt and Co., 1927), p. 184.
16. For an elaboration on these themes, see the Appendix, entitled "Social Science as Public Philosophy," in Bellah et al., *Habits of the Heart.*

17. Erazim Kohak, *The Embers and the Stars: A Philosophical Inquiry into the Moral Sense of Nature* (Chicago: University of Chicago Press, 1984), p. 112.
18. For a survey of some of those developments along with an argument in defense of this "hermeneutical" or interpretive turn in recent thinking, see Norma Haan, Robert N. Bellah, Paul Rabinow, and William M. Sullivan, eds., *Social Science as Moral Inquiry* (New York: Columbia University Press, 1983).
19. This point is explained well by Jurgen Habermas in his *Knowledge and Human Interests* (Boston: Beacon Press, 1971). See especially pp. 309–310.
20. See Bellah et al., especially chapters 2 and 10.
21. Josiah Royce, "The Philosophy of Loyalty," in *The Basic Writings of Josiah Royce*, edited by John J. McDermott (Chicago: University of Chicago Press, 1969), p. 862.

Chapter 5

Linking Science and History: Bridging the "Two Cultures"

BERNARD R. GIFFORD

I write as a professional educator trained in the sciences and devoted to the humanities. Scientists, characteristically, advocate more science and mathematics courses for precollegiate students as the best way of readying them for life. Humanists make the same claim, for the same reason—that more courses in the humanities should be required. More often than not, if any agreements between them are reached, they result from a search for accommodation rather than from mutual understanding.

But such competition tends to present a serious challenge to the teacher of the humanities; all too often advocates, for example, of courses in history find themselves on the defensive. Public pressure it seems, would favor more emphasis on the "urgent need for more mathematics and science experts" to keep the United States from "falling even further behind" other nations in this or that applied science. This situation is treated as if it were a zero-sum game: since schools have finite resources and students have a finite course load, an enhancement of mathematics and sciences poses the threat that critical time and resources will necessarily be subtracted from those of the humanities curriculum.

Teachers of history, fine arts, and literature are well able to defend continuing and increasing support for humanities requirements in the schools. They can cite their central role in guiding an individual's development in creativity and moral maturity, as well as in answering the increasing demand for insight into ways of life foreign to one's own. Usually the argument claims also that those on the "other side"

*An earlier version of this paper was written for *Challenges to the Humanities*, edited by Diane Ravitch, Chester Finn, Jr., and Holley Roberts (Holmes and Meier: New York, 1985).

place too much value on technical training and job preparation, and not enough on affective or evaluative and analytical activities.

While advocates of greater emphasis on science and engineering claim to find humanities "worthwhile" they also warn that, in establishing priorities and allocating limited resources, we must acknowledge a responsibility to provide maximum support for activities that will help to meet society's needs; we must not permit ourselves, they say, to be sidetracked by "attractive fringes and fuzzy niceties." They argue further that the case for the humanities seems difficult to make, set against the manifest benefits—and monetary gain—produced by advances in science and engineering.

What then is the role of the history, fine arts, or literature teacher in assuring fairness in the adjudicating of such debates? As humanists, must they feel always threatened? There are no easy solutions, but, even as a scientist, I argue that any proposal to tip the balance of public support heavily in favor of mathematics and science—if grounded in a belief that scientific knowledge is superior to knowledge in the humanities—is a proposal based on error. Those who lead in history education must help the public learn that studying the humanities provides access to knowledge of a kind quite different from that acquired through learning physics formulas or mastering the elements of numerical analysis. History provides insights into the human condition in all its complexity, imparting the kind of knowledge upon which individuals can base wise, well-grounded choices. This kind of knowledge is what good history teachers help their students to gain.

THE TWO CULTURES

The issues underlying this debate between the proponents of scientific knowledge and the defenders of the humanities are scarcely new. In May 1959, C. P. Snow delivered the Rede Lecture at Cambridge University and took as his title and theme "The Two Cultures and the Scientific Revolution." Snow's celebrated thesis, simply expressed, was that a gulf of mutual incomprehension exists between natural scientists and humanists. Summarizing that lecture, Snow said:

> In our society (that is, advanced western society) we have lost even the pretense of a common culture. Persons educated with the greatest intensity we know can no longer communicate with each other on the plane of their major intellectual concern. This is serious for our creative, intellectual and, above all, our normal life. It is leading us to interpret the past wrongly, to misjudge the present, and to deny our hopes of the future. It is making it difficult or impossible for us to take good action.
>
> I gave the most pointed example of this lack of communication in the shape of two groups of people, representing what I have christened

"the two cultures." One of these contained the scientists, whose weight, achievement and influence did not need stressing. The other contained the literary intellectuals. . . . Literary intellectuals represent, vocalize and to some extent shape and predict the mood of the non-scientific culture: they do not make the decisions, but their words seep into the minds of those who do. Between these two groups—the scientists and the literary intellectuals—there is little communication and, instead of fellow-feeling, something like hostility.[1]

Though, as Snow admitted, the gulf separating the two cultures was more pronounced in Britain than in the United States, the lack of communication was no less a problem. Indeed, in America today, that widening gulf will not easily be narrowed.

Many people know little of science. Stephen R. Graubard, editor of *Daedalus*, notes in a recent special edition on scientific literacy: "To say that science is a mystery for great numbers—that it appears to be largely inaccessible even to men and women who believe themselves educated—that this condition is scarcely improving, is now commonly accepted."[2] Others, well versed in the sciences but estranged from the humanities, are blind to the power of humanistic learning and understanding needed to illuminate the dark corners of our civilization. During the late 1960s, for example, when the social fabric of our country, especially in the nation's urban centers, was being torn by racial, political, and intergenerational conflicts, the Dean of M.I.T.'s College of Engineering proclaimed: "I doubt if there is such a thing as an urban crisis, but if there were, M.I.T. would lick it in the same way we handled the Second World War."[3] There was, and still is, a social crisis. Many have tried to "lick it." The crisis—both then and now—resists approaches used by those who ignore the importance of blending scientific technique with humane intelligence.

Separation of the two cultures has not entirely blocked the possibility of mutually enlightening contacts. On both sides of the gulf communications have been maintained by those who insist upon seeking truth in all its forms. The complex problems of contemporary society require wise judgment coupled with technical proficiency—that is, the active involvement of individuals and groups who have both kinds of knowledge. Snow himself recognized the importance of education for bridging the gulf between the two cultures:

There is, of course, no complete solution. In the conditions of our age, or any age which we can foresee, Renaissance man is not possible. But we can do something. The chief means open to us is education—education mainly in primary and secondary schools, but also in colleges and universities. There is no excuse for letting another generation be as vastly ignorant, or as devoid of understanding and sympathy, as we are ourselves.[4]

As one whose formal academic training is in the sciences and as an administrator and faculty member at a major research university I have thought often about the larger implications of Snow's observations for our society. It is clear that the current trend of encouraging students to specialize earlier and earlier in their education runs counter to the objective of providing a sound education in the humanities *and* the sciences. Unchecked, this trend alone can deepen C. P. Snow's gulf into a permanent chasm across which no bridge of mutual understanding will ever be constructed and maintained.

Such doubters—whose own educations have most likely been limited exclusively to narrow specialization in science or engineering—typically believe that anything worth knowing can be discovered via scientific methods. A look into the history of the split between the sciences and the humanities will show how false is this belief in only one way of knowing; different kinds of objects of knowledge require different methods for their investigation.

Inquiry guided by questions such as "What constitutes a life worth living?" cannot be conducted as though we were investigating the electrical properties of metals, for example. Assessing the quality of life is an entirely different process, built on a different tradition of investigation and another way of "knowing."

Because I believe that both humanist and scientist are seeking true knowledge, I will try to show that it is wrong to regard either way as perfectly suited to understanding the world—one pursuing truth quantifiably and the other, qualitatively. Each approach is valid but incomplete; each serves as a much-needed complement to the other. This insight offers guidance for considering how the rift between the two cultures can be reconciled so that we can develop a comprehensive and critical vision of the world.

IMPLICATIONS FOR THE CLASSROOM

Because the rift between the sciences and the humanities has come to have such far-reaching consequences, it is imperative for educators to take the lead in building bridges that will give all students—regardless of career objective—access to and facility with knowledge on both sides of that rift. We must draw upon Americans' fundamental belief in a broad and balanced vision—that no aspect of our national life should become the exclusive domain of any single group. For example, lay people serve on juries as guarantee that the public can act as a check to assure fairness in the legal system and to guard against tyranny by expertise. Similarly, our system demands that a civilian be the commander-in-chief of the armed services, again to ensure that the wider view is at all times considered. And, as citizens, we are familiar with and understand the system of checks and balances within our government. Without the ability to continue to provide the polity with the knowledge that they need—from the sciences *and* from the humanities—this system cannot function.

It is critical for all students to understand that the search for truth, is *everyone's domain,* and each person's responsibility, regardless of vantage point. Building bridges across the rift is thus especially important because the degree to which we can show students various modes of truth-seeking and various forms of productive behavior is, to a great extent, the degree to which we will be able to succeed in letting them find their own ways to pursue the truth. This process must begin in kindergarten. As students become familiar with the processes and products on both sides of the rift, they can develop both into active users of data and people who respect multiple viewpoints.

Because our society is becoming increasingly technical—some feel at an exponential rate—we must give our students as broad-based an education as possible. If the only constant is change, then those who are narrowly educated, who have only one "way of knowing" (and lack even an understanding of how that tradition developed) are doomed to obsolescence the moment that the next crop of students learns newer developments. No one knows this better than engineers. Thus science students not only must come to understand the history of science—of the interaction between science and the greater society throughout history—but also have to recognize their responsibility to become as well rounded as possible in order to understand themselves and appreciate multiple viewpoints.

Students who lean toward scientific disciplines need instruction in and interaction with the humanities, including languages, art, music, and of course, history. Only then can the scientist develop the necessary understanding of the implications of his or her research. An education that balances scientific knowledge with humanistic knowledge serves to enrich the soul and allows scientists to comprehend more fully the complexity of life in the social sphere. Tolstoi put us all on warning when he said, "Science is meaningless because it gives no answer to our question, the only question important for us: 'What shall we do and how shall we live?'"[5] We must give our future scientists the wherewithal to address Tolstoi's question.

In order to prepare children for a rapidly changing world, we ought to offer them a broad education. To carry this out within the limits of the school curriculum and school year calls for innovations in the content of courses and in the ways they are taught. We may have to surrender the narrow assumption that the teaching of the sciences has no relation to the teaching of the humanities—and vice versa. I do not ask that disciplinary boundaries be ignored. Rather, I urge that knowledge generated within one discipline be used to enhance learning in other fields.

The point can easily be illustrated: it is a fairly simple matter to include some history of science and technology in a history course. The laws of physics as applied to the development of elevation, for example, are a vital part of an urban culture—without elevators we would have no modern cities. The same integration is vital for understanding each historical era. Similarly, history can be incorporated into mathematics classes. Students should learn that Descartes invented coordinate geometry and Newton, calculus, in order to solve particular methodological problems in their scientific investigations. In literature courses, students can profit from reading the writings of scientists who, after all, include some of our greatest humanists. *The Double Helix*, Crick and Watson's exciting account of investigations into the structure of DNA, is but one example of many excellent texts. Lewis Thomas's *Lives of a Cell* is another. Stephen Jay Gould's writings serve as the ideal example of the possibilities and benefits derived from bridging the gap.[6] Moreover, writing ought to be an important part of science classes; learning to make concise, step-by-step outlines of procedures is an analytic skill useful in many contexts. And science can enhance humanities and art classes: introduction to the principles of the geometry of perspective, the chemistry and physics of color, and the physics of musical instruments are some obvious examples.

The success of such a curriculum hinges on the proper preparation of students, beginning in the earliest grades. Teachers themselves will have to be educated broadly enough to be able to nurture beginning skills and knowledge—of science and math, as well as of language, history, social studies, and art—in ways that suggest the complementarity of all knowledge. Without a doubt, this means that we will also have to change the ways we recruit and train teachers. Students cannot be expected to acquire true cultural literacy unless we give them teacher models who are themselves culturally literate. Schools of education have a responsibility to see that teacher-training programs do not encourage narrow specialization to the neglect of broad general knowledge.

Finally, those in decision-making positions must resist the temptation to succumb to prevailing pressures for enlarging science and mathematics curricula at the expense of literature, history, and language courses. Their solemn obligation is to ensure that American education remains well balanced. We cannot expect young people to make well-informed decisions about career specializations until we have given them knowledge of the alternatives and a chance to explore their talents.

This is a tall order. There is already too much to do in school and too little time in which to do it. But when we understand what is at stake, I think that we will all be more than willing to work together. By drawing on knowledge from our own various disciplines, the perspectives of our own vantage points, and the wisdom born of our own experiences, we not only will make the rift easier to bridge but will also be teaching our students by example. There is no better teacher than example, and no more effective lesson than one that exhibits a congruence of message and method. We who care about the schools cannot make the two cultures one. But we can and should take as our solemn responsibility to prepare every student, using the best that each has to offer, and enriching each student's life with the valuable knowledge, ideas, and possibilities contained in each.

NOTES

1. C. P. Snow, *The Two Cultures and the Scientific Revolution* (New York: Cambridge University Press, 1963), pp. 60–61. For a rather vigorous, even vituperative rebuttal to Snow's thesis, see F. R. Leavis, *Two Cultures? The Significance of C. P. Snow,* with an essay by Michael Yudkin (London: Chatto & Windus, 1962). Snow's responses to Leavis's attacks can be found in *The Two Cultures: And a Second Look* (Cambridge, Eng.: Cambridge University Press, 1965) and in *Public Affairs* (New York: Charles Scribner's Sons, 1971).
2. Steven B. Graubard, Preface to special issue, "Scientific Literacy," *Daedalus* 112 (Spring 1983): 5.
3. "Reaching beyond the Rational," *Time,* April 23, 1973, pp. 49–52.
4. C. P. Snow, *The Two Cultures and the Scientific Revolution,* p. 61.
5. Max Weber, *Essays in Sociology,* edited by H. H. Gerth and C. Wright Mills (New York: Oxford University Press, 1973), p. 143.
6. James D. Watson, *The Double Helix: A Personal Account of the Discovery of the Structure of DNA* (New York: Atheneum, 1968); Lewis Thomas, *Lives of a Cell* (New York: Viking Press, 1974); Stephen Jay Gould, *The Mismeasure of Man* (Norton: New York, 1981).

Chapter 6

A Usable History for a Multicultural State

CHARLES WOLLENBERG

A wise observer of this state once noted that California "is like the rest of the United States, only more so." That certainly is true for the ethnic composition of the population. It is also true for its ethnic and cultural history. Just as the United States is and has been a multiethnic, multicultural society, so is California—only very much more so.

Minorities or Third World people now make up 20 percent of the United States' population; and they account for at least one-third of California. This includes about 5.5 million people of Latin American origin, 1.8 million blacks, 1.75 million Asians and Pacific Islanders, and over 200,000 Native Americans. Moreover, minority numbers are growing far more rapidly than is the population as a whole. Between 1940 and 1980, as California's population more than tripled, the numbers of Hispanics and blacks increased more than tenfold. Since the immigration law reforms of 1965 and the establishment of refugee provisions for Indo-Chinese in the 1970s, the Asian population also has exploded. By the year 2000, Asians probably will have passed blacks to become the state's second-largest minority.[1]

The burgeoning of California's ethnic population is a historical development of national as well as state and local significance. The great influx of Asians and the even greater migration of Hispanics into the state have made California the destination of more than a quarter of all foreign immigrants to the United States. This figure, incidentally, is for legal immigration; if undocumented aliens were included, the percentage would be even higher. Early in the twenty-first century, California probably will become the nation's first mainland state to have a majority of minorities. Or, to put it another way, there will be no majority group in California's population.[2] California's two great urban centers, the Los Angeles and San Francisco Bay areas, are for the late twentieth century what New York and Boston were for the late nineteenth: major entry points for a new wave of immigration that is changing the nature of American society.

The schools of California will have a majority of minorities even before the twenty-first century. In the 1981–82 academic year, minorities already comprised over 50 percent of all kindergarten and first-grade public school students. In Los Angeles, by far the state's largest school district, non-Hispanic whites, who accounted for 50 percent of total student enrollment in 1970, made up only 21 percent in 1984. Hispanics alone account for half of the Los Angeles district's 556,000 students; and more than a quarter of those in Los Angeles schools are enrolled in bilingual education programs.[3]

Given these ethnic percentages, the question "What shall we teach?" in the history classrooms in the schools—which is the theme of this study—is an especially appropriate one. Clearly, the history that we teach should help students better understand the dynamic society in which they live. That history should be "multicultural" in that it recognizes and respects social and ethnic diversity, past and present. This emphasis on diversity is derived not from a political or cultural ideology, but from historical and present-day reality. To be sure, the history/social science curriculum must teach both immigrant and non-immigrant students about the origins and applications of American traditions, values, and constitutional and political principles. But in our concern about a new wave of immigration, we must avoid reverting to the "Americanization" curricula of the early twentieth century. These programs, with their uncritical ("my country right or wrong") style of American nationalism and their adherence to a narrow, "white Anglo-Saxon Protestant" view of American culture, unnecessarily denigrated the rich heritages of ethnic and immigrant minorities. Our aim should not be to impose contemporary values and viewpoints upon the past, but to help young people understand the historical roots of modern American society.

State history is an appropriate vehicle for teaching students about the historical roots of the multiethnic, multicultural society in which they live. The history of virtually any state in the United States can serve this purpose—California's only more so. However, to create a usable past through state history, we must avoid the provincialism and romanticism that has characterized so much of the state history traditionally taught in the schools. The traditional, romantic view of California history, enshrined in so many textbooks of a generation ago, is obviously inappropriate. Although the happy pageant of docile Indians, kindly friars, and colorful Forty-Niners may entertain, it certainly does not enlighten. At best this approach produces nostalgia—a perfectly pleasant emotion, but surely not the basis for good history. Dr. J. S. Holliday, Director of the California Historical Society, calls nostalgia "the past without its pain." Good history, however, even as it documents the pleasure of the past, cannot ignore the pain.[5] Nostalgia also presupposes a separation between past and present, making history become a comfortable refuge from contemporary cares and woes. We, on the other hand, seek a history that promotes understanding of present-day problems and conditions.

In the 1960s many young historians, influenced by black and other Third World protest movements, began seriously investigating the role of minorities in California's past. Our results (for I was one of these once-young scholars) stood as a welcome reaction to the Anglo emphasis of much of the state's earlier historiography. But some of the new studies did little more than document the presence of particular ethnic groups at a certain time and place. Minorities were often portrayed only as victims or role models and, while neither portrayal is necessarily inaccurate, neither yields a complete and well-rounded picture of ethnic group experience in California life. Finally, the emphasis on particular minorities has carried with it the danger that California history may become a series of individual, isolated chronicles of group experiences with no unifying social synthesis. In short, as immensely valuable as has been the historical scholarship on California minorities that began in the 1960s, by itself it has not turned out to be the usable, multicultural history that we seek.[6]

Whether such a historical synthesis is even possible is debatable, for the very dynamism and diversity of California's social development makes synthesizing a very difficult task. Since 1849, there probably has never been a time when a majority of California residents actually were natives of the state. Rather, from the Gold Rush to the present, the social history of California in large part has been a series of great, overlapping migrations. Lou Cannon, one of the most perceptive observers of state politics, has made the point that Ronald Reagan, rather than Richard Nixon, is the first true California president, in part precisely because, unlike Nixon, Reagan was *not* born there. He came to California from Illinois, the state that produced the largest number of new California residents during the early thirties.[7] If Reagan, a transplanted midwesterner, is the "true" Californian, then it follows that Californians, as a people, may not have a common history but may instead represent many different histories brought from different parts of the nation and the world.

James Houston, however, has argued that, while the *people* of California may not have a common history, the *place* called California certainly does.[8] I believe that this history of the place can provide, if not a social synthesis, at least common themes and experiences on which to base a useful understanding of the state's past. There is, of course, the natural environment that has dramatically affected the pace of human development. The continuing significance of water as a major political issue is just one obvious illustration of that fact. Another is the ongoing role of climate and landscape in attracting new residents to California.

Human institutions and economic, political, and cultural systems also belong to the place's common history. A Mexican farm worker arriving in the San Joaquin Valley may know or care nothing about the history of California agribusiness, but he is nevertheless affected by it—indeed is an integral part of that history. Similarly, an Asian immigrant family coming to Oakland or Los Angeles may not be aware of the development of urban transportation in California, but that family probably will live in a neighborhood whose character has been shaped by past interurban rail systems and present-day freeways. Of course, all Californians are touched by a political and legal system founded on Anglo-American concepts of government and justice, just as all are affected by the English language and its accompanying heritage of thought, culture, and literature.

All Californians also are influenced by the state's rather exaggerated version of American popular culture. Pop culture, largely the product of our mass consumption capitalist economy, may, for good or ill, be the strongest unifying force in American life. And much of that culture—from network television shows and movies to Levis and ranch-style suburban homes—has a "Made in California" label. Even motels and gas stations were invented in California.

It is not surprising to learn—though unfortunately as a result of a tragic mass murder—that a McDonald's restaurant was a major social center and gathering place in the largely Hispanic community of San Ysidro. Nor, I suppose, would we be surprised that a Los Angeles cafe featuring kosher burritos is owned by a Korean and has a Guatemalan cook. I could argue that popular culture is not "real culture," if by that we mean a series of deep, commonly held values and traditions. But, whatever it is, pop culture does produce common experiences, images, and elements of a lifestyle shared by most Californians, whatever their ethnic and national origin.

Finally, virtually all Californians are united by the common heritage of migration itself. All of us, except those of California Indian background, are here because of past or present migration or immigration from somewhere else. This, of course, is true for the United States as a whole—but in this, as I have said, California is like the rest of the nation, only more so.

Interrelationships among different national and ethnic groups attracted to California during successive waves of migration are, in fact, the underlying dynamic of the state's social history. An economic historian might argue that the economic development necessary to draw millions of newcomers to the state is the foundation of California history;

but, beyond that, migration itself has stimulated vast material growth by creating new human demands and needs and by furnishing new sources of labor, talent, and entrepreneurial ambition. The struggles for power, wealth, and prestige among these groups lie at the root of much of the state's bitter heritage of racial conflict and oppression. Race, national origin, and class have always intersected in California—again, I would argue, to an even greater degree here than in the nation as a whole. Ongoing migration, then—the process that makes it hard to conceive of a common history for the *people* of California—is, ironically, the unifying theme of the social history of the *place* called California.

From this perspective, many familiar events of California's past take on new meaning. The original Spanish-Mexican settlements, for example, are significant in part because they represent the beginning of the area's multicultural heritage. The mission Indians, though a numerical majority, were, in terms of power and economic role, California's first minority group. They were forced into various menial occupations (such as agricultural labor), which ever since have been held primarily by ethnic minorities. Colonial Hispanics also began a migration north from Mexico, which, though periodically waxing and waning, has been a part of California life ever since the eighteenth century.

The Gold Rush, too, is often misunderstood. It, rather than the formal United States conquest in 1846, determined the nature of California's place in the American nation and political union. The issue of California statehood in 1850 produced the last compromise between North and South before the Civil War. The Gold Rush also produced the state's first modern multinational migration. While a majority of new arrivals came from the settled parts of the United States, significant minorities arrived from Europe, Latin America, Asia, and the Pacific Islands as well. San Francisco, a metropolis created by the Gold Rush, has been one of the nation's most ethnically and nationally diverse urban centers ever since. The city's political and social life, as well as the history of its often-powerful labor movement, has always been intimately related to the interplay of the various groups within its diverse population.

Completion of the transcontinental railroad in 1869 is another key event that needs reinterpretation. It dramatically broadened the state's economic and social base, promoting development and settlement of the Central Valley and allowing agriculture to replace mining as California's biggest business. Even more important, railroad construction opened southern California to rapid growth, beginning the process that would result in the nation's second-largest metropolitan region. The rail lines, particularly, attracted to the Southland new arrivals from the Midwest and laborers from Mexico. Even as San Francisco, the far West's first great city, became the center of nineteenth-century Chinese immigration, so Los Angeles, the new metropolis, was the heartland for early twentieth-century arrivals from Japan. Economic development—based on oil, irrigated by agriculture, tourism, and movies—combined with the multiethnic population and a decentralized settlement pattern encouraged electric rail systems, to make Los Angeles the prototype Sunbelt city. In the automobile age, it was to be the model for the new Houstons, Dallases, and Phoenixes (not to mention San Diego and San Jose) that were to emerge after World War II.

The war itself remains another event whose significance to California has been misunderstood or completely ignored. In fact, World War II was to the 1940s, 1950s, and 1960s what the Gold Rush had been to the 1840s, 1850s, and 1860s: an historical watershed of almost revolutionary proportions. More than any other event, that war produced contemporary California.

World War II began a three-decade period of growth that created the nation's most populous state and the world's seventh-largest economy. (The Los Angeles metropolitan region alone has the globe's fourteenth-largest gross product.) The war also laid the base for California's aerospace and high technology industrial economy, its massive higher education system, and its dominant postwar suburban lifestyle. Although World War II did produce the horror of Japanese relocation, it also brought about the beginning of massive increases in black and Hispanic populations. The struggle against Adolf Hitler and Nazism kicked many of the ideological props out from beneath the racist value system that had been so much a part of prewar California life. Without the social, demographic, and economic changes set into motion by World War II, it is difficult to imagine the great protests and countercultural movements of the 1960s occurring as they did.

Again, though certainly I would not claim any of these postwar phenomena to be uniquely Californian, I would argue that in these areas too California was like the rest of the nation—indeed, the rest of western industrial society—only more so. It is precisely this broad perspective of California history, with its multiethnic emphasis and common themes linking past and present, that makes the subject so attractive for classroom use.[9] This kind of California history can teach students a great deal about the nation and the world as well. It can also teach them something about human diversity, the nature of prejudice and oppression, and about the value of democratic tolerance and individual and social justice. Teachers can illustrate these lessons by familiar rather than far-removed or abstract examples.

The history of the *place* called California is a resource to be cherished rather than (as is so often true now) ignored or debased. That history is one of the few things that can be held in common by the diverse residents of this multifaceted and confusing part of the United States. It can help us to understand more deeply ourselves, our neighbors, our society, and even our world. California history need not be provincial; it can be understood as part of the broadest possible framework of human experience.

Developing usable history for a multicultural state can, in fact, be an important part of survival in a multicultural world. I have been talking about California, a state that is probably unique in its diversity among the fifty; each of the others, however, has its own particular ethnic and cultural history. Teachers and educators in those states may, I hope, find this kind of approach a useful springboard for enriching the teaching of state and local history in their areas of the country.

NOTES

1. The most convenient source of demographic information on California is James Fay, Anne G. Lipow, and Stephanie Fay, eds., *California Almanac* (Novato, CA: Presidio Press, 1984), sections 1–3.
2. Ibid. See also "The Optimists: A Survey of California's Economy," *The Economist* (May 19–25, 1984), survey section 1–22.
3. Bernard R. Gifford, *The Good School of Education: Linking Knowledge, Teaching and Learning* (Berkeley: Graduate School of Education, University of California, 1984), table 3, p. 72; Robert Lindsey, "Los Angeles," *New York Times Magazine* (July 22, 1984), pp. 28–31, 62–67.
4. For statewide history guidelines in the schools, see California State Department of Education, *California Framework for History-Social Studies in the K-12 Program* (Sacramento, 1981), and "History Social Sciences SD 013 Model Curriculum Standards" (draft), (Sacramento, 1984).
5. J. S. Holliday, "Resources for Teaching California History" (presentation at Clio Conference, Berkeley, August 1984). For a critique of public school California History texts, see Richard DeLuca "In Search of the Real California: History in the Fourth Grade Textbook" (prepared for the Clio Conference, Berkeley, August 1984).
6. For examples of the treatment of minorities in the late 1960s and early 1970s scholarship, see Roger Daniels and Spencer C. Olin, eds., *Racism in California: A Reader on the History of Oppression* (New York: 1972); George E. Frakes and Curtis B. Solberg, *Minorities in California* (New York: Random House, 1971); Robert F. Heizer and Alan J. Almquist, *The Other Californians* (Berkeley: University of California Press, 1971); Anne Loftis, *California: Where the Twain Did Meet* (New York: Macmillan, 1973); Charles Wollenberg, ed., *Ethnic Conflict in California History* (Los Angeles: Tinnon-Brown, 1970) and Roger Olmsted and Charles Wollenberg, eds., *Neither Separate nor Equal* (San Francisco: California Historical Society, 1971). For a critique of such scholarship, see Lawrence B. DeGraaf, "Recognition, Racism and Reflections on the Writings of Western Black History", *Pacific Historical Review* (February 1975), pp. 22–51. Chicano historians have pioneered in a more sophisticated coverage of California ethnic experience. See Albert Camarillo, *Chicanos in a Changing Society* (Cambridge: Harvard University Press, 1979) and Richard Griswold del Castillo, *The Los Angeles Barrio* (Berkeley: University of California Press, 1979).
7. Lou Cannon, "The Winning of the East," *California Magazine* (August 1984), pp. 106–112.

8. James Houston, *Californians* (New York: Knopf, 1982), p. 272.
9. For discussions of the use of state and local history in the schools, see Fay Metcalf and Matthew Downey, *Using Local Sources in the Classroom* (Nashville: American Society for State and Local History, 1982); also Karen Jorgensen-Esmaili, "Another Look at Community History" (prepared for Clio Conference, Berkeley, August 1984).

Chapter 7

American History and the Idea of Common Culture

NATHAN I. HUGGINS

All history is abstraction, generalizations on human experience. I think none of us would make the mistake of assuming that the history we teach and write about is identical to what happened in the past—the events and experiences themselves. Students and teachers of history have long looked at written history as deliberately selective. The historian chooses his subject, asks what he considers the most crucial and necessary questions, selects his data, and constructs his argument and narrative with an eye toward discriminating between that which he finds compelling and essential and that which appears incidental and of no consequence.

Different moments, we all know, urge different necessities; and in a different time, a different historian will ask different questions, discover significance in data others believed dross, construct different order, and tell a different story.

Generally, those who make these commonplace observations want to remind us of the essentially creative and subjective character of history—at bottom always one of the humanities, even as it borrows heavily from the methodologies and techniques of the social sciences. I wish instead to make a different kind of point, or, rather, to emphasize a different facet. The necessarily discriminatory character of historical writing and teaching makes the product an abstraction of experience, not the comprehensive experience itself.

History orders and gives meaning to experience *because* it is selective. Of course, it is unthinkable to try to be comprehensive and inclusive, even about the smallest slice of history. There are too many angels on the head of a pin, one might say, to count them all individually. As we give meaning and order to the jumble of the past, we should always be aware that something or, rather, some things are being left out—things that are important and meaningful in themselves and important to those who find themselves bound to kindred experiences and destinies. Another kind of historical dispensation may feature what others ignored.

History, then, is in some sense like a road map. It abstracts reality so as to give shape and possible utility. Many towns do not appear on even the best road maps, and it does not really matter to us as we whiz past on the expressway. We can ignore that geographical spot and its inhabitants, all incognito, and we won't lose our way. At the same time, however, we must understand that the place has enormous importance for its residents, who would be lost if they did not exist on their own "maps." Chances are, those townsfolk see the surrounding territory, their state, the nation, and the world in some sense differently from the rest of us precisely because they are not "on the map." Part of the argument for our thinking about them as we contemplate the "big picture" is that their view is likely to be a useful distortion of reality divergent from our own.

At the risk of going on too long with this analogy, we should think about how people at different times have conceived of regions of the world as reflected in cartographical representations. We do not have to go too far back into the past to find on maps of the period vast regions of terra incognita, often thought of as uninhabited. Time, exploration, and knowledge subsequently have filled in those blank spaces with physical characteristics—mountains, rivers, deserts, and even evidence of human habitation. It is important to make conscious note of the obvious: those spaces never were *really* empty except for those who found in them no useful meaning. It is our loss that we are likely never to know what view of the world the inhabitants of those regions had.

Only when we think about the past in this way can we appreciate the chauvinism and ethnocentrism in concepts of discovery. It is more than a clever twist of words to say that native Americans "discovered" Europeans only when the latter landed on these shores. If we could understand both attitudes of that process of mutual discovery, we might gain useful insight into a moment of history unavailable to us who have been taught that the only reality was that as perceived by those considered to be our cultural forebears.

This is of capital importance when we think of how American history has been written and taught. We have allowed vast areas to be dismissed as terra incognita. We have imagined that for all practical purposes the continent was empty until the coming of English settlers—American Indians often being confounded with the wilderness. We have essentially dismissed French and Spanish settlement in the "New World"—even on territory that would later become part of the United States—until contact or westward expansion made it necessary to include in telling the story. Written American history said virtually nothing about Spanish culture in the West and Southwest, not to mention its ignorance of French Louisiana. By now, it is well enough known that blacks, Asians, native Americans, and other ethnics and so-called minorities were treated, until the past decade or so, as "not on the map" of American history. But that is only a small part of the matter. The history we have written, read, and taught has so generally assumed that American history was about New England, New York City, and something generally vague called the South (meaning slavery, plantations, aristocracy, poverty, backwardness, racism, and the like) that we are at a loss to understand regions of our country that are now beginning to determine much of the country's politics and character.

Experience and necessity, however, are determining. Empty spaces in the historical landscape do get filled in when demands of the present—our need to understand our lives, our problems, where we are—compel us to give concrete representation to what we might earlier have dismissed as "not on the map." The reason historians turn their attention to peoples and subjects once ignored is that the problems of our time now demand a knowledge of them that we have not had before. True, some historians may have taken up Afro-American, Asian-American, native American, and other ethnic histories out of a sense of fairness to "victims" of the past; but the reason these studies will continue to have a place (and a growing importance) in American historiography is because we have learned that we must know about them to know anything well. We are told that California in the 1990s will be a "Third World state." If we are to produce good histories of California for that future population, we are going to have to know a lot more than we now do about the experiences of native Americans; peoples from the Pacific; and immigrants from Mexico, Central America, and the Caribbean Basin. It is not merely because it is a nice thing to let such people learn about themselves (a lure for them to learn other important things, too), but because no one can understand the territory without such knowledge.

This is an important distinction because those who wish now to argue for American history as "common culture" do not, to my mind, fully understand the new emphasis on ethnic histories. They assume only some unfair imbalance in past histories that perhaps needed redressing. "Of course," they say, "blacks should not have been left out of American history. But we have gone far enough now to guarantee them visibility and fair treatment. The danger is that we have gone too far; our history is fragmented. By our focus on the particular, we have lost sight of the whole. What is needed now is to rearticulate those common values that make us all Americans. We need the kind of American history we used to have, that told essentially *one* story to *one* people."

The problem is, however, that our social geography is far different from that of two decades ago—spaces we once thought empty are now too insistent and demanding. We do not know enough yet about what fills those spaces to understand fully how they inform our present and future, but we cannot be as complacent in our ignorance as we once were. Understanding what we used to call our pilgrim fathers will help us to understand something about America and California, but in 1990 we will also know a great deal that departs from that tradition.

The history that will best serve the coming generation will be no less an abstraction of the American past than those we have studied and written. What is included will have to give shape and meaning to the past for a population quite different from that of this generation. A shift of focus and emphasis will mean that some values once thought of as dominant will be subordinated to others. Coming generations of Americans are likely to find a reality that discovers meaning and importance more in pluralism than in oneness. The dominant historical questions will naturally reflect that shift even at the cost of presumed common culture. Those who most fear such a result see it as a loss of national unity and identity. What, after all, is the principal reason for studying national history if not to see oneself as part of a large tradition and order?

The problem raised by the question of "common culture" is really the problem of a national history. If by nature history is an abstraction, national histories are so in a special way. The need to define the nation as a coherent whole obliges one to obliterate or subordinate those particular groups who would lay claim to an independent or an alternative generalization. The nation-state came about by subsuming the many into one; and it succeeds best when individual groups are able to submerge themselves comfortably into the large abstraction of the nation.

This has always been an implicit problem in United States history. Always a pluralistic nation, we have become more dramatically and divergently so in the late twentieth century. Historians—and all Americans—have dealt with the problem in various ways. We thought of the frontier as the Americanizing experience. Significantly, historians discovered the power of the frontier only when it was perceived by some to be closing in the face of rising immigration. Then there was the melting pot—the assumption that the crucible of the American experience would produce an "American" from the polyglot population that streamed to these shores. At no time—certainly not since the Civil War—have Americans ever been comfortable with the pluralistic reality of the American nation. That reality notwithstanding, we have tried to fashion a story to serve as the nation's common history—subordinating a great deal of human experience and particularity by the way. A lot of what has happened in the last twenty years attests to the failure of that story. The problem is, can we fashion a new one? Should we?

While the problem of national history has a special force in America, it is certainly not peculiar to Americans. Merely glancing at other national histories with which we might be familiar, we see how the Welsh and the Scots resist being swallowed into a common British history. The same can be said of the Celts in Brittany who want to keep their language and culture from being erased by a dominant French history in the name of nationality. Surely the same point can be made for minorities in Italy, Germany, Eastern Europe, and Russia. Those of us who prefer the superhighways of national history feel no great loss in not knowing much about these groups and their aspirations. But what some would dismiss as mere particularism means a great deal to those involved. History has shown that such groups will not efface themselves for our sakes; indeed, they show universally a remarkable and often annoying tenacity. We would do well to know more about particular ethnic elements in those countries than about some abstraction called the nation. That, too, is true of America. National histories basically are ideological constructions, which rest on the premise that the defined whole is greater than the sum of its parts—an assumption always contradicted by those who feel themselves defined as much by the part as by the whole.

A stress on "common culture" turns history into a tool of national unity, mandated principally by those anxious about national order and coherence. Leaving aside the vague and unscientific use of the term "culture," we see nonetheless that, without some organizing principles, some imposed structure, something we all can assent to as ours, the radical variety of experience threatens chaos.

At a very abstract level, all humankind shares common values, aspirations, and "culture." In the years immediately following World War II, a photographic exhibit at New York's Museum of Modern Art calling itself "The Family of Man" wanted to make exactly that point. But that concept is too abstract and general to serve national needs. That which could serve as a common heritage (values or what have you) must be general enough to cover the kaleidoscopic variety of our social life yet particular enough to distinguish us from others. It is not a simple task. Those pushing for a "common culture," however, seem to believe that repeatedly asserting the need for discovering the formula is enough.

I suspect that advocates of "common culture" do not see their position as debatable because: (1) they do not recognize the sources of their concerns as ideological—like most ideologues, to themselves their arguments are common sense; and (2) they have no problem understanding and defining the shared, common "culture"—it is, simply, what they recognize as their own. I have heard no advocate of "common culture" who did not assume that "everyone should recognize that *my* story is *our* story." During a long part of American history, immigrants and others seemed willing to try it, and there will always be those who will accept whatever is the dominant "culture" as their own. But it will not work for long; and what was accepted as dominant will change.

Until the end of World War II, in one form or another, the Bancroft myth of American history served as a frame within which to build the national myth and history. It defined the common culture in terms of an Anglo-Saxon tradition that, however badly it fit reality, was generally accepted. The first cracks in that structure, that myth, appeared in the 1940s and 1950s—years that saw a growing emphasis on social history and a new focus on particular peoples and their experiences. Some complained, seeing that these changes shattered the common history that had served the nation since the nineteenth century. But the problem was that the children of immigrants, it seemed, wanted to change the story. In 1962 Carl Bridenbaugh voiced these anxieties in his presidential address to the American Historical Association:

> Historians of our Recent Past shared a common culture, a body of literary knowledge to which allusion could be usefully made. . . . Today we must face the discouraging prospect that we all, teachers and pupils alike, have lost much of what this earlier generation possessed, the priceless asset of a shared culture. Today imaginations have become starved or stunted, and wit and humor, let alone laughter and a healthy frivolity, are seldom encountered. Furthermore, many of the younger practitioners of our craft, and those who are still apprentices, are products of lower middle-class or foreign origins, and their emotions not infrequently get in the way of historical reconstruction. They find themselves in a very real sense outsiders of our past and feel themselves shut out. This is certainly not their fault but it is true. They have no experience to assist them, and the chasm between them and the Remote Past widens every hour. . . . What I fear is that the changes observant in the background and training of the present generation will make it impossible for them to communicate to and reconstruct the past for future generations.

Bridenbaugh's anxieties were not unlike those who today are concerned with the "common culture." Now, ironically, the problem is being raised by those very people whom Bridenbaugh described as "outsiders." By birth and class, Bridenbaugh saw himself as conversant with what he called the "Remote Past," which he feared was being lost forever. The present group at least grants the possibility of sharing, within the radical diversity. It is more democratic. Yet, I disagree with them all because I believe they are unaware of what drives their demands—which I see as ideological sets leading to a national and inspirational history. Too many descendants of immigrants would have all students finishing high school American history knowing that they are "American" and exactly why they should be proud of it. "Common culture," in this sense, is an indoctrination into normative standards and "values" (another vague word now in favor).

Though I do not like this rather benign formulation, I sense something even more ominous when I hear casual talk of teaching "our common values." Given its normative implications, it translates into indoctrination into how we *ought* to think about things. I am more comfortable with variety than conformity, and I think our values will manage to get across without being deliberately promoted.

The questions to be raised in history are not so much the values we do or do not share but, rather, how we interpret past events. Those very elements that advocates of "common culture" find most to be taken for granted are the crux of dispute because of differing perspectives on the past. The Declaration of Independence is the most frequently used illustration of values all Americans hold in common: all men are created equal, and so on. Putting aside for the moment a fact that all students of American history should know—that there always were and there continue to be Americans who do not subscribe to those values—and even assuming that all do accept such statements as describing our national ideals, we will nevertheless diverge sharply and reasonably about how those ideals relate to American history.

We might all agree that American history reveals a gap between ideals and reality. Some might say that the important thing is to bridge the gap by accepting such values, taking them seriously and trying, however imperfectly, to live up to them. Others, looking at the same history, would stress the persistence of the gap—that is, the failure of Americans to honor the principle except when forced to by circumstance. The question is whether the glass is half full or half empty—not a matter of values but one of ideological perspective. I do not think it the historian's role to insist, for reasons of national interest, that the more positive perspective is more valid, while the other is mere cynicism. The historian should see questions from as many perspectives as possible. The historian should find it a blessing rather than a burden that variety—ethnic, regional, or what have you—forces him to look at the same problem from different angles. My point is not that the historian should avoid having a personal point of view. But he should recognize that it is but one among several; and he should be willing to give respectful attention to perspectives not his own.

I would argue, rather, that the role of history is not to promote a nation, a people, or a cause. Nor is it the function of history to make us feel good about the accident of our birth in the best of all possible countries. In 1971, in an essay in *Key Issues in the Afro-American Experience*, I wrote of the need to argue that same point against the popular view that the reason for writing and studying Afro-American history was to learn about heroes and heroines in "our" past, to discover "our" identity, and to create alternative myths to those of the dominant culture. Such history serves all America and a "common culture" no better than it does blacks.

Yet, after all of this has been said, a real problem remains for teachers of American history in the schools. Even granting the radical diversity of the country and recognizing the importance, in the school subjects children study, of legitimizing different heritages, should not American youngsters learn something in common? Should not some basis for discourse span ethnic and regional borders? To ask the question is to answer, Yes. Yet, how does one teach American history to a class in San Francisco—the class being made up of Irish-, Italian-, Chinese-, Japanese-, Filipino-, Afro-, Jewish-, and native Americans? Should they not all know something in common with their peers throughout the country? How can one teach that and still be open to the variety of perspectives implicit within that heterogeneous class?

I do believe that there is an irreducible body of information about the American past that all high school graduates ought to know. That "core" should comprise mainly the history of political and social institutions, their development, and their practice. Students ought to know how American institutions developed, and how and why they differed from those in the "Old World," including England. Naturally, this study would expose students to the ideological foundations of American institutions; and through such instruction they would have to become familiar with those values and principles through which American political and social life have found sustenance. Such a core of knowledge is essential to active and constructive life as a citizen in the United States. In that sense, it is a skill—like literacy or practical arithmetic. One can share this kind of knowledge with everyone else in the country, seeing oneself defined either by the generality of America or some particular part of it.

Aside from this core, history has another important role to play, a role peculiar to the discipline and having nothing to do with promoting common cultures. History is one of the humanities because, by studying it, one is forced to look seriously at experiences *other than one's own.* Even when we look at the lives of our forebears, we should understand they *are not ourselves.* It is essential to understand this point. Black Americans, for instance, who fail to recognize that they are not the same as slaves will never understand slavery. The present provides us with a different perspective on as well as a different knowledge of the past, and that distancing makes historical study informative and exciting. Maintaining that distance, we can analyze and attempt to understand the process of change and speculate on cause.

This opportunity to view the past from a continually new vantage point defines, in my view, what is peculiar to history as a discipline, and this is why one studies it—as an intellectual endeavor. It is not to celebrate heroes or the good fortune of our birth. It is not to develop patriotism; and, except as it draws us into the common human experience, it is not to make us feel one with our countrymen. Though these may be good things to do, they are not reasons why one should study, teach, or write history.

The discipline required by history is indifferent to content. Any history will do: Greek, Chinese, African, native American. All that is required is data that can be used for historical analysis and the will on someone's part to organize that data so as to give meaning to the whole. For the American historian, the pluralism of American life could inspire excitement in the possibilities rather than anxiety over the ever-illusory "common culture." There again, it matters whether one sees the glass as half full or half empty.

Part III
WHAT SHALL WE TEACH?

In our third section, a group of three distinguished historians—William McNeill, Peter Stearns, and Harry Scheiber—discuss the problem of history in the schools from the point of view of professional historians. As we have seen, history in the schools differs from history in the university. When university historians argue about what history should be taught in the schools, generally they are arguing about what they believe is good history—that whatever is "good history" is what should be taught. They are not concerned, for example, to promote social efficiency or citizenship. On the other hand, those who do argue that history in the schools ought to serve purposes outside of history itself also want it to be good history; specifically, they wish to concentrate on parts of history judged especially relevant to their concerns. McNeill, Stearns, and Scheiber present the case for sound historical practice and do not seek for justification outside of historical truth. Insofar as the main criterion of good teaching is sound historical practice, they can help us understand how world, social, and constitutional history should be taught.

As Hertzberg pointed out, university historians are separated from the schools by the extremely specialized nature of much of modern historical research as contrasted with the necessarily generalizing character of school-level history. William McNeill is widely recognized as a leading practitioner of generalized history in the historical profession today. In Professor McNeill's historical writings, broad themes that span centuries, indeed millennia, are common, as are themes that cross cultures. This broad view—the view that teachers of world history must adopt—poses inevitable problems.

Are there themes that can unify global history? Or must we be content to teach the different culture areas as if they were separate from one another and could be explained entirely by their internal dynamics? McNeill suggests that to select from among the overwhelming diversity of world history, the teacher of world history might use the theme of power. The teacher should focus on whatever civilization happens to be in the forefront of world civilization, whether it be Western Europe, China, or India. McNeill's view is that mankind has shown a progressive power to dominate his natural and human environment and that the mainstream of human history—which passes from one leading civilization to another—is this accumulating power. Human history thus becomes the cultural continuation of organic evolution. The student of history should learn to think of himself in relationship to an immense evolutionary whole, to put concerns of self or nation into a truly global perspective.

McNeill's view of history is not likely to suit the powerless, who will want to use history to validate their struggles; or those who seek for moral values, such as citizenship; or those who see history as a means by which we broaden ourselves by reexperiencing the cultures of peoples of the past whether or not those peoples enjoyed long periods of dominance. Also, the theme of power and progress is not as well adapted to the history of art or philosophy as it is to technology. Power is a standard that eliminates much. But McNeill is arguing that a world history course *must* be selective and must attempt to search out themes and stories from the vast panorama of world history; otherwise, the student will achieve only fragmentary knowledge. Power is one such standard.

Peter Stearns, one of America's best and most prolific social historians, discusses the vast expansion of the subfield of social history. That area—the history of everyday activity, of young people, of sports, of family life—has proven one means of reconciling the concerns of history with the interests of school children. Social history, however, remains more of a potential than a realized part of most school history programs. This is true in part because many teachers were trained in the era when social history had a very limited place in the larger field. Teachers familiar with social history have had difficulty adding an ambitious program of social history to an already crowded curriculum. Nevertheless, it seems certain that social history will soon become a much larger part of the history program in schools.

The question is not whether social history should be included, but rather how it will be integrated into the basic history course. Stearns offers two models. The first makes social history the core of the subject as a whole, so that, for example, the basic chronology of American history would be determined by social processes rather than by political events. This point of view would have the effect of making political history a satellite of the social history central core—an approach Stearns acknowledges as probably too radical to be readily acceptable. A second, more moderate, approach involves interpolating substantial segments of social history into the basic course of political history. Thus, Stearns suggests a segment on preindustrial economy and society within the history of colonial America; a segment on commercialization within the history of antebellum America; and a segment on industrialization and immigration within the history of late-nineteenth- and twentieth-century America.

Stearns warns of several dangers, many of which flow from the inherent strengths of social history. Its concern with everyday life naturally appeals to students, who come to understand that their own private concerns—with sports, love, and family—are part of history. Stearns warns that in capitalizing on this advantage social history should not degenerate into trivialities.

Stearns' essay is not only a piece of advocacy for social history, it is also, in itself, a sort of introduction to the subject. Teachers will benefit from his discussion of the various topics that fall within social history, from his suggestions on how to teach the subject, and from fascinating *obiter dicta* that indicate relationships between social, economic, and political history. Stearns has also supplied a bibliographical essay for American social history.

The impact of social history on other fields of history may be glimpsed in Harry Scheiber's essay on teaching American constitutional history. Scheiber, a leading American expert in the field, advocates an approach that integrates constitutional history with general American history, particularly with the history of group conflict. The constitution should be taught not only as a long-running debate between judges and high-minded politicians, concerned with philosophical principle and legal nicety; it should be taught also as a battleground on which contending interest groups have sought to use the law to forward their particular aims. Though Scheiber argues from the point of view of sound academic history, his way of looking at constitutional history undoubtedly will make the subject more available to the generalist and to the classroom.

The bicentennial of the United States Constitution and the strongly ideological character of recent American politics ensure that constitutional problems will be in the forefront of public consciousness for the foreseeable future, especially since the bicentennial commemoration will run from 1987 to 1992. Virtually all students will be taught constitutional history in some degree. Scheiber contends that strategies that teach subjects such as checks and balances, the federal system, and the Bill of Rights solely as legal and philosophical doctrines are unlikely to convey an understanding and appreciation of either their origins, influence, or evolution. We must discuss constitutional law in relation to social forces and social change. We must, as Scheiber says, teach the "law-in-action."

Chapter 8

Pursuit of Power: Criteria of Global Relevance

WILLIAM H. MCNEILL

Teachers have long been aware that our inherited pattern of introductory courses in history is ill adapted to the post–World War II world. The combination of courses in American history and Western civilization that we inherited from curriculum-builders of the immediate post–World War I era no longer provides the necessary background for students who will live in a world where Asian, African, and Latin American peoples and nations matter as much as Europeans. Some sort of world history seems the obvious answer to the perceived inadequacies of Western civilization courses; but progress in establishing such courses has been far slower than I, for one, expected. Students and teachers alike are dismayed by the complexity of the task. No clearly agreed-upon model courses have arisen and spread themselves across the country as occurred in the 1930s when Western civilization courses first became general.

The fault has been, at least partially, at the college and university level, where disillusionment and dissatisfaction with Western civilization courses in the 1950s and 1960s led not to constructing a new kind of standard introductory course in history but rather to liberating instructors from any compulsory pattern of teaching. Any course was judged as good as any other; but, as students of the 1970s soon pointed out, this principle implied also that any course was just as irrelevant as any other. So the liberation of the 1960s turned into unemployment in the 1970s—a condition from which the profession of history has yet to recover.

I am not personally familiar with the pattern of curricular evolution in high schools, but I believe a somewhat parallel fragmentation took place there, too. Pressures to find room for other social sciences—economics, anthropology, sociology, and psychology—competed with pressures to do justice to blacks, women, and Hispanics, along with other previously overlooked minorities; and on top of that, harassed teachers were expected to do something about drugs, sex, and citizenship. Under these circumstances, even the familiar basic U.S. history survey threatened to fall apart into a series of diverse fragments, while any coherent sense of the history of peoples beyond national borders became effectively unattainable.

This is a dangerous and socially costly situation in which to find ourselves. It is dangerous because, without the cement of a common past, disruptive group behavior becomes more likely. It is costly because shared knowledge and belief about past actions is the only way for people as a whole to act together and achieve common goals without wholesale resort to force. Indeed, it seems clear to me that the principal role of history as written and taught is to create and sustain public identities—and, on occasion, to destroy them as well. National histories, preeminent in nineteenth-century Europe and America, addressed the question "Who are we?" directly and, as long as national states remain the most important locus of power over human lives, national history surely will remain critically important in answering the questions of our public identity.

But nations are not fully sovereign today and never were so. We also belong to a civilizational tradition; and the civilizations of the world share a global human past as well. Western civilization courses strove to discover and transmit awareness of our own particular civilizational past. World history must aim at discovering the common human past all human beings share. To remain ignorant is costly. It allows, nay compels, us to collide unknowingly with others, to stumble into wars and failures of policy like those we have recently experienced in Asia. Indeed, the public record of our country since 1945 seems to me to show very clearly how the strengths and weaknesses of our educational system register in public experience. In Europe since 1945, on the whole, Americans have known what they were doing and have not been horribly surprised by the reactions Europeans have shown to our initiatives—and vice versa. That is because the American public and our leaders knew a good deal about Europe from their school days. But in Asia our ignorance has revealed itself time and again. Failure in China (1943–49) and failure in Vietnam (1963–73) have not really been compensated for by our relations with Japan and South Korea because mutual ignorance—greater on our side than on theirs—makes our good relations with those two nations far more fragile than it is for their European counterparts.

Knowledge per se is not a sovereign remedy for the world's ills, but it can help one to know what one is doing, and refraining from doing, in relations with others. World history is the obvious way to try to cope with this need; but so far, our attempts to do more than talk about it have stumbled against the all-too-obvious fact that the world is so full of a vast number of things that difficult choices have to be made in defining what to pay attention to and what to leave aside as unimportant or unnecessary for an introductory course. There is no substantive agreement whatever on this vitally necessary step. Until historians and teachers come closer to agreeing about what matters, world history will continue to linger in the wings, coyly refusing to come center stage and to assume the role its advocates wish for it in our schools and colleges.

Radical selection of what to pay attention to from amidst a buzzing, blooming confusion is at the heart of all intelligent behavior. Humanity's great triumph is to have invented words as a way of channeling attention to what really matters in a given situation. Our problem for world history, therefore, is to find the right words for the necessary organizing terms and concepts, so that we may focus on what truly is significant in human affairs as a whole and around the globe.

Initial efforts at world history in our classrooms tended to overlook this principle. It seemed easier to add information about the rest of the world to existing Western civilization courses and textbooks than to think of a new way to present the history of all humanity. Wallbank and Taylor's text is the great monument to this approach.[1] According to this view, history is what happened in Europe and in the lands overseas that participate in modern Western civilization. That story, however, must be interrupted once in a while with a "meanwhile in Asia, Africa, and America" until, with the great discoveries of the sixteenth century, the rest of the world was finally united with Europe and joined history in a suitably subordinate and submissive condition! Of course I caricature the approach. It was and is in fact a very substantial improvement on my generation's portion of information about the non-Western world, which was nothing at all.

Still, a Europocentric vision of the past is fundamentally unsatisfactory. It does not express the way things were through most of recorded history. Europe remained a backwater in medieval times when first Indian, then Moslem, and next Chinese civilizations exercised a sort of world primacy. Only about 1450 or 1500 did Europe begin to assume the centrality it enjoyed until about 1950. Now it looks as though other parts of the globe will take over the primacy European states exercised securely for only about two hundred years, 1750 to 1950. It makes no sense to retroject that passing phase of world history onto all the past. We need a better perspective, a more truly global viewpoint than that.

Yet remarkably little effort has been made in such a direction. The main energy of research and thinking across the past thirty years has been devoted to exploring subnational identities and experiences, broadening the range of historical inquiry, reaching down to the oppressed and poor, and in other ways repairing omissions in older visions of the past. This is laudable enough, and I do not mean to denigrate the very real accomplishments of my fellow historians. But, for the most part, their efforts have left world history high and dry. Adding new complexities and further details to the record makes the task of deciding what to put into and what to leave out of a world history course more difficult and, many would say, impossible.

World history is indeed an impossible subject if one assumes that historians must deal with the documents of the past by reproducing the record of what men and women were conscious of during their lifetimes. Some historians sometimes speak and act as though they believed this to be so. It is one kind of history and an often interesting, fascinating kind at that. But world history that aspires to reproduce past human consciousness in all its multiplicity is infinitely cacophonous and therefore unintelligible. So many voices, with so many discordant opinions and feelings and hopes and fears, repeating the same themes over and over, with variations, sometimes abrupt, sometimes so subtly modulated that only minute statistical analysis could reveal alterations! No one can write world history on that basis.

But in fact many important aspects of our lives remain beyond our contemporary consciousness and become visible only in retrospect. This is true of personal lives, as Freud pointed out. It is true of societies also, not because of subconscious drives and motives, as in individual lives, but because large-scale changes often occur without anyone's intending or planning them or even being able to recognize them until the passage of time makes the results apparent to some keen observer—who then gives the phenomenon a name and allows others to recognize what "really" happened. Such an important change as the Industrial Revolution, for example, came about without anyone's knowing it at the time. The term itself was introduced to England a century later, in the 1880s, by Arnold Toynbee, uncle of the more famous historian Arnold J. Toynbee. Other unnoticed changes—demographic, climatic, ecological—also take place without contemporaries' understanding their significance. Climates of opinion likewise come and go. And even though we are conscious of opinions at the time, general patterns of their rise and fall (in which we participate as individuals) assuredly remain beyond our awareness until the perspective of time perhaps lets us begin to see ourselves from outside, as it were—to recognize our own past opinions as part of a statistical rise and fall of a historical complex of beliefs, now gone forever.

This other dimension of history is discoverable through documents, to be sure, but only by asking generalizing questions about what the authors of the documents had to say. Instead of trying to reproduce the authors' consciousnesses, we may seek to make sense of the past by using concepts meaningful to us, making the documents answer questions which, like as not, never crossed the minds of those who wrote the words down in the first place.

Historians have always done this, sometimes without being fully aware of how they went about it. For the effort to make the world make sense requires us to use our own words to set forth our own best and most adequate system of meanings and to reject the errors of the past as active guides to the truth. Here lies the only hope for world history.

Perhaps it is worth pointing out that any change in scale involves a shift in criteria of relevance. Our national history is not the sum of fifty separate state histories; and the history of the State of California is not a history of each of its counties set side by side and bound into a single volume. By the same token, world history is not the sum of national histories, and not even of civilizational histories.

Moreover, one can see that most of what was to matter for humanity as a whole happened without anyone's being aware of it at the time. In past ages, communications were slow and weak. The "world" of which anyone could be conscious was, in fact, only a small portion of the whole globe. The historic importance of agriculture and iron smelting, for example, or of Salamis and Thermopylae, or of Confucius's teaching and Buddha's example remained largely or completely hidden from contemporaries. If we wish to take global humanity seriously, therefore, we must find our own criterion of relevancy. We will have to ask our own questions and find our own answers. Only so can we address the needs of our time and create a meaningful, useful history of the world with room for all the different sorts of people who actually share it with us.

But where are the organizing ideas, terms, concepts that we need? How can we know what to leave out? I do not want to appear dogmatic or more certain than I am, but I can declare to you that having spent ten years writing my principal work, *The Rise of the West*,[2] I discovered, rather to my surprise, that I had written an account of cumulating human power—power over nature and over fellow humans, to be sure, but also power of ideas to make sense of experience and what I can only call aesthetic power, too. This, I submit, is a great theme and worth imparting to the young, if only because it dignifies human hands and minds—emphasizing progress and valuing the net result of innumerable actual human choices across past time made by individuals and groups who nearly always preferred wealth and power to poverty and powerlessness.

Cumulative technology is the most obvious form of human power. In this realm, no one is likely to dispute the reality of progress. Setbacks and temporary losses of skills have occurred in some places and are worth looking into and remembering; but, overall and on a global basis, there is no doubt whatever that human skills have cumulated and increased, thanks to sporadic breakthroughs—now here, now there, but always tending to spread from their place of origin, as neighbors and neighbors' neighbors imitated and adjusted for their own use some new, superior way of accomplishing human purposes.

Technological advances, however admirable and important, ought not to be isolated from the side effects and unforeseen costs of innovation. We are familiar with this in our discussion of the Industrial Revolution. By now, the fate of hand-weavers and spinners faced with competition from machines is familiar enough. Other new technologies involved similar displacements of old skills. Gains always have to be weighed against losses. Creation involves destruction—always, inevitably. This we need to impress on our students and on ourselves. My celebration of human power, heartfelt though it be, must find room for losers and winners alike: for every new form of power came into being surrounded by a cloud of ambivalent side effects—even a new art style! But when costs and gains have been duly weighed, the net judgment I come to is positive. Human intelligence and ability have produced marvels, and we have every right to admire the cumulative achievement of our species.

I feel also that we should admire the way in which the record of cumulating human power over nature appears as part of a much larger evolutionary trend, going back to the Big Bang itself and forward toward who knows what? Human cultural evolution seems to be a continuation by other means of organic evolution; and organic evolution is itself part of the evolution of the universe, reaching back for billions of years. This scientific worldview, completed in my lifetime with the historization of astronomy, strikes me as grand and genuinely awe-inspiring. It shrinks self, nation, and all humanity to minute proportions. We become tiny, yet simultaneously great: atoms, but conscious atoms; each of us a thinking reed, but with an amazingly sharp point for penetrating the mysteries around us.

To convey such a worldview to the young is a challenge indeed, since matters of the moment and of the self loom so very large for all of us, especially for children and adolescents. But that very fact makes the effort to fit everyday experience into the larger frame of historical reality worthwhile. We can hope to correct unthinking myopia by offering a broader view, a truer view, and a view in which personal disappointments and temporary failures loom less large and may even become more bearable. The consolations of philosophy are real enough; and this sort of grand historical worldview is a kind of philosophy worth having. Or so I believe.

Cumulative power over other human beings is rather more controversial than cumulative power over nature because, on the face of it, some persons gain while others lose from such an evolution. Dislike of subordination is a common human trait. As a result, economic, military, and political power systems are liable to occasional breakdown. Yet, over time and space, I think it undeniable that the size of human organizations has increased and their capacity to control behavior has widened. This is because there are enormous gains from working together, which benefit all concerned, managers and managed alike. Managers may gain more: the poor have often been exploited by their masters. But cooperation, inequitable or no, still brings results that cannot be attained without organization of effort through the exercise of power.

Civilizations are, in fact, distinguished from simpler and more egalitarian forms of society by the division of labor, which involves subordinating some to the commands of others within hierarchical social structures. And across time, civilizations have tended to expand because the results of action within such social structures satisfied human wants more adequately on the whole than alternative forms of society were able to do. This is an elaborate way of saying that civilizations were powerful—capable of imposing their will on others by a combination of compulsion and attraction. Setbacks and breakdowns occurred, as with technology; but overall and in the long run, the direction of human history seems unambiguous. Our organizing power has increased and continues to grow; and weaker societies, less well organized, have never been able to stop the expansion of better-organized human groups.

Contemplating this process, a historian need not lack sympathy for the weak and marginal communities that, from time to time, were overrun by military force or disrupted by epidemiological ravages as a result of contact with civilized, disease-experienced, and power-experienced populations. But to deny this aspect of the record of the past or seek to arrest historical process at some particular time and condemn further aggression as wicked seems to me, well, naive and unhistorical. We ought to accept the harsh and bitter sides of human experience on earth along with the sweet, and find room for human aggression and violence as well as for the finer and more admirable sides of civilized life. Anything else is self-deception and fails to prepare our students for life in the real world.

Finally, my vision of cumulative human power emphasizes and values thought and art. It is fashionable to declare that no cumulation takes place in these realms—especially in art. Yet it seems clear to me that a world in which we can encounter many different art forms and attain some level of familiarity with many different literary and religious traditions is a richer and more powerful world than one in which only a single, local form of cultural expression is available. Development of communications allows this. That sort of enrichment, which has become so very marked in our own time, runs back to the beginning of civilization. Civilizations always brought strangers into touch and mingled cultural traditions, allowing choices and provoking innovations in art, literature, and thought through the stimulus of contact with outsiders and their different ways. Perhaps the quality of art has not improved since cave paintings, but our knowledge of art and our experience of it surely has cumulated in much the same way as have other dimensions of human culture and skills.

Progress, if understood as a persistent growth of human power over nature, over one another, and over ideas and works of art, is surely real. In teaching world history, this, I believe, is what we should tell our students.

No doubt, there are other ways of organizing the human record. One can simply invert values and deplore the decline and fall of primitive equality and freedom. Or one can point to the equality between the sexes which (perhaps) existed in neolithic villages before civilization began. Or some other past age may be invested with a rosy hue from which all that follows is reckoned as decay. Many historians have, in fact, done something like this. But such posturing strikes me as a kind of romantic folly. Those who think contemporary life is inferior to some past age want to have their cake and eat it too: want to enjoy the wealth and power we have and, at the same time, scorn it. This is mere childish petulance.

Another, more serious, alternative is to compartmentalize the world into a series of separate civilizations or continents or some other spatial segmentation. Stavrianos wrote a widely used textbook on this principle.[3] For some purposes, perhaps it is best to divide the world up into parts and treat each by itself. In former times, America and Australia were isolated from the Eurasian ecumene where the main action of human history was concentrated, if one uses my criterion of power. Africa, too, remained marginal through most of recorded history. There may be circumstances under which separate attention to these very considerable parts of the modern world is justified. Africans and Amerindians want their own history somewhat in the same way that Americans (or citizens of any other nation) also want a history that is their own. To satisfy that want, it is natural and necessary to carve out separate histories—national or continental, as it may be—from the warp and woof of global history.

Yet, if what matters in world history is the accumulation of skills and knowledge and of the wealth and power that skills and knowledge bring, then it is a mistake to try to give equal attention to places where critical innovation lagged. Choices must be made; and a year's course has only so many weeks and days. In most circumstances, therefore, it seems best, at least to me, to devote attention mainly to the Eurasian ecumene and, within that complex, to shift attention among the great metropolitan centers as first one and then another took precedence over the rest of the world in generating advances in human skills and knowledge. Ebb and flow of cultural influences among the main centers, consequent upon such innovation, may then provide a framework for world history that makes sense and treats the outlying regions as outliers of the main action.

Obviously, I speak as a single and, I sometimes feel, oddly isolated Individual. The past, the whole human past, is indeed before us. Teachers ought to want very badly to make sense of it all, for themselves as well as for their students. We can do so only by striking out boldly on new lines, deciding what matters for humanity as a whole, and putting that into our courses to the exclusion of all else. Only so can we teach world history; and only world history is adequate to prepare the young for living in the world of instant communication that our technology has already created.

NOTES

1. Thomas W. Wallbank and Alistair M. Taylor, *Civilization Past and Present*, 6th ed. (Glenview, Il.: Scott Foresman and Company, 1969).
2. William H. McNeill, *The Rise of the West: A History of the Human Community* (Chicago: University of Chicago Press, 1963).
3. Leften Stavros Stavrianos, *The World since 1500: A Global History* (Englewood Cliffs, NJ: Prentice-Hall, 1966).

Chapter 9

Social History in the American History Course: Whats, Whys, and Hows

PETER N. STEARNS

The writing of American history has in many ways been transformed during the past twenty-five years through the growing influence of social history. Not by any means an entirely new subject in the 1960s, social history nonetheless gained increasing prominence and definition from a growing band of researchers, who gave to their subject something of a pioneering passion.

The rise of social history, on the part of American scholars dealing both with United States history and with the history of other areas, can be documented in several ways. First, one can see how the sheer volume of sociohistorical research has impinged on other topical fields. In reviewing an assessment of the state of historical writing in the United States in 1980, Gertrude Himmelfarb wrote that virtually all historical research has become, directly or indirectly, social history.[1] She exaggerated somewhat; conventional military, diplomatic, and intellectual histories continue to be written. But in terms of research that has made the most lasting mark, her judgment seems largely valid. Aside from the uncovering by historians of new documentary sources that alter the factual account of political or diplomatic history—particularly some historians working in recent periods where the empirical record remains to be fully established—social historians have increasingly ruled the roost. From the pioneer band of the 1960s, intent on challenging established themes, social historians became a dominant group in the 1970s, penetrating leading journals and establishing new outlets of their own. Revealingly, all of the new historical journals founded in the United States since the late 1960s that claim any wide prominence have been devoted to social history entirely or in large part.[2]

The success of social history spills over easily into conventional topical areas. Intellectual historians today are less likely to treat formal ideas in isolation from broader social currents, striving instead to anchor intellectual developments in particular social contexts, or to chart the impact of new ideas on a wider public. And the history of religion now becomes less a comment on formal theology, more an attempt to assess the interaction between religious leaders and defined social groupings.[3] "New" political history and labor history show similar trends. The new labor history quite simply moves from the political account of trade union or socialist party policy to an attempt to study workers themselves and to see protest movements as emanating from the lives and values of the working class. New political historians concentrate particularly on assessments, often highly quantitative, of the social basis of electoral behavior.[4] Even military history has been touched by the new current, rather recently, in a number of valuable studies of the social conditions of military life in the Revolutionary and Civil Wars.[5] Of the major traditional topical branches, diplomatic history alone remains substantially unaltered by the social history thrust, in part because of the difficulty of escaping the diplomatic orbit in assessing cause and impact of change in foreign affairs; but here the result has been a substantial decline in the vitality of this branch of historical inquiry.

A second way to chart the impact of social history is to note how many conventional subjects in United States history have been altered by new findings and emphases. Seventeenth-century witchcraft, once an unhappy Puritan oddity, now becomes an index of deep cultural tensions in seventeenth-century society on both sides of the Atlantic; it needs serious attention because it was central to the experience of the time.[6] Early federal history from about 1780 to 1820 now must involve more than a study of building a new political structure because this was also the time of crucial transformations in American agriculture, of the rise of commercial transactions, and of change in American attitudes on subjects as diverse as emotional expectations in the family or the importance and definition of youth.[7] American liberalism and nineteenth-century reform have to be reviewed in light of findings on the complex motivations that resulted in changes in schools, prisons, and asylums; glib optimism about liberal motives and impact will no longer suffice.[8] Other concepts once blithely accepted as part of a definition of a distinctive American character—such as untrammeled opportunity for mobility or a passion for the uplifting qualities of education[9]—have been substantially redefined through the findings of social history. It turns out, for example, that while rates of social mobility in the United States were somewhat greater than in Europe during most of the nineteenth century, they were not very high; and that in the twentieth century the lead of United States over Europe dwindled.[10] It remains interesting that many Americans believed and still believe in the idea of a distinctive land of opportunity; but now this finding must be integrated with other vital aspects of the social reality.

Finally, the rise of social history can be charted through the development of substantially new topics as part of mainstream research. Family history has become a complex and fascinating specialty, far removed from mere genealogical or antiquarian interest, as historians try to grapple with changes in family structure and function, in emotional relationships and basic stability. The history of leisure activities and purposes turns out to reveal major changes in American society—and some fascinating problems of interpretation as well.[11]

The impact of social history on the list of topics now significant in assessing the past of the United States leads up to an inescapable conclusion: American history isn't what it used to be. At the research level, at least, its contours have been substantially redefined. Revealingly, no approach to history since the rise of social history two decades ago has come close to rivaling the influence of this new subfield.

This new approach has, almost inevitably, widened the gap between history as researchers define it and history as taught at all levels in the schools. Research historians are always inclined, of course, to look for weaknesses in the teaching of their own hobbyhorse. Even as he counted his royalties, Bruce Catton may well have bemoaned the ignorance of most high school students about Civil War tactics. Furthermore, some lag between research trends and teaching trends is inevitable, particularly in a period when declining student enrollments have forced textbook publishers into unusual conservatism and, simultaneously, reduced the number of newly trained teachers entering the lists. The limits on the cognitive abilities of precollege students, along with the necessity for high school social studies to deal with civic education and to project a standardized image of the American past for purposes of citizenship, unquestionably dictate that the enthusiasms of research historians and college teachers be tempered somewhat in devising an acceptable school curriculum.

But the gap between the research interests of professional historians and the content of high school history has become too wide. When the College Board tried to define appropriate standards for high school social studies—as part of its Equality Project on criteria for training middle-ability, college-bound students—it stressed a strong social history component, particularly in the United States history course, as one of the two curricular emphases (along with serious attention to world history).[12] This same redefinition has altered the balance of questions asked on the various Achievement and Advanced Placement tests, again with an increasing percentage of attention allocated to social history. A group of Pennsylvania educators, not primarily social historians, agreed quite readily that social history was the key emphasis needed in a projected series of institutes on the teaching of history.[13] A variety of projects, many funded by the National Endowment for the Humanities, have been set up to try to develop curricula and training appropriate for fuller use of social history in the classroom. Many individual teachers, finally, as well as some entire school districts, have radically revised their history courses during the past five years, again toward the same end.[14] So the lag between traditional history teaching and the rise of social history has been increasingly identified and widely deplored. It is not mere imperialism on the part of dedicated specialists to suggest that introducing a substantial social history element into the teaching of United States history has become a leading challenge.

This fact, in turn, leads to a threefold agenda: pinpointing what social history is; explaining why its serious inclusion into the teaching of history is indeed significant, not merely faddish or whimsical; and, with increasing urgency, talking about how this may be accomplished. The first two portions of the agenda are not novel since a number of history teachers and researchers already have devoted considerable attention to offering a usable definition and justification for social history as a teaching component. But the task commands attention still because the impression of newness and unfamiliarity still hovers around social history in the minds of many interested teachers. Though the approach is no longer novel, the nature of social history involves certain complexities that help explain the lag in widespread curricula adoption and that must inform any successful implementation. But it is vital to emphasize, as against discussions in years past when the subject was indeed newly broached to school teachers, that the leading issue has become not what or why, but how—and to this question the final section of the present essay will be devoted.

WHAT SOCIAL HISTORY IS

The easiest way to envisage what social history is all about (and accurate enough to a point) is to see it as a new set of topical interests.[15] This topical definition, in turn, has two overlapping segments. The burst of enthusiasm for social history research that developed in the 1960s most clearly pointed to social history as the study of "inarticulate" groups. It quickly turned out that sufficiently abundant sources existed, and the label "inarticulate" was rendered somewhat misleading. The basic argument here was that groups outside the mainstream of conventional history—that is, groups that were not producers of formal or higher culture or did not include individually identifiable actors on the political scene—had an interesting past in their own right. Further, such groups

were not simply acted upon by leaders or society or even by anony-
mous forces such as economic cycles. Though lacking an equal share
of society's power and wealth, the inarticulate definitely played a role
in shaping their own values and habits. Thus workers did not tamely
bow to industrial work methods or middle-class reformers' ideas about
leisure; in part workers shaped their own environment. Thus slavery
was not wholly an imposition on the slaves; slaves themselves played
an active role in their own lives, and indeed in their masters' lives, even
when they did not actively protest their lot.[16]

The history of the inarticulate (or "history from the bottom up,"
in one graphic description)[17] has usually involved attention to one or
more groupings in past society: lower classes, such as workers, peas-
ants, or farmers; ethnic or racial groupings; gender groupings, particularly women; and age groupings, with particularly fruitful attention
in American social history, to children, youth, and the aged.[18] Many
individuals, of course, fit into several groupings, and an ideal social history would capture ordinary people through social, ethnic, gender, and
age-group status, recognizing that the importance of each grouping may
change somewhat over time. Scholars, teachers, and readers who are
not themselves social historians have given this topical aspect of social
history the widest attention because its emphasis coincided, not acci-
dentally, with growing political attention to women, blacks, other ethnic
minorities, and even the elderly.

But there is a second topical aspect to social history—closely related
to the study of ordinary people but with somewhat different, even
wider, implications. Social historians study not only ordinary people but
also the ordinary aspects of life. They have moved increasingly to this
emphasis for several reasons. First, the number of groupings of ordinary
people is finite. While the map has not been completely filled in—we are
still getting pioneering social-group studies of men,[19] of homosexuals,[20]
and of the middle-aged[21]—its outlines, at least, are now fairly clear.
Further, even in studying the most familiar groupings, such as women,
it soon became obvious that serious attention must be paid to roles
in families and to activities as consumers and workers; social history
could not be simply an effort to demonstrate the political or ideological
influence of the inarticulate—although some practitioners continue to
wish that this were so—for the simple reason that ordinary people
did not define their lives exclusively in these conventional categories.
Finally, attention to ordinary activities, even of upper-class groups,[22]
rounds out a picture of past society and provides historical perspective
on a host of issues by which we judge society in our own lives. Thus
social historians have added a historical dimension to topics such as
alcoholism, crime, or the meaning of modern leisure, subjects that in
fact cannot be coherently discussed as contemporary issues without

some understanding of their evolution over time. Social history in this sense represents an attempt to deal historically with topics that concern most Americans currently—and while this list of topics most certainly includes politics and formal culture, it also includes family stability, the process of education, and shifts in the patterns of crime.

Social history as a set of topics, then, states that all groups in society deserve historical study in their own right and as contributors to the broader process of social change; and that all human behaviors (save as immutably fixed by species biology) subject to social influence, and therefore to change over time, similarly demand historical inquiry. These include health practices, social mobility, leisure, work, important aspects of feeding, sleeping, and lovemaking, and even—in one of the latest topical extensions—emotional experience.[23] A number of social historians recently have summarized their interest in life's ordinary experiences and institutions by urging a central interest in the mentalities, the basic values of a whole society or of major groupings within society.[24] These mentalities would apply not only to political life but also to family expectations, assessments of the desirability and possibility of mobility, work experience—the whole gamut of activities that in fact define social life at any period of time.

Going far beyond the "how they lived their daily lives" approach that once confined social history to what was aptly dubbed a "pots and pans" agenda, social historians have expanded the list of topics subject to serious historical analysis. And, relatedly, they have expanded the sources open to historical research. Social historians have used census materials and other quantitative data to get at the demographic, occupational, and family structure of ordinary people.[25] They have found hundreds of diaries and thousands of letters written by relatively ordinary people that describe a wide variety of aspects of life.[26] They have begun to use evidence from material culture (the design of housing and available artifacts) for the light that such evidence sheds, not just on how people in the past got through their daily routines, but also on what their values were.[27] Thus these scholars explore definitions of privacy and individuality through an examination of when social groups in the nineteenth century decided that it was vital for children to sleep apart from their parents. Oral history evidence also looms large for recent periods. Finally, social historians milk a distinctive array of published sources, such as manuals on childrearing or sermons, and look for distinctive features even in familiar published sources, such as law codes, for what they reveal about ordinary people and ordinary life.

Social history, involving such a major increase in the number of topics and sources open to historical investigation, already poses a challenge for history teaching. Quite simply, if a number of additional topics must now be added to the standard American history course in order to cover major trends among "inarticulate" groups and other major themes of American social history, it is essential to reshuffle the curriculum. This involves some hard choices. When, for example, Advanced Placement programs proclaim that 25 percent of their questions will cover social history, what are they suggesting be left out?[28] Whatever omissions are made will necessarily grieve teachers, who understandably rely on routine and develop attachments to certain standard topics; or parents, who expect American history to cover what it always covered, lest it seem soft or trendy; or civic authorities, concerned that American history provide an agreed upon record of the past as part of creating necessary national consensus—all can lament the need to curtail or lop off certain portions of the standard coverage in the interest of making room for the social history interloper. Yet this kind of choice is exactly what social historians and others who now agree that social history must become part of the school curriculum are insisting upon.

But there is more; and this is where the particular confusion over teaching social history becomes acute. If social history were merely a new set of topics, debate might range vigorously over how much to introduce and about what to leave out, but the parameters of discussion would be fairly clear. Unhappily, social history is more than a topical addition; it is also a distinctive approach to the past. Herein lies the real challenge for the history teacher.

For the conventional historian the key unit in describing the past is of course the event: so and so was born April 22, 1827; the United States and Liechtenstein sealed their historic agreement on November 19, 1799. Not so for the social historian. Events are not emphasized in social history, and some critics indeed argue that they are so ignored as to make history's narrative role virtually disappear. There are facts aplenty in social history, but they involve processes or patterns of behavior as the key unit. Thus the social historian inquires into a particular pattern of birthrates and the spacing of children, noting when this pattern yields to a different pattern and, if possible, why.[29] Or the social historian describes a pattern of reactions to the imposition of a new work system, as evidenced in rates of absenteeism or job-changing.[30]

Patterns of this sort are of course composed of large numbers of individual events, but the events in themselves—too small, sometimes individually too hard to detect—cannot tell the social historian's story of what a particular historical period was like and how change occurred. Major events may well play a role in the social historian's processes, illustrating certain patterns (for example, class structure during revolutions) or causing new patterns (for example, new demographic behavior produced by a major war). But there can be no gainsaying that the social historian's emphasis involves a different basic unit. Similarly, social history entails a distinctive kind of chronology, which deals with shifts taking place over a decade rather than events or individual actions that can be neatly pinpointed to a given year or a given day. This is a genuine chronology despite its seeming looseness. Social historians are historians in that they seek to demarcate, categorize, and explain change. But the nature of their subject matter dictates a different method of handling time. Hence social historians argue with conventional historians not only about what kinds of change are important in broadening history's topical coverage, but also about how to portray change, regardless of topic.

One illustration of this kind of tension is rather familiar to history teachers. The Industrial Revolution has been hard to handle in most conventional history courses because, once the parade of inventions has been mustered, few specific single events were involved and because it occurred over stretches of time longer and vaguer than the more familiar time units of presidencies and wars. Thus not a few history teachers have advised students to avoid questions dealing with the Industrial Revolution, implicitly recognizing that the phenomenon does not readily fit the conventional narrative. Yet the Industrial Revolution is a key phenomenon—indeed the *central* phenomenon—in shaping modern history in the United States and Western Europe. To a social historian, any treatment that forces the Industrial Revolution into the background is inadequate on its face. Social historians argue hotly over a host of interpretive issues wrapped up in the Industrial Revolution, but they have little trouble visualizing and portraying many basic features of the process. This is precisely the kind of development that, to a social historian, does organize the record of the past.[31]

The difference between social and conventional history in the way the past is visualized really lies at the heart of the problem of using social history seriously in a standard history course, including that quintessential survey course, United States history. It has often proved easier to alter courses in Western civilization, or even world history, to include the social historian's vision than to tamper with the United States history course—precisely because the narrative line in our own past has long seemed so fundamental. To use social history is possible, as we will argue in a moment. But it is difficult. It involves not simply pruning existing coverage but also engaging in some serious rethinking. This means work and, without question, nuisance. In the face of this kind of effort, it is particularly tempting to reassert the virtues of the conventional approach, which means that the social historian in the classroom must directly confront the question (that teachers in most subjects can usually duck on grounds of routine or the obvious need to keep pace with the Japanese): Why bother?

JUSTIFYING SOCIAL HISTORY TEACHING

Many teachers, confronted with the pleasant opportunity of improving a high school history course, think in terms of extending the treatment of conventional history—piling on more work, for example, about United States political development—rather than experimenting with social history. Many Advanced Placement teachers, for example, given the guidelines for the test itself, see their course as an exercise in traditional basics, updated in interpretations but not in subject matter or approach. A course in United States history for gifted students, initiated in the Pittsburgh school district in 1983–84, operated at an appropriately high level in terms of length and assignments but excluded social history in favor of retaining the more comfortable political emphasis.

As a matter of fact, a number of academic historians have not accepted the seriousness of social history and have even in recent years mounted a counterattack. Though social history courses now do hold a prominent place in most leading university history departments, many important state universities and colleges offer no distinct social emphasis at all. Thus a precollege teacher who might argue against social history (given all the other problems facing social studies teaching) would have respectable company; and the view of this group is certainly understandable since most secondary teachers themselves received little or no training in social history.

Criticism of social history differs from sheer neglect but still adds up to a case against major innovation. Some comments are simply frivolous or grumpy. Tudor historian Geoffrey Elton, for example, recently accused social historians of being essentially *voyeurs,* prying into matters that should be concealed under Victorian veils.[32] Others stem from particular interests: thus several American and English social historians have castigated colleagues for drifting from social history's roots in radicalism and its real purpose in demonstrating the political awareness of the masses and the need for revolution. But several other kinds of criticism do warrant attention from researchers and teachers and do have implications for the classroom. Gertrude Himmelfarb, recanting her praises in 1980, recently blasted social history for distracting from the basic knowledge of political institutions that forms the only coherent thread in the past. She specifically pointed to test items on Advanced Placement examinations (which have indeed tried to prod education into greater attention to social history), arguing that essays on changes in women's roles simply cannot compare in significance to comparable exercises on the constitution.[33] Himmelfarb goes on to claim that social historians have wallowed in numbers without attention to human context—here she is simply inaccurate in terms of the field as a whole—and that social history denigrates the idea that human affairs can be rationally managed, which is just plain silly given social historians' attention to showing capabilities for rational action inherent in ordinary people. Himmelfarb essentially believes that the actions of elites are the only serious causes of historical change and that elites (alone?) behave rationally and so illustrate human responsibility and the value of human choice. These propositions are dubious in the extreme, but they do illustrate a kind of conventional historical thinking that has resisted, and that will certainly go on opposing, any increase in social history teaching. Further, a number of social historians themselves have become concerned about social history's lack of grand syntheses and of a clear narrative line. Eminent social historians, such as Lawrence Stone, have therefore pleaded for a return of event-filled storytelling on grounds that this alone gives coherence to the past.[34] Without question, social historians do face important issues in modes of presentation and in the ability to organize the topics that they have staked out; and here their problems relate closely to the difficulties of translating social history into meaningful teaching.

So much for this aspect of truth-telling: teaching social history is difficult; social historians have not worked out all the features of their own genre; and there are, readily available, both some rather poor and some rather good arguments against translating the undeniable research enthusiasm for social history into the precollege classroom.

With due regard to the various problems, however, social history should be more widely taught. The fact that a variety of groups, many emanating from the ranks of teachers themselves (for example, in the preparation for College Board social studies criteria) have so concluded does offer some support for this claim. But outside authority is not needed to defend social history. Here is why:

1. Social history topics, although analytically demanding, involve aspects of students' immediate experience, such as the history of adolescence or leisure, and thus often develop critical thinking skills better than conventional political topics. This is not an either-or proposition. Certainly students should be encouraged to develop historical perspective on political institutions and processes. But social history topics that are literally closer to home are cognitively more accessible to many high school students and facilitate that vital transition from history as memorization of concrete facts to history as a means of categorizing and explaining change.[35] Moreover, social history materials and themes, such as local records and artifacts, provide a wealth of activities and projects that can help move history teaching from excessive reliance on teacher-talk instruction to student-participant or hands-on learning.[36] In other words, this newly developed body of factual material should be taught along with other factual material from the past. But social historians have also, if sometimes unwittingly, created themes and materials particularly appropriate to the development of new thinking skills and student-involved projects. Teachers who have used social history materials in high school courses, while not reporting uniform enthusiasm or a magical quantum leap in student insight, do produce a fairly consistent record of heightened student involvement and interest at all ability levels.

2. Social history teaching extends the possibility of relating history courses to other aspects of the school curriculum. Here again the claim is not that social history alone can link disciplines but that it can enhance such linkages in important ways. In course segments dealing with social history, for example, there is ample room to call upon basic statistical skills as well as upon knowledge of literary and artistic sources. Studying basic trends in demography or social structure presents obvious opportunities for using student abilities in applied mathematics, with great benefit arising from developing the capacity to transfer learning from one portion of the curriculum to another. Although the connection between history and literature courses is better established, the themes of social history so parallel the concerns of many modern novelists (and, indeed, artists) that the transfer can be significantly enhanced. Still more obviously, social history's topical and methodological interests overlap with sociology, anthropology, and social psychology and so extend the possibility of coordination among the various disciplinary ingredients of social studies programs even when history courses remain the dominant element. With a strong social history component of the American history course the interchange with social studies segments on family, criminal justice, and a host of other topics is immensely facilitated, as a number of imaginative teachers have already realized.[37]

3. Aside from its value to the learning process and its interdisciplinary advantages, social history quite simply has altered the framework of United States history in ways that must affect teaching the subject. This is so despite the undeniable problems that social history poses and the lack of full coordination within the subfield itself. As argued above, many familiar topics in United States history have been recast because of social history from the origins of the American revolution[38] to the basis and complex impact of progressivism.[39] Central developments long evoked, but often haltingly treated, such as the Industrial Revolution or the immigrant experience, have been given richness and centrality. Finally, certain new themes have been sufficiently explored as basic parts of the American experience, such as evolution of the family and women's roles, to command inclusion even in a quick overview of the past history of the United States. To be sure, not all of social history's new topics fit the survey approach, and detailed empirical findings and even certain interpretive debates must be slighted as in other branches of history. But the parade of leaders and political institutions cannot be understood without reference to social history; and, at the same time, the conventional approach can no longer be seen as the only standard by which the American experience must be measured.

4. Moreover, social history has extended and improved our understanding of historical change. The result is new complexity, inevitably, but a complexity that at some levels must be mastered in order to advance Americans' grasp of what their society is all about. Thanks in substantial part to social history, we know more now about how American society is constrained and shaped by past experience than was true twenty years ago. The gains of social history within the historical discipline are not accidental or faddish; indeed, a somewhat parallel interest in historical sociology, as a means of giving coherence to a discipline rather lacking in direction at present, has similar roots. Social history has not unlocked all doors and often seems more productive of good questions than of hard answers about social change and the relationship between past and present societies. But that it has advanced knowledge constitutes the fundamental reason for students to be exposed to major findings and approaches. Many social historians have had the experience of speaking to adult groups—interested, say, in family or community history—only to be confronted with the poignant reaction: I didn't know *that* was history. This reaction must become unnecessary in the future. History has a richness and relevance wider than what most of us were taught.

Quite simply, social history has generated excitement in a discipline often regarded as hopelessly stagnant and under siege during the past two decades. Social history will not bring panaceas for classroom boredom or social studies teacher blues. Nor can it resolve all the genuine problems anyone must have in trying to figure out what makes people and societies tick. But it can help.

HOW TO TEACH SOCIAL HISTORY: DOS AND DON'TS

If social history has such obvious teaching promise, why has it not been widely introduced? The answer has several parts. First, it can be legitimately noted that the question is slightly off the mark. Many courses have long had a social history component, whether so labeled or not. Recent enthusiasms for the history of blacks, women, native Americans, and other groups have prompted some serious social history infusions. A number of teachers, some benefiting from various institutes or the advice of agencies such as the Advanced Placement program, have experimented with social history in American history, Western civilization, and social studies courses.

But it remains true that social history's march into the schools has

been slower and more uneven than its research gains or its utilization at
the level of college teaching. Innovation has traditionally come slowly to
social studies teaching, as the fate of various experiments in the 1960s
attests. The timidity of textbook publishers and other such current re-
tardants slow change. Social historians themselves have compounded
the problem by concentrating on often-narrow monographs, failing to
consider a wide nonacademic audience, and frequently avoiding the
kind of synthesis of findings that would lend itself to classroom use.
Only fairly recently, indeed, have significant numbers of social historians reached out toward larger numbers of teachers and other relevant
educators, including museum specialists.[40] Only recently, indeed, have
social historians ventured anything like a textbook on United States history or offered sweeping chronological statements on such key topics
as the social history of women.[41] But practical problems, though real,
do not alone explain the lag in widespread introduction of the new approach into the schools. There is also the underlying difficulty of linking
new topics and distinctive views of historical fact and historical chronology to what already exists in the United States history course.

It is not enough, clearly, to invoke the importance of social history
or to define it for the uninitiated. A variety of experiments are needed,
involving initiatives from active teachers and collaboration between social historian/researchers and the teaching corps. It is neither possible
nor desirable to provide a detailed prescription on how to treat social history adequately within the confines of the United States survey
course. What is possible, and indeed essential, is to indicate some guidelines for actual curriculum work and for ongoing discussion. These
follow from the results of practical, often quite successful, efforts to
introduce social history into high school (and, to a lesser extent, middle school) curricula in a number of schools and school districts. Social
history teaching, in other words, has been widely enough attempted to
allow discussion to move beyond the preliminaries—which have tended
to produce a sense of "That's nice, but what do I do on Monday?"—to
implementation strategies that can rest on certain guidelines or at least
use these guidelines as the basis for further debate.[42] Implementation,
in turn, involves a few fundamental principles—two essential tasks and
two temptations to avoid. It also involves choice between two acceptable strategies, each of which meets key tests of taking social history
seriously.

THE DOS

To introduce a social history component into the American history
course, it is essential, obviously, to reevaluate current curriculum
content—and to leave some standard topics out or at least to reduce

their coverage. There is abundant room for debate over what to drop, but the necessity must be clear. Teachers of survey courses might usefully recognize that certain periods of American political history are not, in fact, terribly significant because they did not bring about serious change in the political process or the institutional structure. Concepts of critical elections (there have not been many),[43] borrowed from the "new" political historians, can aid in winnowing through political history. Some presidential administrations may be lumped into larger periods, some even ignored altogether. Detailed attention to ultimately transient issues, such as the bank reforms of the 1830s, might be scaled down. A number of important developments in American politics and diplomacy might be handled with broader strokes than are currently applied—with loss of detail but not necessarily of emphasis.

A second fundamental in introducing social history teaching is a firm grasp of certain social processes with ramifications that must be traced among a number of groups and a number of aspects of life. Again, there can and should be debate over how many social processes to emphasize, but the principle of defining a manageable number is essential to coherent teaching. The Industrial Revolution seems one obvious candidate. The rise of mass schooling, the reduction of the birthrate, and the rise of corporate bureaucracies are other likely possibilities from the nineteenth century.[44] Developments such as these touched a variety of social groupings, both high and low on the scale; they altered work, leisure, family life, social structure, even health and crime, while also affecting the political process and formal culture. They provide benchmarks for change; they provide essential focus.

THE DON'TS

Almost as fundamental, in approaching the teaching of social history, are two negatives: don't think of social history as teachable with any real effect in isolated snippets; and don't concentrate social history teaching on an endless array of mistreated groups.

Many teachers, confronted with social history topics that they find interesting or important but aware also of the real problems of integrating social history into the standard American history curriculum, are tempted to a one-day, once-in-a-while format. The result can be a lesson on the factory work experience here, one on late-nineteenth-century leisure opportunities there. Textbook publishers, in their most characteristic response to pressure for more social history, have responded in kind. The result is a host of standard American history texts with new feature sections—on women and racial minorities or more generally on "how they lived." The sections may be quite good in themselves but, like the occasional class days on social history topics, stand rather obviously apart from the conventional center of the survey.

Confronted with this limited kind of integration, a social historian is tempted at first to find the new materials better than nothing, a useful if halting first step in an admittedly difficult process. But with rare exceptions this kind of approach is not really adequate, involves no serious rethinking, and signals to students that social history materials are mainly designed to serve as light relief to the serious stuff of American history. If an occasional class day or reading assignment on social history is indeed a first step, an initial experiment designed to lead to fuller integration later on, fine. But if, as has obviously been true with many textbooks, the result induces a self-satisfied sense of adequacy, then it actually does more harm than good. A random class (or even an entire week) on social history is not an appropriate goal, unless the plan is to dispose of social history as meaninglessly as possible.

The temptation to convert substantial sections of the American history survey into a treatment of minority groups also should raise warning flags. But here the problems are more subtle. An important feature of social history is the study of various groupings that have been far from the sources of power in American society. An important, and to a point legitimate, pressure has been applied to social studies curricula during the past two decades to win more attention to the identity and dignity of groups usually ignored or downplayed in American history courses. Here, it might seem, is a marriage made in heaven: the social history approach, enriched by a host of research findings produced by social historians, allows the history teacher to pay serious attention to women, blacks, ethnic groups, native Americans, the elderly, and so on. Unquestionably, the pressure to give such groups more attention has provided the leading entry for social history into survey courses and texts. The result can be some solid, stimulating social history teaching.

But there are three dangers in this approach. First, not every kind of attention to "minorities" involves real social history. Efforts to focus on leading figures or especially politically active individuals among various minorities can produce a kind of political history that ignores ordinary people almost as fully as does conventional political history. Second, a social history that takes up only one particular group after another fails to deal with larger patterns of social and individual behavior in ordinary life. It also omits the social history of Americans who do not fall in any clear minority camp. It is thus valid but incomplete. Third, a group-after-group approach to American history, social or otherwise, risks unnecessary incoherence. And an attempt to deal with too many minorities risks losing central threads in the American experience—a loss that probably makes for an inaccurate portrayal of our past and that certainly is a pedagogical mistake.

The solution to the problem takes several forms. First: while each group does indeed have a valid, usually interesting social history, some groups of regional importance are best treated primarily in state or local history courses. Second, the experiences of a number of groups can be treated in the United States history survey in relation to some central developments in social history, such as the impact of the Industrial Revolution or the results of the mid-twentieth-century rise of a service-based occupational structure. The general points about these developments remain central, but they can and should be traced in their particular impact on key ethnic or social class groups.[45] Third, specific groups can be evoked at chronological points where their social experience was particularly dramatic, and particularly important, in terms of the larger American society.[46] Such groups need not be separately identified at other chronological points—not because they had become insignificant or trivial but because recurrent treatment would distract from more important themes. Finally, some groups—most obviously women and blacks, because of their size and because of the particular dilemma they regularly posed to American values—must be studied seriously and consistently as part of the basic fabric of United States social history.

Thus, there are strategies that can deal successfully with the challenge of group histories, but the central warning must stand: the response of the survey course to the challenge of social history cannot consist solely of a procession of groups. The ultimate formula proposed by some advocates of the group approach—that the key to American history is the position, at any given time, of classes, races, ethnic groups, the two genders, and age groups—may in a sense be valid; but the formula is too complex to be used with any success in the American history survey. Further, social historians must insist that American social history not be seen as a uniform experience around universally held values. We know that the melting-pot vision, which assumed rapid integration of each group into a single mainstream, is not valid. American social history consists thus of a series of tensions, some of them—as for women or blacks or propertyless workers—virtually continuous over time in the national experience. But while these tensions require treatment from the various sides involved, they do not require complete nominalism, such that American social history becomes an almost random procession of separate group histories. Certainly, the demands of a coherent social history (and certainly of a coherent survey course) warn against any assumption that occasional forays into teaching about the condition of women or immigrants or blacks—the most likely result of the "snippets" impulse combined with the desire to placate group identity demands—will produce meaningful curricula.

But if social history in the American history course does not consist of an occasional snippet or even of serious attention to great numbers of variously disadvantaged groups, what does it involve? There are at least two strategies that promise success. Both allow emphasis on some social and conventional history topics over others. Both, certainly, allow serious attention to minorities' and women's history. Finally, both meet simple but important tests that any meaningful attempt to integrate social history into the survey course must pass.

The first strategy, hardly humble from the standpoint of the social historian, involves converting the basic organization of the survey course into key periods of social development.[47] American history is to be seen as a set of processes rather than a series of events, with the processes broken at definable points in time by significant forces of change. Colonial society is thus viewed as a particular kind (or more properly, given major regional diversities, particular kinds) of preindustrial society, in which political institutions and intellectual developments, along with family forms and social structure, are studied as illustrations of preindustrial life in the American environment. Political and commercial change then led (between about 1780 and 1820) to a new kind of society, in which different political, social, and cultural processes must be defined and, in turn, illustrated through key events. Development of a more fully industrial society, beginning in the later nineteenth century, could represent another breaking point, with attention again paid to changes in institutional and behavioral patterns in the various facets of American life and the impact of such changes on key groups. Lines of cleavage for the twentieth century may seem less obvious; but the revolution in occupational structure, government functions, and women's roles that happened around the mid–twentieth century seem obvious choices. The point is not to insist on a standard set of time periods per se but to urge exploration of certain periods as part of a full merger of social and political-intellectual history in terms of basic patterns of life and response to major change.

A survey course thus radically revised might be particularly appropriate as a follow-up to middle school American history courses, which could stick with a more standard, narrative format. Integration of social history into the survey definitely provides a useful challenge toward a more careful sequencing of effort through the student's career. American history should not be presented all down the school years in terms of the same factual parade.[48]

The second approach toward integrating social history—and for most teachers, doubtless, the more realistic path at this point—admits a considerable bifurcation in approach. Here, a substantial part of the survey remains organized around a political narrative. But periodically a two- or three-week segment will explore the nature of American society at those same key points of time that in the first strategy were basic organizational units. These segments combine attention to changes in basic life experiences (work and family patterns, demography, mobility) with studying diversity of impact among key groupings in American society. By their length, these periodic units avoid the "snippets" approach. Also they call for a consistent attempt at integration with the narrative section that follows. Jacksonian democracy, for example, is seen not only as a series of political events and personalities, or even as an ideological issue, but also as a political expression of changes occurring in the work experience, ethnic balance, even leisure habits of the wider society.

A survey course organized as an alternation between political and social emphases, between event-based and process-based chronologies, is obviously not a tidy package. But American history has not involved a lockstep march with all ranks in order, anyway. This alternating emphasis can be a pedagogical advantage. And it represents an accurate rendering of the admittedly divided state of American historical research at present. No scholar, without largely ignoring one kind of history—either social or conventional—has put together a fully integrated picture of the national past. Despite the feasibility of the first, more radical strategy for some existing survey courses, the idea of an alternating curriculum probably more accurately indicates the state of our knowledge at present.

An alternating strategy, or indeed any strategy that purports to use social history seriously in teaching, must meet a few final standards, lest it degenerate into a barely altered narrative style. First, the social history segments must be given serious weight on examinations. Students must learn (and perceive that the teacher intends to screen) social history facts and concepts as thoroughly as the more conventional elements. This is not a burden on students, who usually have fewer preconceptions about what history should consist of than do their teachers. But it is an essential because students readily sense where the real emphasis lies and respond accordingly.

Second, whatever the strategy, teachers and students alike must try seriously to interrelate the various facets of national experience. If history is presented in hybrid social and political segments, they must be linked. Thus a social history segment on the twentieth century cannot consist merely of studying lifestyles or even changes in women's roles. It must attend also to the impact of changing government functions on family patterns, race relations, even crime. And students must seek, in examining changes in the social experience, some clues for changing political behavior, including new party alignments and declining rates of voter participation.[49]

Third, in all segments of the survey course, major themes must be traced over time. We are accustomed, at least in any course that is not a mindless series of events, to look for continuities in political experience: to ask, for example, what relationship political expectations in the colonies had to the political forms of the new republic; or to see what link there was between early reform experience, Progressivism, and the New Deal. We must ask similar questions of the social history segments, so that students sense both continuity and change in American family forms and functions, crime rates and perceptions, or approaches to leisure.[50] Through this insistence on recurrent topics over time, the student can gain a sense of ongoing historical perspective applied not only to American political culture but to the social experience as a whole. Through this, the expanded window on the past that social history has built becomes an opening toward real historical analysis.

CONCLUSION

Teaching social history in the United States survey is a challenge; it also provides an exciting payoff. General strategies based on actual classroom experiences can be suggested. Of course, these strategies must be discussed, must be filled in, and may be usefully supplemented by additional approaches. Opportunity for further collaboration among teachers in preparing both the curricula and tests still so badly needed is not the least of the exciting challenges in the discipline.

And there is a final perspective from which to view the challenge. Essential aspects of social history, both as topic and as approach, broaden the effort to deal with the United States history survey as an analysis of key civic values. Social history adds new factual dimensions to this analysis and usefully complicates the analysis by noting additional areas of conflict and inadequacy where values are invoked or disputed but not applied. Attempts to define an American impulse to tolerance or individualism or due process can only gain by serious examination of the evolution of the American family or the American workplace as well as by studying the patterns of Supreme Court decisions. The addition of social history will, unquestionably, uncover new areas in which rhetoric has in the past departed from reality,[51] but it will also point to areas, such as the treatment of children,[52] where some distinctive American values reached rather deep into everyday experience. The social historian indeed must insist that only by looking at a wide spectrum of the American experience over time, and not simply at the political/legal strand, can we understand key values and value dilemmas.

NOTES

1. Gertrude Himmelfarb, review of *The Past before Us*, edited by Michael Kammen, in *The New York Times Book Review*, 18 May 1980.
2. Such journals include *Social Science History, Journal of Social History, Journal of Interdisciplinary History, Societas,* and *Journal of Family History*.
3. Paul E. Johnson, *A Shopkeeper's Millennium: Society and Revivals in Rochester, New York, 1815–1837* (New York: Hill & Wang, 1978).

4. Michael Kammen, ed., *The Past before Us* (Ithaca, NY: Cornell University Press, 1980).
5. See, for example, Sylvia Frey, *The British Soldier in America: A Social History of Military Life in the Revolutionary Period* (Austin: University of Texas Press, 1981).
6. John Demos, *Entertaining Satan: Witchcraft and the Culture of Early New England* (New York: Oxford University Press, 1983); and Keith Thomas, *Religion and the Decline of Magic* (New York: Scribner, 1971).
7. Philip J. Greven, Jr., ed., *Childrearing Concepts, 1628–1861* (Itasca, IL: Peacock, 1973); David Hackett Fischer, *Growing Old in America* (New York: Oxford University Press, 1978), pp. 77–112; and Christopher Clark, "The Household Economy, Market Exchange and the Rise of Capitalism in the Connecticut Valley, 1800–1860," *Journal of Social History* 13 (1979): 169–190.
8. David Rothman, *The Discovery of the Asylum* (Boston: Little, 1971); Michael Katz, *Class, Bureaucracy and the Schools: The Illusion of Educational Change in America* (New York: Praeger, 1975).
9. Stephan Thernstrom, *Poverty and Progress: Social Mobility in a Nineteenth Century City* (Cambridge, MA: Harvard University Press, 1964).
10. Hartmut Kaelble, "Long-Term Changes in the Recruitment of the Business Elite: Germany Compared to the U.S., Britain, and France since the Industrial Revolution," *Journal of Social History* 13 (1980): 404–423.
11. See the coverage of the *Journal of Family History*, 1976ff.; Benjamin Rader, *American Sports: From the Age of Folk Games to the Age of Spectators* (Englewood Cliffs, NJ: Prentice Hall, 1982); and Christopher Lasch, *The Culture of Narcissism: American Life in an Age of Diminishing Expectations* (New York: Norton, 1979), pp. 181–220.
12. The College Board, *Academic Preparation for College* (New York: College Board, 1983) and *Academic Preparation in Social Studies* (New York: College Board, 1986).
13. Richard Traina (Franklin and Marshall College), Twelve (Pennsylvania) Colleges' Application for a Training Grant in History, English and Modern Languages, submitted to National Endowment for the Humanities, Spring, 1984.
14. "Teaching Social History," *Social Education* 46, special issue (1982), edited by Linda W. Rosenzweig; see also Linda W. Rosenzweig and Peter N. Stearns, eds., *Project on Social History Newsletters and Curricula* (Carnegie-Mellon University Press, 1980–1982), and *Themes in Modern Social History* (Pittsburgh: Carnegie Mellon University Press, 1985).
15. Harold Perkin, "Social History," in *Approaches to History*, edited by H. Finberg (Toronto: University of Toronto Press, 1962).
16. See Eugene D. Genovese, *Roll, Jordan, Roll: The World the Slaves Made* (New York: Pantheon Books, 1974); and John Blassingame, *The Slave Community: Plantation Life in the Antebellum South* (New York: Oxford University Press, 1972).
17. Jesse Lemisch, "The American Revolution Seen from the Bottom Up," in *Towards a New Past*, edited by Barton Bernstein (New York: Pantheon Books, 1968), pp. 3–45.
18. See the bibliography for leading histories of the various social groups; on women, see also Barbara Sicherman et al., *Recent United States Scholarship on the History of Women* (Washington, DC: American Historical Association, 1980).
19. Joe Dubbert, *A Man's Place: Masculinity in Transition* (Englewood Cliffs, NJ: Prentice Hall, 1979); Peter N. Stearns, *Be a Man! Males in Modern Society* (New York: Holmes & Meier, 1979); and Peter Filene, *Him/Herself: Sex Roles in Urban America* (New York: Harcourt, 1974).

20. Jonathan Katz, ed., *Gay American History* (New York: Discus Books/Avon Books, 1978).
21. Tamara Hareven, ed., *Family Transitions and the Life Course in Historical Perspective* (New York: Academic Press, 1979).
22. Frederic Cople Jaher, ed., *The Rich, the Well-Born, and the Powerful* (Urbana: University of Illinois Press, 1973).
23. *Journal of Social History* 16, no. 3 (1983), special issue on the history of love; Peter N. Stearns, "Emotionology: Clarifying the History of Emotions," *American Historical Review* 90 (1985):1085 ff., and Randolph Trumbach, *The Rise of the Egalitarian Family* (New York: Academic Press, 1979).
24. James Henretta, "Social History as Lived and Written," *American Historical Review* 84 (1979): 1293–1323.
25. Charles Tilly, ed., *Historical Studies of Changing Fertility* (Princeton, NJ: Princeton University Press, 1979).
26. Ellen K. Rothman, *Hands and Hearts: A History of Courtship in America* (New York: Basic Books, 1984).
27. Thomas J. Schlereth, "Material Culture Studies and Social History Research," *Journal of Social History* 16 (1983): 111–144; and Barbara G. Carson and Cary Carson, "Things Unspoken: Learning Social History from Artifacts," in *Ordinary People and Everyday Life*, edited by James B. Gardner and George Rollie Adams (Nashville: American Association for State and Local History, 1983), pp. 181–204.
28. College Entrance Examination Board, *Advanced Placement History* (New York, 1979).
29. Robert Wells, *Revolutions in Americans' Lives: A Demographic Perspective* (Westport, CT: Greenwood Press, 1982).
30. Stephen Meyer, *The Five Dollar Day: Labor Management and Social Control in the Ford Motor Company* (Albany: State University of New York Press, 1981); Alan Dawley, *The Industrial Revolution in Lynn* (Cambridge, MA: Harvard University Press, 1976).
31. Charles Tilly, "The Old New Social History and the New Old Social History," *Review—Fernand Braudel Center for the Study of Economics, Historical Systems, and Civilizations* 7 (1984): 363–406; Raymond Grew, "Modernization and Its Discontents," *American Behavioral Scientist* 12 (1977): 301.
32. Geoffrey Elton, review of *When Fathers Ruled*, by Steven Ozment, in *New York Review of Books*, 8 May 1984.
33. Gertrude Himmelfarb, "Denigrating the Rule of Reason: The 'New History' Goes Bottoms Up," *Harper's Magazine*, April 1984.
34. Lawrence Stone, *Past and Present* (Boston: Routledge & Kegan Paul, 1981); see also Eric Hobsbawm, "The Revival of Narrative: Some Comments," *Past and Present* 86 (1980): 3–8.
35. Matthew Downey, ed., *Teaching American History: New Directions* (Washington, DC: National Council for the Social Studies, 1982); see also *Social Education* 46 (1982), special issue.
36. College Board, *Achieving the Social Studies Outcomes*.
37. *Social Education* 46 (1982), special issue; see particularly Deborah L. Pleasant and Douglas A. Haskell, "Using Social History in Social Sciences Courses," pp. 327–330.
38. Gary Nash, *The Urban Crucible: Social Change, Political Consciousness and the Origin of the American Revolution* (Cambridge, MA: Harvard University Press, 1979); Pauline Maier, *From Resistance to Revolution: Colonial Radicals and the Development of American Opposition to Britain* (New York: Knopf, 1972).

39. Dominick Cavallo, *Muscles and Morals: Organized Playgrounds and Urban Reform* (Philadelphia: University of Pennsylvania Press, 1981); Anthony Platt, *The Child Savers: The Invention of Delinquency* (Chicago: University of Chicago Press, 1969).
40. Downey, ed., *Teaching American History;* Gardner and Adams, eds., *Ordinary People.*
41. See paragraph on textbooks in Bibliography.
42. *Social Education* 46 (1982), special issue; Peter N. Stearns, "Clio contra Cassandra," *History Teacher* (1977).
43. Allan J. Lichtman, "Political Realignment and 'Ethnocultural' Voting in Late Nineteenth Century America," *Journal of Social History* 16 (1983): 55–82; Jerome Clubb et al., *Partisan Realignment: Voters, Parties and Government in American History* (Beverly Hills: Sage Publications, 1980). See especially pp. 252–253.
44. Tilly, "Old New Social History," passim.
45. Generalizations about major social classes can indeed help to group distinctive ethnic experiences, allowing clearer focus on where ethnicity really counted; see Daniel Walkowitz, *Worker City, Company Town: Iron and Cotton Worker Protest in Troy and Cohoes, New York, 1855–1884* (Urbana: University of Illinois Press, 1978), and Herbert Gutman, *Work, Culture and Society in Industrializing America* (New York: Vintage Books, 1976).
46. Leonard Dinnerstein et al., *Natives and Strangers: Ethnic Groups and the Building of America* (New York: Oxford University Press, 1979).
47. Rosenzweig and Stearns, *Themes in Modern Social History;* Richard D. Brown, *Modernization: The Transformation of American Life* (New York: Hill & Wang, 1976).
48. College Board, *Academic Preparation,* on the need for sequencing; see also Peter N. Stearns, "Educational Equality Project: New Standards in the Social Studies," *The Social Studies* 75 (1984): 5–8.
49. Christopher Lasch, *Haven in a Heartless World: The Family Besieged* (New York, 1977); and Morris Janowitz, *The Last Half Century* (Chicago: University of Chicago Press, 1976).
50. Rosenzweig and Stearns, *Themes in Modern Social History;* Eric Monkennen, "From Cop History to Social History: The Significance of the Police in American History," *Journal of Social History* 15 (1982): 575–592; Rader, *Sports;* and Carl Degler, *At Odds: Women and Family Life* (New York: Oxford University Press, 1980).
51. For example, the workplace: see Meyer, *Five Dollar Day,* and Loren Baritz, *Servants of Power: A History of the Use of Social Science in American Industry* (Middletown, CT: Wesleyan University Press, 1960).
52. John Demos, *Little Commonwealth: Family Life in Plymouth Colony* (New York: Oxford University Press, 1971); Degler, *At Odds;* and Bernard Wishy, *The Child and the Republic: The Dawn of Modern American Child Nurture* (Philadelphia: University of Pennsylvania Press, 1968).

BIBLIOGRAPHY

Main trends in social history are discussed in several essays in Michael Kammen, ed., *The Past before Us* (Ithaca, 1980), which also provide extensive research bibliographies. For comments on social history in the classroom, see Matthew T. Downey, ed., *Teaching American History: New Directions* (Washington, 1982) and *Social Education* 46, no. 5 (May 1982), edited by Linda W. Rosenzweig. Both these collections contain sample lessons and curricula, and discussions of classroom experience. Another volume, intended for museum educators, is also relevant: James B. Gardner and George Rollie Adams, eds., *Ordinary People and Everyday Life: Perspectives on the New Social History* (Nashville, 1983). A fine definition is Harold Perkin, "Social History," in H. Finberg, ed., *Approaches to History* (Toronto, 1962).

Many leading developments in social history can be followed through key journals in the field: *Journal of Social History, Comparative Studies in Society and History, Journal of Interdisciplinary History,* and *Past and Present.*

College Board work on social studies criteria can be followed in *Academic Preparation for College* (the Equality Project statement, New York, 1985). See also Peter N. Stearns, "Educational Equality Project: New Standards in the Social Studies," *The Social Studies* 75 (1984): 5–8.

Critiques of social history include Gertrude Himmelfarb, "Denigrating the Rule of Reason: The 'new history' goes bottoms up," *Harper's Magazine,* April 1984; Lawrence Stone, *Past and Present* (Boston, 1981); and Tony Judt, "'A Clown in Regal Purple': Social History and the Historians," *History Workshop* (1979): 66–94.

Leading United States history texts at the college level that include substantial social history segments have proliferated in recent years. They can be invaluable in preparing high school curricula and materials. Such texts include Gary Nash, *Red, White and Black: The Peoples of Early America* (Englewood Cliffs, NJ, 1982); Stephan Thernstrom, *A History of the American People* (New York, 1984); Mary Beth Norton and others, *A People and a Nation,* 2 vols. (New York, 1983); Robert Wiebe, *The Segmented Society* (New York, 1975); Thomas Bender and Edwin Rozwenc, *The Nature of American Society* (New York, 1978); Bernard Bailyn and others, *The Great Republic* (Lexington, MA, 1981); Gary B. Nash and Thomas R. Frazier, *The Private Side of American History,* 2 vols. (San Diego, 1984). A United States social history text and document collection intended for the secondary schools is Linda W. Rosenzweig and Peter N. Stearns, *Themes in Modern Social History* (Pittsburgh, 1985).

While many of the most exciting developments in American social history lie in monographic studies, there are some wider interpretive treatments covering a longer chronological span; the titles that follow do not venture an exhaustive list but suggest starting points on major topics and approaches. On women's and family history, see William Chafee, *Women and Equality: Changing Patterns in American Culture* (New York, 1977); Robert Wells, *Revolution in Americans' Lives: A Demographic Perspective* (Westport, CT, 1982); Nancy Cott, *The Bonds of Womanhood: "Women's Sphere" in New England 1780–1835* (New Haven, 1977); Carl Degler, *At Odds: Women and Family Life* (New York, 1980); Herbert Gutman, *The Black Family in Slavery and Freedom* (New York, 1976); Andrew Cherlin, *Marriage, Divorce, Remarriage* (Cambridge, MA, 1983); and Christopher Lasch, *Haven in a Heartless World: The Family Besieged* (New York, 1977).

On childrearing and the emotions, Philip J. Greven, Jr., *The Protestant Temperament* (New York, 1978) and Carol Z. Stearns and Peter N. Stearns, *Anger: The Struggle for Emotional Control in America's History* (Chicago, 1986). On age groups and experience, Bernard Wishy, *The Child and the Republic: The Dawn of Modern American Child Nurture* (Philadelphia, 1968); Joseph Kett, *Rites of Passage: Adolescence in America 1790 to the Present* (New York, 1977); W. Andrew Achenbaum, *Old Age in the New Land* (Baltimore, 1979).

On the working class and mobility, Stephan Thernstrom, *Poverty and Progress: Social Mobility in a Nineteenth Century City* (Cambridge, MA, 1964) and *The Other Bostonians: Poverty and Progress in the American Metropolis* (Cambridge, MA, 1973); John Bodnar, Roger Simon and Michael Weber, *Lives of Their Own: Blacks, Italians and Poles in Pittsburgh, 1900–1960* (Urbana, 1962); Herbert Gutman, *Work, Culture and Society in Industrializing America* (New York, 1976); and David Montgomery, *Workers' Control in America: Studies in the History of Work, Technology and Labor Struggle* (Cambridge, Eng., 1979). On slavery, Eugene D. Genovese, *Roll, Jordan, Roll: The World the Slaves Made* (New York, 1974). On ethnicity, Leonard Dinnerstein and others, *Natives and Strangers: Ethnic Groups and the Building of America* (New York, 1979); and Dinnerstein and David Reimers, *Ethnic America* (New York, 1981).

On leisure, Benjamin Rader, *American Sports: From the Age of Folk Games to the Age of Spectators* (Englewood Cliffs, NJ, 1982) and Mark Lender and James K. Martin, *Drinking in America* (New York, 1982).

On special topics, David R. Johnson, *American Law Enforcement: A History* (St. Louis, 1981); Eric Monkkenen, *Police in Urban America, 1860–1920* (Cambridge, Eng., 1981); Michael Katz, *Class, Bureaucracy and the Schools: The Illusion of Educational Change in America* (New York, 1975); Susan Reversby and David R. Romer, eds., *Health Care in America: Essays in Social History* (Philadelphia, 1978); Paul Starr, *The Social Transformation of American Medicine* (New York, 1983); David Stannard, ed., *Death in America* (Philadelphia, 1975); Hugh Davis Graham and Ted Gurr, eds., *Violence in America* (New York, 1969; rev. ed., Beverly Hills, 1979).

Finally, two exceptional studies in colonial social history also deserve mention: John Demos, *The Little Commonwealth: Family Life in Plymouth Colony* (New York, 1971) and Rhys Isaac, *The Transformation of Virginia, 1740–1790* (Chapel Hill, 1982).

The social history of the West, including California, is frankly not as rich to date as that of other key regions. But there are some important special studies, including: Julie Jeffrey, *Frontier Women and the Trans-Mississippi West, 1840–1880* (New York, 1970); Elaine Tyler May, *Great Expectations: Marriage and Divorce in Post-Victorian America* (Chicago, 1980); Robert Griswold, *Family and Divorce in California, 1850–1890* (Albany, NY, 1982); Richard W. Fox, *So Far Disordered in Mind: Insanity in California, 1870–1930* (Berkeley, 1979); Peter R. Decker, *Fortunes and Failures: White-Collar Mobility in 19th Century San Francisco* (Cambridge, MA, 1978); Frederic C. Jaher, *The Urban Establishment: Upper Strata in Boston, New York, Charleston, Chicago and Los Angeles* (Urbana, 1981); Walter Stein, *California and the Dust Bowl Migration* (Westport, CT, 1973); Alexander Saxton, *The Indispensable Enemy: Labor and the Anti-Chinese Movement in California* (Berkeley, 1971); Carey McWilliams, *Factories in the Field: The Story of Migratory Farm Labor in California* (reprint, New York, 1969); Manuel Gamio, *The Life Story of the Mexican Immigrant* (New York, 1972); John Caughey and LaRee Caughey, *Los Angeles: Biography of a City* (Berkeley, 1976); Robert M. Fogelson, *The Fragmented Metropolis: Los Angeles, 1850–1930* (Cambridge, MA, 1967); and Richard Bernard and Bradley Rice, eds., *Sunbelt Cities: Politics and Growth since World War II* (Austin, 1983).

Chapter 10

The Constitution in the School Curriculum: A Proposal for the 1987 Bicentennial

HARRY N. SCHEIBER

A gathering tide of scholarly projects, "outreach" programs, and the like has been set in motion by the bicentennial of the United States Constitution. Many of these efforts bespeak a serious determination to make this an occasion of significance transcending the commercialism that dominated so much of the American Revolution bicentennial a decade ago. There seems now to be a widely shared concern to engage in *cerebration,* and not only *celebration;* there is a seriousness abroad with regard to reappraising American constitutionalism in all its aspects.[1]

This mood is reinforced, no doubt, by the way in which the current political scene in the United States has been colored lately by a return to ideology. Debates over the Reagan administration's "New Federalism" initiatives, over budget-balancing and other proposed constitutional amendments, and over state rights versus centralism all have raised issues of far-reaching potential consequence for our constitutional form of government.[2] From all segments of the political arena come signs of what Robert Hawkins, chairman of the Advisory Commission on Intergovernmental Relations, has termed an earnestness about our "developing the capacity to understand the capabilities and limitations of alternative constitutional, political, organizational, and regulatory strategies for governing America."[3] No political movement that involves so searching a set of inquiries can fail to affect the schools deeply. Moreover, the general concern for reappraising the public schools and their performance, sparked by the Gardner Commission Report, has contributed to efforts, as in the State of California, to examine the fundamental structure of teaching of American history and governance.

This is a time, then, of enormous promise for the study of American law and history in the school curriculum.[4]

How should the Constitution and the constitutional tradition be presented in this nation's classrooms? To what purposes and with what departures from traditional approaches to teaching constitutionalism should legal and constitutional issues be considered as we teach American history and government?

A dark shadow is cast over the inquiry by the hard statistical fact that less than half this nation's citizenry choose to participate in the processes of governance by exercising their right to vote. This is a challenge to the educational system just as it is to the cherished republican and democratic values of the nation. Any inquiry into teaching the Constitution in the schools is rendered urgent by the repeated findings of pollsters that the citizenry are generally unlearned regarding even the most prominent features of the Constitution's text—and that there is neither an informed understanding nor anything like a consensus on some of the most important provisions of the Bill of Rights.[5]

Viewed from another perspective, the question of how to teach the Constitution and our legal heritage—and for what larger purposes of civic education—is lent urgency by the current-day fascination of educators with teaching "values" to students in the public schools. Unfortunately, many advocates of instruction in "values" and "value development" have completely stripped such matters of their historical context. For many educational reformers and doctrinaires, the teaching of values has been made a concomitant of teaching "skills" or else a hobby of developmental psychology—not even of political philosophy, let alone of history.[6]

Viewed by some others, instruction in constitutional history and values offers a signal opportunity for ideological indoctrination. Professor Sidney Hook, for example, has recently called for such an approach, contending that the schools have an obligation to inculcate the great and eternal truths about freedom.[7] What happens when there is profound disagreement on some of the eternal truths, as we know must be inevitable, is a troubling issue. To know how Professor Hook's forthright advocacy of indoctrination can roil the waters today, we need only recall moments in our history when received values were challenged for purposes of repression or purposes of expanding liberty—in World War I's repressive superpatriotic campaign, or during the McCarthy red hunt, for example; or in the course of the civil rights movement, when civil disobedience became a matter that touched the lives of thousands of students directly. Still, one must sympathize with the view that, at the very least, basic values of liberty must be confronted in the classroom. We may hope that students can be taught how to arrive rationally and with integrity at their own answers, even if we do not agree outright on the necessity for "indoctrination." It is difficult, in fact, to know how one can escape confronting basic values in the course of introducing students to the Constitution, its meaning, and history.

All this brings us back to the larger question of how to integrate constitutional law and legal history into the standard curriculum. I want to propose here a framework that departs in many ways from the standard, accustomed ways of dealing with the Constitution. The proposed framework will, I hope, point a way toward giving vitality and immediacy to the teaching of law and constitutionalism—but at the same time integrating those subjects usefully into the American history course.

A word first about what this framework is *not:* it is not the history of Supreme Court cases. That is, I do not advocate teaching constitutional history exclusively as the growth of doctrines articulated by judges over time. This doctrinal history is an important subject—and it must be included—but it is not the whole of the larger enterprise. The great cases of constitutional law deal only with the tip of the iceberg: they illustrate high principle and reveal conflicting versions of our basic law in the hands of responsible actors. But to concentrate upon those great cases alone—engaging in the classic process of playing a sort of follow-the-dots game with doctrine, tracing the commerce clause or the First Amendment from one decision to another through time—is not the way to give students an accurate map of the whole terrain. It does not tell us enough of *law as a working system.*

The framework for teaching the Constitution ought, I think, to be a three-part structure:

1. The first conceptual element in the structure should be the traditional one, with a focus on Supreme Court doctrine. This will be concerned with the rules and ideology that inform the constitutional system of governance. But the stress is on *governance* and not solely on doctrine: this permits a broadening of focus to embrace the legal system and legal process, not merely "law" as a set of abstractions.

There is a certain "core" factual content with regard to this element of the structure that warrants consideration. Certainly students ought to be asked to consider some major expressions of American political theory. It is difficult to use *The Federalist* papers, both because they are so voluminous and because their unity as an argument for the Constitution is too easily lost from view when only excerpts are considered; still, surely at least the essays on federal division of powers, on size and democracy, and on the projected dynamics of the new government and its politics all ought to be read. The writings of theorists and political giants so diverse as Frederick Douglass, John C. Calhoun, Abraham Lincoln, and Stephen Field are essential. Moderns, from Theodore Roosevelt and Martin Luther King, Jr., to various contemporary political voices also require consideration. Themes such as individualism and ideas of the community good, illustrated by reference to thinkers such as Thoreau, Chief Justice Shaw of Massachusetts, Lincoln and the radical abolitionists, and the framers of the Fourteenth Amendment, all can be profitably interwoven with formal constitutional themes. Alongside the contract clause and its importance for property concepts, we want to develop the meaning of police power and community values—abundantly expressed in our law, but not exclusively in the decisions of the Supreme Court. Moreover, the normative standards that are applied to the governmental system, historically and in our own day, require a basis in doctrine. To say whether our system, in various periods of history, has worked to advance or to frustrate such ideals as "due process of law" and "freedom of speech" requires, as a prior undertaking, a development of what those phrases have been understood to mean.[8]

This part of the framework for teaching, as I have said, is the most familiar one to us. But it is not only law as doctrine and in relation to theory that students ought to understand; it is also law as a working system. Thus we come to the second element of the structure, one that deals not with "law in books," not with the great parchment documents and the law cases, but instead with "law in action."[9]

2. The processes of constitutional and legal change, law in action, constitute this second conceptual element of the structure. Law does not evolve in a kind of intellectual outer space populated only by orbiting jurists, theorists, and an occasional president: law is the product of social change and also an autonomous force that shapes institutional content and dynamics. Our courses in American history ought to consider such questions as how the law has defined such institutions (their powers, immunities, limitations, and functions) as the judiciary, the corporation, the voluntary association, the college and university, agencies of local government, and the public schools themselves.[10] The competing claims of public interest and community values, on the one side, and private desires and vested interest, on the other, need to be explored in all these different institutional contexts.[11]

To understand the legal process, it is also necessary to consider how law can channel and establish the pace of change. After all, if a legal system is needed in order to have "rules of the game"—and this is what a legal system does, both in its role of establishing social controls and in its role of defining rights—the outcomes lead to interesting questions. Does change proceed as law designs it? Or does it frustrate the intentions of the designers? Who are the losers and winners when the legal system allocates privilege, largess, or immunity?

In recent years these questions have become the center of enormous controversy in the community of legal historians. Some, taking rather a radical posture, begin with the premise that the legal system has always worked principally to protect the "advantaged" and advance their interests; even the concept of "rule of law" is said to be a smokescreen, for in fact legislatures and courts work (at times almost conspiratorially) to prevent the enactment of truly transforming change that will help the powerless and the poor. This is an extreme view, and one that is difficult to defend—I may add—when one confronts the complexity of historical realities, let alone such developments as the modern extension of civil rights and liberties by the federal courts![12] Other legal historians take constitutionalism more at face value, and they regard "rule of law" as a major contribution of our legal culture to ordering human affairs in ways that have corrected abuses, protected the weak (not always, but certainly with good effect at major junctures), and served the cause of making power responsible. Still other legal historians find that the main theme is tension in the law: pressures for protection and extension of privilege and counterpressures for reform. The legal system mediates the tension, sometimes performing in accord with constitutional ideals, at other times failing to do so and perpetuating anomalies and even such incontestable wrongs as human slavery.[13]

Teaching "law in action" in this way is an especially challenging undertaking, one must admit at the outset. To know what Chief Justice Roger B. Taney said about technology and clearing the ways for innovation as well as about the contract clause in the Charles River Bridge case—posed against what Justice Joseph Story said in dissent—is no longer enough. To be sure, the confrontation of these two great figures in constitutional discourse is a fascinating matchup; there is high drama and eloquence on both sides, something one hopes can capture students' attention and spark the imagination. But there is a different sort of high drama in the relevant, underlying confrontations in American society of the 1830s. To deal adequately with the Charles River Bridge matter means understanding the importance of corporate charters in the economy of that day, knowing something of the struggle that was underway over the definition of privileges for business firms and over the public-private distinction.[14] One would welcome the introduction of such challenging concerns into the study of legal development and constitutionalism in our classrooms.

More generally, in fact, modern historical scholarship dealing with the period 1820–1860 has illustrated that there was a truly fundamental confrontation in the political sphere over the proper limitations on private property rights—a confrontation that eventually had important implications for the rising challenge to slavery. In this period there was also an expansion of governmental activities, including both promotional and regulatory measures by government at all levels. Those developments (really constituting the beginnings of modern active government) revealed changes in federalism as an element of law in action, changes in the structure of private-sector power and influence, and innovations in use of public resources that exacted costs as well as distributed benefits. All were an important part of the context of that era's "great law cases." The state legislatures were framing regulatory laws and devolving privileges in a great variety of patterns within a federal system that provided great latitude for such activism. At the state level, meanwhile, the courts were exercising broad discretionary powers over definition of property rights, over business law generally, and other private law in the tort and contract areas. Who benefited, and whose interests were damaged? How did the results square with constitutional ideals?[15]

A similar line of inquiry, broadening the field of investigation and the context to embrace the major issues of law in relation to social change, can be pursued for other subjects entirely familiar to a good American history curriculum. To cite only a few subjects amenable to such treatment, consider black slavery—upheld by both state law and constitutionalism, eventually challenged by "agitators," who were later recognized as heroes who exposed the dilemma of ideals in conflict with inhumane custom and writ. For another example, consider the emergence of "consumer interests" as an identifiable focus of law's concerns and of pressure-group politics in the Progressive Era. Consumer interests must be seen in relation not only to constitutional reform but also to the rise of expertise in government and the expanding capacities of the public sector in the face of private-sector giantism that had outrun government's effective reach in regulation.[16] Or, for the more modern period, consider the emergence of "civil liberties" as a discrete concern of an organized pressure group, their travails in the political arena and in the courts, the emergence of new legal and constitutional norms, the fragility of those norms in the face of social pressures for repression, and the relationship to later civil-rights movements in a similar cause.[17]

When the processes of change are considered, both high drama and a vital concern with values are inherent in the history of the Constitution as a changing document. How the basic instrument of government itself has undergone transformation is a subject that must be part of any reasonable definition of the "core" matter of legal history. The processes prescribed for amendment are themselves prominent subjects of study: the student ought to know how the framers envisioned amendment, how truly radical the very idea was at the time, under what widely varying circumstances amendments of key importance have been approved, and what have been the substantive effects on the legal-constitutional order. How "dual federalism" and substantial state autonomy prevailed before 1861, when control of the question of slave versus free labor was only one of a large number of issues left to the states; how a virtually new charter (what Laurence Tribe calls precepts of the Constitution Model II) was created by adoption of the Thirteenth, Fourteenth, and Fifteenth Amendments; and how far-reaching constitutional change in the New Deal era was spearheaded not by formal amendment but by "ordinary legislation" later validated by the Supreme Court—all these themes ought to be central to classroom presentation of the nation's legal heritage.[18]

Moreover, as I will argue later in this paper, parallel phenomena in state law merit similarly close attention when we examine the history and impact of constitutional change. At the least our students ought to know the differences between constitutional law and ordinary legislative and judicial measures; the differences between public and private law; and the ways in which social, economic, and political change have been pursued through a variety of combinations of law in these forms. To be so comprehensive, as I have indicated, is a challenging matter for teachers. It brings us into areas of historical scholarship that are truly controversial, and it requires a keen appreciation for the difficulties in "getting the law straight" (no one wants teachers, let alone students, to become bogged down in the difficult technicalities of law or to transform themselves into dilettante attorneys-at-law). Yet it is a venture worth undertaking, and it cannot be done effectively without some effort at grappling with the materials of both the law and disciplines such as economic history or public administration—fields not usually part of the instructor's standard training or within the arsenal of readily available methodologies in the schools.

3. The third element of the framework proposed here extends beyond the formal content of rules and doctrine, and complements "law in action" concerns: it is study of *values as expressed in the actual behavior of the society.*

How constitutional and legal norms—the values that are given priority and that influence the acting-out of individual lives and group functions—have been expressed in actual behavior is an intriguing and difficult question. To illustrate how to approach this question in ways that integrate readily with main themes of a well-structured American history course, the following examples are offered:

First, the theme of civil liberties. Introducing the history of doctrine is important but not sufficient. Students ought to know, for example, something of the "clear and present danger" principle—when it was first formulated, how its champions wished to apply it as an interpretation of "freedom of speech" requirements, and how the Supreme Court did or did not actually apply it. It is of at least equal importance, however, for students to be guided through an informed inquiry into the circumstances that gave rise to the concern with doctrine, to know of the record of repression and of pressure for free speech, to understand some of the perplexities involved in determining the proper limits of speech, and to inquire into the basic interpretive question: what constitutes a "civil liberties crisis?"

Thus dealing with "law" not as an abstraction but as a reflection of social and political realities would indicate the importance of surveying the history of civil liberties as well as tracing constitutional free-speech doctrines. Interesting comparisons can be drawn with regard to the Alien and Sedition Acts crisis, with the issues it brought forth concerning the relationship of common-law libel and First Amendment constraints; with the campaign against the abolitionists, including the refusal of Congress to accept antislavery petitions, the practice of Southern postmasters in not distributing abolitionist mail, and the ways in which society first branded antislavery proponents as "agitators" and permitted ostracism and violence against them, yet later heeded their appeals and (at least in the North) elevated them to positions of power; and with other clearly defined "episodes" in which free speech was curtailed.[19] Of equal interest is the subtler problem of conformist tendencies expressed not through uses of law in a formal way but through exertion of social pressure. Indeed, the historian John Roche has contended that the degree of freedom to dissent in small nineteenth-century communities was circumscribed severely by such pressures—to the extent that conformism might have exceeded all but the worst of efforts to force conformity through law.[20]

Against such a background, the notorious World War I period—in which freedom of speech and press were widely denied, violence condoned, academic freedom curtailed both in schools and universities, and all efforts to oppose the war policy put down by the Wilson administration (at the time the "clear and present danger" standard was germinating)—becomes an integral element of concern with teaching the Constitution. Vital issues emerge from such an integration of law and political history. How effectively has the Supreme Court protected civil liberties in the midst of deep crises and widespread hysteria, as opposed to protecting liberties by formulating new constitutional standards after the crisis has receded? How important is presidential leadership in forming public opinion in such crises? And does the complex of events in a crisis such as World War I (including the postwar red scare) reveal popular commitment to, or rejection of, values embodied in our constitutional law?[21]

The history of natural resource use and control in American history offers another example. Law—including constitutional law and both public and private law in the states—has influenced every phase of the history of natural resources. When we speak of the market—supply and demand—as playing the central role in allocating resources, we do well to remind students that law establishes the rules for the market:

law defines private rights and duties, it establishes the dimensions of governmental power, and, not least, it can serve as an expression of society's legal values. Under the Constitution in the nineteenth century, the federal government pursued a variety of policies through control of public lands. The goal of settlement was served, the complementary goal (albeit one that often involved conflict of interests with settlers) of promoting development through exploitation of forests and mineral resources was pursued, and revenues were raised. Constitutional law sustained both a system of land legislation geared to alienation of public property (sales on liberal terms to private individuals and firms) and to free or low-cost distribution (as under the 1862 Homestead Act); and both selective subsidies (railroad land grants and other special grants) as well as support of public education, transportation improvements, and other public programs by grants directly to state governments in the West.[22] When public policy underwent a sea change in the 1890s, however, the precepts of constitutional law—even in a period of conservatism for a property-minded Supreme Court—legitimated creation of national forests, a strong federal role in reclamation, and a variety of resource conservation measures.[23]

The way the federal system—as a working system—functioned in resource allocation and conservation can serve to illustrate vividly the legal and constitutional values held by the electorate. Revealed in political behavior, from the early struggles over land laws in the 1787–1800 period down to the Sagebrush Rebellion of our own day, are views of state rights, federal authority and its proper limits, and the interplay of privatistic goals and public purpose. In the development of resources and in the struggles over conservation, regionalism and sectionalism (including some themes of "frontier history," long a staple in American history courses) confronted constitutional principle.[24]

Why not ask students to confront both this rich historical record in light of constitutional law and also the modern-day permutations of age-old conflicts—for example, the contemporary debate over whether trees and animals should have rights, just as people do, and whether there is a "constitutional right to a habitable environment"? The quest for the public interest and its proper constitutional context continues to involve basic issues of federalism. The society's behavior in such matters expresses legal values, no less than in court decisions in great cases. To trace the record brings students face to face with the history of economic individualism, changing concepts of property rights, and fundamental legal questions regarding use and preservation of nature's bounty.

In discussing the three-part framework for teaching the Constitution and American legal development, I have drawn from examples—the Charles River Bridge case, issues of civil liberties in World War I, natural resources—that are embedded in the standard core of American history courses that attempt minimal coverage of the subject. Teachers will find many other staple topics similarly adaptable to dealing historically with the hard questions of law in action: the constitutional order in rules and doctrine, the working legal system in relation to formal rules, and the expression of legal values through behavior of the society.

In conclusion, I wish to propose another perspective on teaching constitutional issues. This approach is based on a creative fusion of the history of state law, on the one hand, and national law, on the other. In our fascination with the 1787 bicentennial, it is tempting to overlook the fact that even in our own day of powerfully centralized federalism the operation of the constitutional system leaves to the states (with their own separate constitutions) vital areas of property, family, criminal, business, and educational law. To a remarkable degree, the ordinary transactions of life are still conducted under laws enacted and enforced under authority of the states. Moreover, many state supreme courts in recent years have been interpreting their state constitutions' bills of rights in a fashion independent of the U.S. Supreme Court's adjudication of similar or identical language in the national Constitution.[25]

In California, for example, where the state supreme court has taken the lead in developing independent state grounds for interpretation of rights, some of the most divisive issues in recent politics have centered on this issue. In addition, the U.S. Supreme Court in recent years has handed down some of its most important decisions in cases arising from California law—notably in the areas of federalism, proper reach of the state policy power (especially in land-use regulation), and the public trust doctrine (affecting limits of private ownership in shorelands, navigable inland waters, and other property). The resulting patterns of interplay between California law and national law—with similar patterns discernible in the other states of the union, though of course with varying substantive content—offer a fascinating opportunity, I think, for classroom teaching on constitutional law and legal history. Although I speak of California here, it is only one example among fifty.[26] One hopes that in all fifty states a renewed interest in constitutional history and law in action will lead to creation of new teaching materials—paralleling what Project '87 and the American Historical Association are producing for teachers on the subject of national constitutional law—that will bring state law alive for our students.[27]

A recognition of "law in action" in the curriculum will help educate the coming generation to both the diverse heritage and the fundamental values of our evolving legal system. Students ought to be asked to probe into how popular values can be identified and their effects on behavior understood; how values expressed by the courts and constitution writers influence the course of social change; and how rules and doctrine bear on the realities of historical developments and contemporary law. If there is enduring validity—as I think there is—in Justice Holmes's adage that the life of the law is not logic but experience, then our history teaching ought to reflect that reality.[28]

NOTES

1. The National Endowment for the Humanities has fostered individual research, new editions, and other publications, media projects, and conferences; there is a forthcoming *Encyclopedia of the American Constitution*, edited by Leonard W. Levy and Kenneth Karst (New York: Macmillan); the American Historical Association and the American Political Science Association have created Project '87 to encourage public programs and scholarly projects on the Bicentennial, and Project '87 has launched a quarterly journal, *This Constitution;* and many state governments and historical societies, as well as scholarly and bar groups, have announced Bicentennial activities. All these activities are apart from what the federal government will undertake.

2. See, for example, the symposium entitled "Renewing Federalism: A Continuing Appraisal," *National Civic Review* 71 (1982); and publications since 1980 of the U.S. Advisory Commission on Intergovernmental Relations. ACIR's magazine, *Intergovernmental Perspective,* has been a source of provocative current commentary on federalism themes.

3. Statement of Robert B. Hawkins, Jr., before the Joint Oversight Hearing of the Intergovernmental Relations Subcommittee of the U.S. Senate and the Intergovernmental Relations and Human Resources Subcommittee of the U.S. House of Representatives, July 25, 1984 (to appear in published Hearings volume).

4. The preface to this volume notes efforts by the California legislature, the office of the state superintendent of instruction, and the University of California to respond to public and professional concern regarding the educational system and especially curricular content.

5. The results of extensive polling of both "elite groups" and a representative segment of the electorate is presented in the important new work by Herbert McClosky and Alida Brill, *Dimensions of Tolerance: What Americans Believe about Civil Liberties* (New York: Russell Sage Foundation, 1983).

6. See Harry N. Scheiber, "Recapturing a Usable Past: Knowledge and Skills in the High School American History Curriculum," *The History Teacher* 12 (August 1979): 481–492, in which I present a set of strongly held objections to the "skills" and "values" approaches stripped of rigorous historical content. For views sympathetic to the ahistorical approach, see Allan O. Kownslar, "Is History Relevant?" in *Teaching American History: The Quest for Relevancy.* Forty-fourth Yearbook of the National Council for the Social Studies (Washington, DC: National Council for the Social Studies, 1974). See, inter alia, Mark M. Krug, "The Social Studies—Search for New Directions," in *What Will be Taught?—The Next Decade,* edited by Krug (Itasca, IL: F. E. Peacock, 1972).

7. Sidney Hook, 1984 Jefferson Lecture, reported in *Chronicle of Higher Education,* 16 May 1984, pp. 7–9.

8. Unfortunately, few of the general works on legal history successfully range

beyond judicial decisions to deal with doctrine on this kind of broad can-
vas. Bernard Schwartz, *From Confederation to Nation: The American Constitution, 1835–1877* (Baltimore, MD: Johns Hopkins University Press, 1973)
makes the attempt quite successfully for a confined period of constitutional
history. The work of Willard Hurst (cited in notes 11 and 25 below) consistently seeks to deal with doctrinal foundations beyond the courts; see also
Don E. Fehrenbacher, *Slavery, Law, and Politics: The Dred Scott Case in Historical Perspective* (New York: Oxford University Press, 1981), an examplary
study in regard to analysis of doctrine.

9. I borrow these phrases from the famous work by Roscoe Pound, "The Law
in Books and Law in Action," *American Law Review* 44 (1910); see also
Wilfrid Rumble, Jr., "Law as the Effective Decisions of Officials: A 'New
Look' at Legal Realism," *Journal of Public Law* 20 (1971). The journal *Law
and Society Review*, now in its seventeenth year of publication, has given
continuing attention in its editorial coverage to scholarship on law as a
working system.

10. See Harry N. Scheiber, "American Constitutional History and the New
Legal History: Complementary Themes in Two Modes," *Journal of American
History* 68 (1981). An excellent overview, too difficult for all but the most
advanced high school students, but a useful and challenging guide for
teachers, is the classic work by Willard Hurst, *Law and the Conditions
of Freedom in the Nineteenth Century United States* (reprint, Madison:
University of Wisconsin Press, 1978).

11. See text at note 29 and citations, note 19, below. Processes of constitutional
and legal change form a main theme of essays originally presented as
lectures at a public conference in April 1983, entitled *The New Deal Legacy
and the Constitution: A Half-Century Retrospect* (Berkeley, CA: Boalt Hall
School of Law, 1984).

12. This extreme view is given in Morton Horwitz, "The Rule of Law: An
Unqualified Good?" *Yale Law Journal* 86 (1977): 566. This presumption
also underlies much of his book, *The Transformation of American Law,
1780–1860* (Cambridge: Harvard University Press, 1977).

13. Willard Hurst, "Old and New Dimensions of Research in United States Legal
History," *American Journal of Legal History* 25 (1979); Harry N. Scheiber,
"Back to the Legal Mind? Doctrinal Analysis and the History of Law,"
Reviews in American History 5 (1977); Jamil Zainaldin, "The 'New Legal
History': A Review Essay," *Northwestern University Law Review* 73 (1978).

Lawrence M. Friedman, *A History of American Law* (New York: Simon
& Schuster, 1973; new edition forthcoming) is the standard introduction to
the history of law. A learned and useful synthesis of major themes in social
history of law and in doctrinal development of the common law, it is less
useful as an introduction to constitutional themes.

14. A lively study, on the Charles River Bridge case and its social and political
context, accessible to advanced students in the schools, is Stanley I. Kut-
ler's well-known work, *Privilege and Creative Destruction: The Charles River
Bridge Case* (Philadelphia: Lippincott, 1971). A new book, Jamil Zainaldin,
Law in Antebellum Society (New York: Knopf, 1983) is adaptable to advanced high school use and offers a broad perspective and many useful
documents on the themes of federalism, economic change, and constitutional and legal innovation.

15. Apart from Hurst's writings, an excellent introduction to these issues is
the classic judicial biography by Leonard W. Levy, *The Law of the Commonwealth and Chief Justice Shaw* (Cambridge: Harvard University Press,

1954). Friedman, *History of American Law,* is particularly strong on law and the economy. Analysis of the state governments' role in economic development is in Harry N. Scheiber, "Government and the Economy: Studies of the 'Commonwealth' Policy in 19th-Century America," *Journal of Interdisciplinary History* 3 (1972); and the theme is pursued further in Albro Martin, "Uneasy Partners: Government-Business Relations in Twentieth Century American History," *Prologue: The Journal of the National Archives* (Summer 1979).

16. Slavery issues are treated well in a fine, brief analysis by R. Kent Newmyer, *The Supreme Court under Marshall and Taney* (Arlington Heights, IL: Crowell, 1968); see also A. E. Keir Nash, "Reason of Slavery: Understanding the Judicial Role in the Peculiar Institution," *Vanderbilt Law Review* 32 (1979). Consumerism in its political context is examined for one state by David Thelen, *The New Citizenship: Origins of Progressivism in Wisconsin, 1885–1900* (Columbia: University of Missouri Press, 1972). On the history of regulation more generally, see the essays in *Regulation in Perspective,* edited by Thomas K. McCraw (Cambridge: Harvard University Press, 1981).

17. Paul Murphy, *The Constitution in Crisis Times, 1918–1969* (New York: Harper, 1972).

18. The phrase "the Constitution Model II" comes from Laurence H. Tribe, *American Constitutional Law* (Mineola, New York: Foundation Press, 1978). My own view has been that dual federalism prevailed in practice as well as constitutional theory until 1861. See Scheiber, "American Federalism and the Diffusion of Power," Symposium on Federalism, *University of Toledo Law Review* 9 (1978); also Scheiber, "Federalism and Legal Process," *Law and Society Review* 14 (1980).

19. See James Morton Smith, *Freedom's Fetters: The Alien and Sedition Acts and American Civil Liberties* (Ithaca, NY: Cornell University Press, 1956); Russel B. Nye, *Fettered Freedom: Civil Liberties and the Slavery Controversy, 1830–1860* (Urbana: University of Illinois Press, 1972); and William M. Wiecek, *The Sources of Antislavery Constitutionalism in America, 1760–1848* (Ithaca, NY: Cornell University Press, 1977).

20. John Roche, *The Quest for the Dream* (New York: Macmillan, 1963).

21. Studies of the World War I and red scare episodes include: H. C. Peterson and Gilbert C. Fite, *Opponents of War, 1917–1918* (Madison: University of Wisconsin Press, 1957); Robert K. Murray, *Red Scare: A Study in National Hysteria, 1919–20* (Minneapolis: University of Minnesota Press, 1955); Harry N. Scheiber, *The Wilson Administration and Civil Liberties, 1917–21* (Ithaca, NY: Cornell University Press, 1960); and Paul F. Murphy, *World War I and the Origin of Civil Liberties in the United States* (New York: Norton, 1979).

22. Paul Wallace Gates, "An Overview of American Land Policy," *Agricultural History* 50 (1976), reprinted in *American Law and the Constitutional Order: Historical Perspectives,* edited by Lawrence Friedman and Harry N. Scheiber (Cambridge: Harvard University Press, 1978). For a full treatment of land history, see Gates, *History of Public Land Law Development* (Washington, DC: Zenger Publishing Co., 1968).

23. Samuel P. Hays, *Conservation and the Gospel of Efficiency: The Progressive Conservation Movement, 1890–1920* (Cambridge: Harvard University Press, 1959); and Donald C. Swain, *Federal Conservation Policy, 1921–1933* (Berkeley: University of California Press, 1963).

24. See generally the articles on law, conservation, and related themes in the *Encyclopedia of American Forest and Conservation History,* edited by Richard C. Davis, 2 vols. (New York: Macmillan, 1983).

25. Justice William Brennan provides an introduction to the subject and an

argument for reliance on independent state grounds to define liberties of citizens against government, beyond what the Supreme Court does in interpreting federal constitutional language, in "State Constitutions and the Protection of Individual Rights," *Harvard Law Review* 90 (1977).

The state courts may not define liberties *less* broadly under their own constitutions than the Supreme Court has done. For a survey of state decisions and the general problem, see the symposium on the subject of independent and adequate state grounds in the *Harvard Law Review* 95 (April 1982).

26. The political magazine *California Journal* routinely covers the referenda and initiatives and has occasional analyses of California legal and constitutional questions in the federal courts. Among cases in the Supreme Court of major importance have been: *Agins v. Tiburon*, 447 U.S. 255 (1980), affirming 24 Cal. 3d 266 (1979), on zoning power and property rights; *Summa Corp. v. California*, 104 Sup. Ct. 1751 (1984), regarding the state's public trust doctrine; *Pruneyard Shopping Center v. Robins*, 447 U.S. 74 (1980), on free speech and federally protected property rights.

On the history of referenda and political analysis thereof, see Eugene Lee, "California," in *Referendums, A Comparative Study of Practice and Theory*, edited by D. Butler and A. Ranney (Washington, DC: American Enterprise Institute for Public Policy Research, 1978).

27. The magazine *This Constitution*, published by Project '87, carries information regularly of newly available teaching materials; in addition, *This Constitution* has in each issue an edited set of documents, designed for classroom use, on constitutional history and issues.

28. Additional readings that treat historiography of constitutional and legal history include: Robert W. Gordon, "J. Willard Hurst and the Common Law Tradition in American Legal History," *Law & Society Review* 10 (1975); Harry N. Scheiber, "Doctrinal Legacies and Institutional Innovation: Law and the Economy in the United States," *Law in Context* (Australia), 2 (1984); Lawrence M. Friedman, "The State of American Legal History," *The History Teacher* 17 (1983); Stephen B. Presser, "'Legal History' or the History of Law: A Primer on Bringing the Law's Past into the Present," *Vanderbilt Law Review* 35 (1982); the full bibliographic essay in Alfred H. Kelly, Winfred A. Harbison, and Herman Belz, *The American Constitution: Its Origins and Development*, 6th ed. (New York: Norton, 1983); Wythe Holt, "Then and Now: The Uncertain State of Nineteenth-Century American Legal History," *Indiana Law Review* 7 (1974); and, for colonial legal development, Herbert A. Johnson, "American Colonial Legal History," in *Perspectives on Early American History*, edited by Alden Vaughan and George A. Billias (New York: Harper, 1973). An invaluable general study of governmental institutions and public policy, providing a rich contextual background for analysis of both national constitutional law and state law, is Morton Keller, *Affairs of State: Public Life in Late Nineteenth Century America* (Cambridge: Belknap Press of Harvard University Press, 1977).

Friedman and Scheiber, eds., *American Law and the Constitutional Order* (Cambridge: Harvard University Press, 1978) is a volume of interpretive articles on legal and constitutional development from the colonial era to the 1970s. Stephen B. Presser and Jamil S. Zainaldin, *Law and American History* (St. Paul, Minn.: West Publishing Co., 1980) is a volume mainly of cases but with supplementary materials ranging beyond judicial decisions. Unfortunately there is no adequate history of the criminal justice system in the United States, nor is there an adequate overview of twentieth-century legal development available as yet.

Part IV
TEACHING STRATEGIES AND CURRICULUM REFORM

While all the essays are concerned at least indirectly with classroom teaching, those presented in the fourth section bear directly on teaching strategies and the school curriculum. They seek to make history vivid and enjoyable for the young student and take the tack that students learn best when their subject is made relevant to their particular world and when it can be examined in sufficient depth.

John Anthony Scott, a prolific historian as well as a high school teacher, recommends using the wealth of materials produced by American popular culture. What comes from the direct experience of living, Scott believes, can convey that liveliness to students—for example, the diary of a settler woman carried off in an Indian raid, an account that will "touch the hearts of youth today and win a most receptive audience in our classroom."

Scott not only advocates using such vivid primary materials; he also discusses, through examples, how these materials should be used. The literary quality of a work is important. Because a primary purpose of these documents is to engage the imagination, they must tell their story well. Scott wishes to use private lives, experienced within the great movements and moments of history, to illustrate the tangible reality of events. Folk songs are rich in such examples; thus, he suggests the using of "General Lee's Wooing" as a dramatic way to teach the battle of Antietam. Of course, "General Lee's Wooing" does not exhaust Antietam, much less the Civil War; but it does introduce them in a dramatic way. As Scott notes, folk songs are a traditional means through which views of American values and history have been passed along. He concludes his essay by proposing the creation of an "historical literature center," which would collect and publish primary historical materials of special interest to young people.

In his chapter on the history curriculum, Matthew T. Downey calls attention to yet another dimension of the history education problem. Choices about what teachers will teach and their selection of teaching strategies are limited by the organization of the curriculum. The present school curriculum, Downey points out, relies heavily upon repeated surveys of United States and world history. As a result, teachers find themselves under a great deal of pressure to cover the whole of American or world history each time it is taught. This leads to a superficial skimming of the surface that students find so deadening. The survey approach, he contends, is especially out of place in the teaching of world history. Attempts to cover whole civilizations in a few days or a week or two result in treatments too superficial for much permanent learning to take place. Textbooks written for these courses consistently sacrifice depth and interesting detail for the sake of broad coverage. The result, he observes, is a stultifying cycle of survey courses that frustrates teachers and kills student interest in the study of history.

To break out of this cycle, Downey proposes a reorganization of the history curriculum. His alternative focuses on a particular chronological period at each grade level. By limiting the chronology to be covered each year, teachers will be able to devote more time to in-depth study. However, this alternative does not abandon the survey principle altogether. Each year of instruction should begin with a look backward at what came before and conclude by touching base with the present. But the emphasis would be on the in-depth study of a manageable period of time. This, he concludes, could provide the teachers with the time they need to involve students imaginatively and creatively in the study of the past.

Another way to capture young people's interest in the past is through local history. Karen Jorgensen-Esmaili, who has written a teacher's guide to the local history of Berkeley, California, describes the pedagogical value of local materials. Like primary sources, local materials make historical abstractions concrete and manageable. They are easy for students to identify with, especially the very young who still have an undeveloped sense of time. Jorgensen-Esmaili argues that local history also may be used to teach basic skills such as map reading, oral and written communication, and critical thinking.

The case-study method is a useful way to integrate community history into a history or social studies program. Here, a smaller, more manageable unit—the local community—is studied as a particular manifestation of the larger entity; local history thus is also saved from being "merely" local. Family history, old photographs and memoirs, oral histories, and architectural walks may be useful teaching aids. Jorgensen-Esmaili provides a number of suggestions to teachers for the classroom use of these materials.

Though each community has its own history, it may lack local historians or curriculum specialists willing and able to provide teachers with local history materials. Teachers often will have to find and prepare their own materials. The difficulty of this task is one reason, according to

Jorgensen-Esmaili, that the frequent recommendations to use local materials have produced relatively few results. Local amateur historians can be of great value to the teacher here. In addition, universities should be more active in training teachers in the preparation and use of local materials.

Chapter 11

How Shall We Humanize the Teaching of History?

JOHN ANTHONY SCOTT

How shall we humanize the teaching of history? Where shall we look for materials more creative and exciting than we find in standard texts? For some time these threshold questions have faced history teachers at every level of the educational system.

Young people acquire knowledge and learn to think by using their own independent powers of observation as they explore the world around them. They need access to sources of information that provide direct or primary evidence about reality. Those who would learn must go to the fountain of knowledge themselves and touch the waters with their own lips.

But standard history texts are not primary sources of information. Insofar as history is concerned, primary sources are those records that people of the past have *themselves* created. Such sources, the sum total of our historical heritage, may be divided broadly into two groups. There are, first, works of art and artifacts—paintings, drawings, sculptures, buildings, tools, toys, musical instruments, stone walls, and so on. To use such materials is indispensable for the study of history, but this is a subject that merits a separate paper. Here we shall be concerned with the second great category of original sources—literature.

Literature is created both in written form—manuscripts and printed matter—and in oral form—sermons, speeches, stories, and songs. The United States possesses this historical record in manifold forms and in unrivaled abundance. The challenge confronting us is to fashion concepts and criteria to guide us in selecting appropriate materials for the history classroom from this great literary heritage. How shall we choose offerings that will enable the teacher to humanize the classroom presentation and to expand the range and variety of its scope?

PRIMARY SOURCE MATERIALS

We do not need to look very far to find original sources that are both vivid and fascinating. Our libraries bulge with such materials created throughout American history. Given this rich heritage, it is remarkable how little of it thus far has been tapped for teaching history—not only in elementary and high schools but even at the college level.

One reason for this neglect is the modern educational obsession with commercially packaged texts. It was not this way in the past; historical scholars used to believe that ordinary people were capable of telling their own story and of doing so supremely well. They believed that historians should compile archives of people's own diaries, memoirs, letters, and other writings. Such archives would constitute a heritage from which not only future historians but also future populations might learn. Such was the belief and the practice, for example, of the great nineteenth-century historian, Frank Moore (1828–1904); he made huge documentary collections of the writings, letters, and songs of the common people. During the Civil War, Moore collected thousands of letters written by soldiers at the front. He characterized these as "marvelous. As a monument to the educated intelligence of the rank and file they have no parallel."[1]

We need to return to and learn from Frank Moore's tradition of humane scholarship and democratic education. We must build into our philosophy of teaching the vision of the classroom as a forum where, at long last, the voices of the past will be heard; as a writing room where the present generation may record its own experiences and dreams so that these writings, too, may be preserved for posterity. Beyond the voices of the teacher and the text, we must people the classroom with all those voices that can make the experience of the past live again today. This literary heritage can empower the dead to talk with us, the living. In this way, we will contribute toward linking the generations, forging a vision of a common life, a sharing of past and present, a common destiny.

An approach such as this also may give students fresh opportunities for self-expression. It is desirable not merely to read the message of the past but also to recreate it in *sound*. There is an opportunity here to dramatize the history classroom through the spoken (as well as the written) word, to discover the beautiful sonorities that echo down the corridors of history, to paint the past with our utterance even as an artist paints with color.

I would like to illustrate this point with a few examples from the historical record provided by ordinary people. I have chosen passages written by young people; it may well be that such stories will most immediately touch the hearts of youth today and win a most receptive audience in our classrooms.

It is the morning of a freezing winter's day, February 10, 1676. A band of Nipmuck Indians is attacking the village of Lancaster, Massachusetts, in one of many encounters between native Americans and colonists during King Philip's War (1676–77). Mary Rowlandson, the village minister's wife, tells of the experience. "Now," she wrote,

> the dreadful hour is come that I have often heard of, but now mine eyes see it. Some in our house were fighting for their lives, others wallowing in their blood, the house on fire over our heads. I took my children to go forth, but as soon as we came to the door, the Indians shot so thick that the bullets rattled against the house, so that we must go back.

Mary was taken prisoner with her six-year-old daughter, who had been wounded in the attack and was, in fact, dying. The Indians placed the child upon a horse, and Mary tells us, "It went moaning along 'I shall die! I shall die!' I went on foot after it with a sorrow that cannot be expressed."

The Nipmucks fled through the snow-covered forest with New England militia hard upon their heels. In spite of the terror and the tragedy of her own situation, Mary Rowlandson still retained the capacity to observe and to provide a vivid picture of the Nipmuck people. Here is how she described the fugitive band: "Old and young, some sick, some lame, many with papooses on their backs. The greatest number at this time with us were squaws, and they travelled with all they had, bag and baggage."

The whites had sought out and had destroyed the corn supplies that the Indians had stored away for the winter; reducing native Americans to starvation was the time-honored frontier way of destroying resistance to European encroachment. Thus, the Nipmuck women and children were suffering the pangs of hunger, and these Mary shared. Their food, she tells us, was "groundnuts, acorns, artichokes, lily roots, onions, horses' guts, all sorts of wild birds . . . bear, beaver, tortoises, frogs, squirrels, skunks, rattlesnakes, yea, the very bark off the trees."[2]

Now, exactly one hundred years later, a tiny episode from the war of the Revolution as told by a British soldier, Roger Lamb: the scene is Saratoga, just after the British surrender following the battle of Stillwater, October 17, 1777. The British troops were on one side of the Hudson river and the Americans on the other. The river at that point being neither wide nor deep, the soldiers hailed each other across it and talked together. Here is what happened on one such occasion. A British soldier, wrote Lamb,

> suddenly darted like lightning from his companions and plunged into the stream. At the very same moment, one of the American soldiers dashed into the water from the opposite shore [they swam to the middle of the river and met] and they hung on each others' necks and wept: and the loud cries of 'My brother! My dear brother!!' . . . soon cleared up the mystery. . . . [One

was an immigrant to the colonies, the other had remained in his native Britain. They were] ignorant until that hour that they were engaged in hostile combat against each other's life.[3]

Similar episodes took place in other wars in which Americans fought, notably the Civil War and World War II. Such passages raise interesting questions for classroom exploration. Why should it be worse for blood brothers to kill each other than for other men to do so? If indeed all men are brothers, why do brothers fight?

Now for scene 3: eighty-three years have passed since the brothers' encounter described by Lamb. The speaker here is Delicia Patterson, a young black woman of fifteen, born in Missouri in 1845. She stands upon the auction block set up before a Missouri courthouse; she is for sale. Among the crowd of buyers she spots Judge Miller, a man she knows, and she starts to speak. Here, Delicia herself describes the scene: "I knew him well," she said,

> because he was one of the wealthiest slave owners in the county, and the meanest one. He saw me on the block for sale, and he knew I was a good worker. So when he bid for me I spoke right out on the auction block and told him: "Old Judge Miller, don't you bid for me, 'cause if you do . . . I will take a knife and cut my throat from ear to ear before I would be owned by you."[4]

Hundreds of black people have left us recollections of their child-hood when they were raised in slavery. Many hundreds of these narratives of youth from the lips of the old-timers were taken down in the 1930s during the New Deal era. They represent the first effort ever made by the federal government to create an archive devoted to the experiences of Americans during early youth.

Both before and after the Civil War, people moving out West toiled over long, weary, and dangerous continental trails. They left their stories not only in memoirs but also in messages scratched upon markers set above the graves of those who had died along the way. One such marker said it all in eighteen words: "John Hoover, died June 18, 1849, aged 12. Rest in peace, sweet boy, for thy travels are over." Note the lovely wordplay with "travels." Travels are the journeys which we undertake on earth, and travails are the sufferings of life; both sound the same. With this one word, the parents communicate their own heartbroken comment: John's wanderings are over, his sufferings are at an end.

Our historical literature expresses not only tragedy but also captures with equal skill the happier, sparkling surface of reality. Here is a picture of an Indian encampment from the pen of Francis Parkman, two years after he graduated from Harvard University in 1846 and went west over the Oregon Trail. "Warriors, women, and children," he wrote, "swarmed like bees. Hundreds of dogs, of all sizes and colors, ran restlessly about: and close at hand the wide shallow stream was alive with boys, girls, and young squaws, splashing, screaming and laughing in the water."[5]

We move on into the twentieth century. The United States, in the throes of a mammoth industrial transformation, is emerging as a world power. Hundreds of little boys are working deep below ground in the mines of West Virginia and Pennsylvania to help provide the fuel that keeps factory wheels turning and that converts iron ore into steel. John Spargo, who had himself worked as a child in the mines of his native England, describes the scene:

> Think of what it means to be a trap boy at ten years of age. It means to sit alone in a dark mine passage hour after hour, with no human soul near; to see no living creature except the mules as they pass with their loads, or a rat or two seeking to share one's meal; to stand in water or mud that covers the ankles, chilled to the marrow by the cold draughts that rush in when you open the trapdoor for the mules to pass through; to work for fourteen hours—waiting—opening and shutting a door—then waiting again—for sixty cents; to reach the surface when all is wrapped in the mantle of night, and to fall to earth exhausted and have to be carried away to the nearest shack to be revived before it is possible to walk to the farther shack called "home."[6]

These sources, in their endless variety, introduce students to the wonders of the American past, letting them possess it as their own. Such literature enables students to take a first serious step in the study of history. Validating the past as something real, intensely alive, and profoundly human arouses curiosity. Such curiosity, in turn, creates an emotional commitment that is the first condition of disciplined work.

What criteria might guide us in selecting materials? Obviously enough, we should choose pieces suited to the students' reading levels and to the time allotted for classroom assignments. Here, the documents themselves present few difficulties. They are of varying lengths; within a given piece there are portions that have their own unity and coherence, and even may be used as independent assignments. A great deal of flexibility is possible in selecting classroom readings.

The same is true of content. We may use different viewpoints on one given problem or event. We may choose individual descriptions that let the student enter into the situation as though he himself were there—on the battlefield or sailing ship, at a camp meeting, in the mine, in the gardens or fields, on the trail, in the woods.

We may use documents containing concepts that illuminate the process of conflict and change in society itself. A classic example of this type of "conceptual" document is William Lloyd Garrison's address in the Park Street Church, Boston, on July 4, 1829. On that occasion he set forth for the first time in American history the concept that black people were citizens of the United States, entitled to the full enjoyment of the liberties and rights guaranteed by the American Constitution.

Documents of this sweep and power have great value in the modern classroom. They illuminate not only the struggles of a given era but the course of history itself.

We must choose documents that, though written with clarity and grace, use only the simplest of words. This enormously facilitates the learning process. Indeed, we insult our students if we impose upon them *any* material that is turgid or pompous in style and obscure in meaning.

Original sources, finally, must be presented in the appropriate chronological context; here the input of the teacher is indispensable. In learning to listen to the voices of the past, the student will begin to develop a stereoscopic view of American history that he could never see in a mere text. As the past itself begins to emerge in the round, the student will begin to form his own picture, to see with an informed and engaged eye.

The search for fresh teaching materials may generate not only a fresh approach to teaching history but may also inspire a new breed of texts arising out of the collective work of the educational community itself—of teachers, students, research workers, consultants—who together will confront the tasks of history education. This would be a contrast to the process by which most contemporary history texts are produced. As we know, they are put together for the most part by college specialists and editorial writers who are more or less isolated from the educational community that they are supposed to serve and who too often have had little or no personal experience in educating young people.

FOLK SONGS OF THE AMERICAN PAST

The American musical heritage also provides a body of historical literature that ought to be put before students. In the past, millions learned the story, the traditions, and the values of American culture through singing folk songs. Here, if anywhere, we shall find primary sources of simplicity and compelling power.

American folk songs address the great themes of our history—seafaring, immigration, frontier and farm life, human effort and struggle in its manifold forms, freedom and slavery, religion, and the trade union movement. From the start men, women, and children have composed and loved these songs. The songs tell what ordinary people saw with their own eyes and heard with their own ears; how they felt about the sufferings that they endured and the joys that lightened their days. Because songs often represent the experience not just of one singer but of many others, they are both deeply personal and inescapably historical. More than that, they place human beings where they belong, at the very center of historical reality.

Again and again folk songs introduce an historical episode briefly but vividly. Here it is the *introductory* quality of the song that is so useful for students just beginning to read history. These songs can illuminate an entire historical landscape like a flash of lightning. Much of the research and reading on the topic that may follow does little more than embroider and verify the dimensions of that first insight.

"General Lee's Wooing" is a fine example of a folk song which is also a significant primary source. An unknown Northern soldier wrote it following the battle of Antietam Creek, September 17, 1862; he set it to the tune of *Tannenbaum.*

General Lee's Wooing[7]

My Maryland, my Maryland,
 I bring thee presents fine,
A dazzling sword with jewelled hilt,
 A flask of Bourbon wine;
I bring thee sheets of ghostly white
 To deck thy bridal bed,
With curtains of the purple eve
 And garlands gory red.

My Maryland, my Maryland,
 Sweet land upon the shore,
Bring out thy stalwart yeomanry,
 Make clean the threshing floor.
My ready wains lie stretching far
 Across the fertile plain,
And I among the reapers stand
 To gather in the grain.

My Maryland, my Maryland,
 I fondly wait to see,
Thy banner flaunting in the breeze,
 Beneath the trysting tree.

While all my gallant company
 Of gentlemen with spurs,
Come tramping tramping o'er the hills,
 And tramping through the furze.

My Maryland, my Maryland,
 I feel the leaden rain,
I see the winged messenger
 Come hurling to my brain.
I feathered with thy golden hair,
 'Tis feathered now in vain,
I spurn the hand that loosed the shaft,
 And curse thee in my pain.

My Maryland, my Maryland,
 Alas the ruthless day,
That sees my gallant buttonwoods
 Ride galloping away;
And ruthless for my chivalry,
 Proud gentlemen with spurs,
Whose bones lie stark upon the hills,
 And stark among the furze.

More than twenty thousand Americans lost their lives in a single day at Antietam, but in spite of this vast sacrifice, the encounter was a stand-off. It was, nonetheless, a decisive battle of the Civil War, for it led directly to Lincoln's First Emancipation Proclamation. That great event changed the fortunes of war and made a Northern victory, though still far in the future, practically inevitable.

The Maryland battle took place when Lee himself, having blunted McClellan's offensive against Virginia in the Seven Days' Fight (summer 1862), went over to the attack and moved against the North. Defeating Pope at Manassas, Lee placed himself astride the Potomac west of Washington, D.C. The world held its breath: if Lee could not be stopped as he headed toward Maryland and Pennsylvania, a Southern triumph was at hand. Union prospects of victory would fade, perhaps forever.

Such is the climactic moment of the war presented in "General Lee's Wooing." Lee is portrayed as a grim lover wooing Maryland and bringing with him gifts appropriate to war and death—a shining sword, white sheets that symbolize both love and the grave, blood-red flowers, the curtains of night. But the wooer meets a harsh rebuff; bullets sting his flesh. The gallant men who rode with him turn back, leaving bloody tracks in the dust; the bodies of the fallen rot in the fields and their gleaming bones litter the hills.

On September 17, Lincoln's union escaped disaster by a hair's breadth. The president now made the great decision from which, so far, he had shrunk; he decided to free the slaves and to tell the world that freedom itself was the aim of the American war. Four days after the carnage ended, Lincoln issued the Emancipation Proclamation, declaring that all slaves—whose owners were still at that time in rebellion—would be freed on January 1, 1863. The proclamation, too, opened the way for tens of thousands of black people to participate actively in the war. This black intervention, as Lincoln later recognized, proved a major factor in securing the final union victory.

Students today *must* grasp the meaning of Antietam if they wish to understand what the Civil War was about. "General Lee's Wooing" links a personal battle experience with mighty and impersonal historical forces. At the same time, it is a poetic gem, a tiny example of what is meant by historical literature—a document that is at one and the same time a work of art and a first-rate primary historical source.

During the Civil War soldiers and civilians composed literally thousands of songs; there is a song for every battle and, for some battles, dozens. This enormous creativity was not accidental. From the beginning, folk song had played a big role in the life of Americans—they had indeed literally sung their way through history. There were good reasons for this prominence of song. Hard work dominated the lives of men, women, and children in preindustrial America. Song lightened the monotony of much of this labor and speeded the leaden hours; it provided food for thought and pleasure for the mind; it set in motion magical rhythms to conserve energy and ward off exhaustion.

Men and women did different kinds of work and sang different kinds of songs. Each gender expressed feelings and viewpoints specific to itself. Such songs constitute a fundamental source for the history of men and women alike; women's songs, in particular, may be numbered amongst the most articulate utterances in our documentary heritage. It is doubtful whether we can achieve a first-rate introduction to America's human history if we do not draw upon this musical treasury.

As one example, we may cite the traditional woman's lament, "The Lowlands of Holland." This song, inherited from the English past, was brought to America during colonial times. It continued to be sung and loved by American women—it represented, evidently, the feelings and the experiences of many.

The Lowlands of Holland[8]

The love that I have chosen,
  I'll therewith be content,
The salt sea shall be frozen,
  Before I do repent.
Repent it shall I never,
  Until the day I die,
And the raging sea and the stormy winds
  Have parted my love and me.

My love lies in the salt sea,
  And I am on the side,
Enough to break a young thing's heart,
  Who lately was a bride;
Who lately was a bonny bride,
  With pleasure in her eye,
But the raging sea and the stormy winds
  Have parted my love and me.

My love he built a gallant ship,
  A ship of noted fame,
With four and twenty seamen bold,
  To box her about the main;

To box her about the main, my boys,
  Without a fear or doubt,
'Twas then my love and his gallant ship
  Were sorely tossed about.

"Oh daughter, dearest daughter,
  What makes you so lament,
Is there never a man in all our town,
  Can give your heart content?"
"There is no lad in all our town,
  No lord nor duke for me.
I never had but one true love,
  And he was drowned at sea."

"There shall no mantle cross my back,
  Nor comb go in my hair,
Neither shall coal nor candlelight
  Shine in my bower more.
Nor shall I choose another love
  Until the day I die,
For I never, never had but one true love,
  And he was drowned at sea."

According to tradition, "The Lowlands of Holland" was composed early in the eighteenth century by a young woman whose husband was drowned on a voyage to Holland. The song highlights an important aspect of seafaring in the early modern world; all who sailed in ships—soldiers, sailors, emigrants—lived in daily peril. The song reminds us, too, that women shared the dangers of the sea even if they themselves did not venture on board ship. To sing this song today is to feel afresh the impact of ancient sorrow and to share the agonizing grief of final loss.

Folk songs such as "The Lowlands of Holland" unfold their stories with vividness, speed, and penetrating vision. Here they strike a responsive chord in human nature because most human beings are endowed with the capacity for empathy. Millions of people need to know what they inherit from the past. They need to know what is worth striving for and what imparts dignity and meaning to every human life. On the whole, our history texts contribute little to satisfying this need; however rich they may be in fact, too often such texts are threadbare in meaning; no broad vision sustains them. But a presentation of history that lacks this visionary quality can hardly be called history at all.

It cannot be said that the contemporary media compensate for this lack of stimulus to creative imagination. In long hours of passive viewing, television thrusts before the young images in enormous quantity and overwhelming detail; this media fare is unlikely to stimulate the independent creative imagination.[9]

The folk song approach is quite different from that of visual media or text. The songs, indeed, tell a story and throw forth images, but *only in outline*. Words and melody merely provide clues with the help of which each listener is invited to build a unique picture of the events being described. Such songs, therefore, fulfill the first rule of effective teaching: students themselves must participate actively in the educational process. Young people may join in singing these songs—a highly enjoyable learning experience.

Folk songs stimulate the imaginative life in endless ways, from the simplest to the most sophisticated. "A Paper of Pins" provides one very simple example of this process. Courting songs such as this were popular in colonial days when small houses and crowded cabins provided little privacy, and where in winter young people had to do their courting in public or not at all; they might pass a pleasant time by singing with each other. In "A Paper of Pins" the young man lays out all kinds of tempting gifts for his girlfriend; but she will not be tempted if she cannot imagine the lovely things that he is offering. Both then and now the song, as it were, compels us to visualize the young man's gifts. No two listeners will see the song in exactly the same way; each person's vision will be unique. Why does the tempter begin with a mere paper of pins?—In the subsistence economy of colonial times, most families had to be content with things they themselves could produce; pins were costly and had to be imported from Europe.

A Paper of Pins[10]

"I'll give to you a paper of pins,
    And that's the way our love begins,
If you will marry, marry me,
    If you will marry me."
"I'll not accept your paper of pins,
    If that's the way our love begins,
And I'll not marry, marry you,
    And I'll not marry you."

"I'll give to you a dress of red,
    Stitched all around with golden thread,
If you will marry, marry me,
    If you will marry me."
"I'll not accept your dress of red,
    Stitched all around with golden thread,
And I'll not marry, marry you,
    And I'll not marry you."

"I'll give to you a coach and four,
    That you may visit from door to door,
If you will marry, marry me,
    If you will marry me."

"I'll not accept your coach and four,
    That I may visit from door to door,
And I'll not marry, marry you,
    And I'll not marry you."

"I'll give to you the keys to my chest
    That you may have money at your request,
If you will marry, marry me,
    If you will marry me."
"I will accept the keys to your chest,
    That I may have money at my request,
And I will marry, marry you,
    And I will marry you."

"Sugar and spices, coffee and tea,
    You love my money but you don't love me,
And I'll not marry, marry you,
    And I'll not marry you."

Folk songs evoke not only imagination but also empathy. As students come to know the people in these songs, they learn also to share their joy and pain. The element of compassion so lacking in texts is an ever-present accompaniment of this musical approach to the past.

Folk song literature, finally, meets the criteria for selecting classroom material sketched above both in terms of flexibility and historical content and in terms of literary style. We can examine hundreds of these songs and find that all use only the simplest words. Such songs defy analysis in terms of reading levels: they are at everybody's reading level from the cradle to the grave. Yet, though couched in simple language, the songs are anything but simplistic; they cut to the bone of human experience. Often these songs—as witness "General Lee's Wooing" or "The Lowlands of Holland"—are literary gems, providing models of style from which many students may benefit. And, as may be seen from "A Paper of Pins" the songs are filled with people who talk to each other and who come into conflict. Dialogue accords with the maxim set forth years ago by Jacques Barzun in his *American Teacher:* of two methods of presentation, other things being equal, the more dramatic will be the more effective.

We cite here, as an example of exquisite verbal simplicity, "No More My Lord," a work song of black people that almost certainly dates back to the days of slavery. Men and women are in the woods, clearing away trees where one day cotton will be grown. Each downbeat is the stroke of an ax, striking again and again throughout the long day; in counterpoint is the lovely vision of the slave that sustains life and transcends toil.

No More, My Lord[11]

Refrain: No more, my Lord, no more,
      my Lord
      Lord I'll never turn back no
      more.

1. I found in Him
    A resting place,
    And He have made me glad.

2. Jesus the man
    I am looking for,
    Can you tell me
    Where He's gone?

3. Go down, go down
    Among floweryard,
    And perhaps you may find,
    Find Him there.

The songs—a cherished part of our literary and historical heritage—have found their way into our texts no more than other wonderful materials discussed in the first part of this article. Here, too, we teachers need to explore the challenge. Until well into the twentieth century most Americans lived in a traditional rural culture. Children and young people learned about their society and its history in a variety of settings, mostly informal: at their parent's knees, in winter evenings around the family hearth; in meetinghouse and village school; and at work—in the fields, at the lathe, the last, or the loom. The songs were part of this core of popular education. From childhood, song eased the strain of work, giving consolation and providing entertainment during leisure hours. Beyond that, the songs were models for new creation. Each generation absorbed the tradition and then went on to make its own contribution, to tell its own story. Each successive generation first learned, then created—the two processes were intertwined. The sum of this creative work provides a many-sided picture of American experience over the centuries.

Over the past three-quarters of a century all this has changed. Work, particularly factory and office work, has become regimented and depersonalized. Both the factorylike workplace and the city streets where millions pass their lives generate a ceaseless, unmusical racket; the human voice can hardly prevail about the uproar. Family life, too, in the olden days nourished and stimulated communication through song; but during the twentieth century, family structure has been undergoing a change and a disintegration that we barely understand. Older people used to be precious to a family, both as educators and as singers; their lot in our modern world is an increasing and tragic estrangement from the young. As for music-making itself, commercialism now dominates the field; the oral heritage embodied in folk songs is fast becoming an endangered species.

What does this mean? American children are no longer being taught their traditional heritage. In principle, of course, there is no reason why the media should not include this in its presentations; but in practice it does not happen often. Take, for example, the heritage of cowboy music: over the years such pioneer scholars as John and Alan Lomax, Margaret Larkin, Carl Sandburg, and Americo Paredes have collected and transcribed cowboy songs. There emerges a picture of men who were not only workers, wanderers, and horsemen but poets as well. Unfortunately, the media has shown little interest in exploring this heritage in its profundity and beauty; over the years, instead, the public has been spoonfed a stereotype of mindless violence, a cheaply created lowest common denominator with which to link the inevitable sales message.

What, then, can be done if we wish to preserve and hand on the American song tradition? Perhaps the time has come for the teaching profession, and for historians in particular, to grasp the significance of the oral heritage as a central component of historical literature and to incorporate it at all levels in the history classroom—not excluding, of course, classrooms in colleges of education.

PROPOSAL FOR A HISTORICAL LITERATURE CENTER

Original sources for illuminating the American past are available in almost inexhaustible variety; teachers are challenged to use these materials and render them directly accessible to the rising generation. But the mere existence of these sources is not enough to ensure their use; further conditions must be met. What kind of bridges, we may ask, need to be built between the source collections on the one side and the schools on the other if the nation's literary heritage is to enter the mainstream of its intellectual life and become a fund upon which teachers may draw?

As an indispensable first step, we would suggest setting up a "historical literature center" to service high school and elementary school teachers in California. Such a center, financed by both public and private money, might be conducted under the auspices of the School of Education at Berkeley in collaboration with other university departments; and it might draw upon the scholarly resources of the state university system. A center of this kind would not duplicate others now in existence and would in some ways be unique. Most archival collections have as their main function the gathering together, classifying, and storage of books and manuscripts and the provision of facilities for visiting research workers. The center under consideration here would have as its main purpose not only assembling documentary sources—with special emphasis on a "youth archive"—but also systematically disseminating them to teachers and students throughout the state.

This could be accomplished through the medium of a (weekly, monthly) bulletin to teachers, libraries, and schools; the bulletin should also include background material on the circumstances under which such documents came to be written, analysis of their contents, and suggestions for their use in the classroom. In addition, the bulletin could also serve as a clearinghouse for recording teacher experience in using the documents and for an exchange of views.

Let me explore a few implications that such a center might have for California history teachers.

THE CENTER AS YOUTH ARCHIVE AND ARCHIVE FOR THE USE OF YOUTH

As suggested above, this collection of materials would need to embody the concept of a "youth archive"—an archive preserving the record of how youth, over the long years of American history, has shaped its experience, its spiritual life, its work and play. To preserve records generated by youth itself may be thought of as a frontier of the historian's work in the late twentieth century.*

---

*The suggestion that our young people may be especially intrigued by the experience of youth during earlier times is developed by Matthew T. Downey in "Childhood: The Way It Was," *Teacher*, October 1980, pp. 59 ff. "For students today," writes Downey, "historical childhood memoirs make more than just diverting reading. They can become a primary resource for involving students in the process of history on a personal level."

California today is in the midst of a revolution in immigration patterns profoundly affecting the ethnic composition of the state. Social history is here being made under our very eyes; it needs to be recorded by the people themselves who are making that history—and, above all, by young people.[12] California, therefore, must encourage its youthful immigrants to write, to record their experiences, and to preserve that record. We must begin to conceive of the classroom as a place where history is not merely taught but also written. A youth archive that cherished and conserved such writings might be an incomparable contribution not only to state history but also to that of the nation itself. Such new records could begin to enrich America's history classrooms at once and for all time.

For the contemporary period ample materials exist from which to build a youth archive. But how much could be found from earlier times? It is not yet possible to say because so few historians have ever really looked. At the very least, two types of sources cast light upon the life and experience of youth: the testimony of young people themselves in the form of diaries, letters, reminiscences, art work, and songs; and descriptions of the youth scene recorded by contemporary observers. Some indication of the abundance of the sources in the first of these two categories has been discussed in this article. With regard to the second category, a little more must be said.

Many collections of materials generated by public and private agencies ought to find a place in a youth archive. Such sources would include the papers of Child Labor Committees, of Societies for the Prevention of Cruelty to Children, and similar organizations. There should be a place also to hold records of hearings conducted by federal and state authorities in connection with the investigation of young people's living and working conditions. Although this article has not been concerned with pictorial art as a historical source, it might not be out of place at this point to mention photographic documentation of the life of working youth that was produced by people such as Lewis Hine. Most of the great Hine collection is located in Washington, D.C. Duplicating, reviewing, and cataloguing this material in order to create a youth archive easily accessible to teachers and would in itself be a major contribution to studying and teaching about America's industrial revolution.

THE CENTER AS PUBLISHER

Documents might be distributed through publication of a review of historical literature. This could be issued at regular intervals and mailed to a list that included librarians, schools of education, graduate students, teachers, and consultants. Regular dissemination of materials soon would bear fruit in the form of a file of first-rate primary sources easily available to students and teachers throughout the state.

Documents in themselves are indispensable tools of historical study; but they cannot be properly understood or evaluated unless the reader is familiar with the context in which they were created. We need to know something about the writers and about the specific circumstances that were the occasion for the creation of each document. All of us, too, need help in examining the words and formulations that they used, and in eliciting the proper meaning from each part of the document. Exegesis, in both the broadest and narrowest sense of the word, is a function that has to be linked with the dissemination of source materials; such background material can be invaluable to teachers and to students alike, particularly if accompanied by bibliographical aids and suggestions for further reading. And such a review would be particularly helpful if it indicated ways in which the historian might use a given document in the classroom itself.

THE CENTER AS CLEARINGHOUSE

The history center should act as a clearinghouse through which teachers may communicate with each other, describing experiences using the documents and passing along techniques and conclusions to others. Not the least of the challenges facing the center would be to find ways to elicit this type of information from busy teachers and to make it generally available. It is doubtful if we shall see much advance in the art of history teaching unless practitioners develop a sense of collective interest and involvement—of the value both of learning from others in the field and of making personal contributions to the growth of a collective expertise.

THE CENTER AS LOCUS FOR SEMINARS ON DOCUMENTATION

Personnel of such a history center would be able to organize seminars of a type different from those available to teaching historians in the past. Such seminars might take as their main concern the problem of the selection of sources, including song, for classroom use and the pedagogy of such documents.

One such seminar topic, for example, might be "textbook documentation," that is, a study of topics in the text that needed independent documentation, of the sources available for this, and of the folder of documentary material that would result. People attending this seminar would be asked to bring with them copies of the history or social studies text being used in their own classrooms. The seminar would explore the question: "Which topics treated in these texts are so important that they merit elaboration and documentation from original sources?" Having divided the topics up among themselves, members of the seminar would then proceed to conduct a search for materials. Subsequent meetings would examine and discuss the results of this research, organized by topic. Thus, strengthened with the fruits of a four-week seminar (for which, of course, they would have to be paid), high school historians would return to the classroom. The final phase of the work would be a report on classroom use of the sources and *publication* of the sources so researched and used.

A seminar of this type might help teachers take the first step in moving away from the text and in substituting independent work for the ready-made commercial product. The final phase would focus upon preparing reports on classroom use of the sources that had been generated. These reports might then be published in the center's review. Based upon the work outlined above, the center itself might consider preparing and publishing a documentary text or a series of such texts. For elementary models, one may examine the volumes of the *Living History Library* (Alfred A. Knopf, 1967–76). Individual research and experience would in this way be exploited to enrich the resources available to history teachers throughout the state.

It is worth stressing that members of the seminar would produce documentary packages quite different from each other's. Such seminars, effectively organized, might be able to generate as many packages, almost, as there were participants. Materials for a new type of history teaching would begin to emerge from the educational community itself as opposed to the textbook establishment.

NOTES

1. Letter to James A. Garfield, New York City, 4 May 1874. New York Historical Society, Frank Moore mss. Moore told Garfield that Abraham Lincoln had followed his work with great interest and had passed on to him Confederate papers, from which he had clipped letters.
2. The passages are taken from *The Narrative of Mary Rowlandson*, reproduced in Charles Lincoln, ed., *Narratives of the Indian Wars, 1675–99* (New York, 1959).
3. Roger Lamb, *An Original and Authentic Journal of Occurrences during the Late American War* (1809; reissued, New York, 1968), pp. 193–194.
4. Norman R. Yetman, ed., *Voices from Slavery* (New York, 1970), pp. 239–240.
5. Francis Parkman, *The Oregon Trail* (1949; reissued, New York: Signet Classic edition, 1950).
6. John Spargo, *The Bitter Cry of the Children* (1906; reissued, New York, 1968), p. 166.
7. Frank Moore, *The Civil War in Song and Story, 1860–1865* (New York, 1889), p. 338. Slightly abridged. "Wain" is a wagon or cart; "furze" is a synonym for gorse, yellow-flowered shrubs of the species *genista*. The substitution for the modern classroom of "firs" would make equally good sense.

8. John A. Scott, Child #92, reproduced in *Settlers on the Eastern Shore* (New York, 1967), pp. 194–195; For variants, see Bertrand Harris Bronson, *Traditional Tunes of the Child Ballads*, vol. 2 (Princeton, NJ, 1959–1972), 418ff. For the American variant, *The Yankee Man of War*, see H. M. Belden, ed., *Ballads and Songs Collected by the Missouri Folk-Lore Society* (Columbia, MO, 1955), pp. 379–380.

9. For studies that begin to probe the depressing effects of television on children's creativity, see Dorothy G. Singer, "Television and the Developing Imagination of the Child," in National Institute of Mental Health, *Television and Behavior*, vol. 2 (Washington, DC, 1982), pp. 39ff.

10. John A. and Alan Lomax, *American Ballads and Folk Songs* (New York, 1934), pp. 323–324.

11. Collected, adapted, and arranged by Alan Lomax. Copyright 1947 Essex Music Ltd., London, England. All publication rights controlled by Ludlow Music, Inc., New York, NY for the U.S.A. and Canada. Transcribed by John Anthony Scott from "Negro Prison Songs," Tradition Records 1020. Used by permission.

12. See Carol Younglove's brilliant contribution, *Reflections: Young Immigrants Tell Their Stories* (Hayward, California, 1982). This is a collection of life stories by more than forty young immigrants from Vietnam, Cambodia, Pakistan, Mexico, the Philippines, and other nations. The students prepared their autobiographies as class assignments in Westlake Junior High School.

Chapter 12

Reforming the History Curriculum

MATTHEW T. DOWNEY

The current effort to revitalize history teaching in the schools must include a fundamental rethinking of what history and social studies instruction should encompass and how it should be organized. A basic restructuring of that curriculum is essential if the movement now underway to reform history education is to have lasting impact. Necessary steps toward this goal should include more inservice training for teachers; helping teachers broaden their repertoire of teaching strategies; improved textbooks; a broader range of supplementary materials; and increased graduation requirements in history/social studies. But, because many of the problems that confront history as a school subject are rooted in the present organization of the curriculum, such developments will have little lasting effect if the curriculum itself remains unchanged.

Although curriculum decisions in the United States are made on a state and local basis, something approaching an unofficial, national history-social studies curriculum does exist. The sequence of courses varies somewhat from one school district or state to another, but the programs do have much in common. One will, predictably, find instruction in grades K–6 organized according to the so-called "expanding environments" model. Beginning with the study of family, school, neighborhood, and community in the primary grades, the focus broadens in the middle grades to include state history, United States history, and world history, geography, and cultures. The pattern is less predictable at grades 7, 8, and 9, but usually includes another course in United States history at grade 8. The high school curriculum typically includes a second course in world history at grade 10; another United States history course at grade 11; and some combination of United States government and social science electives at grade 12. A combination of factors holds this informal national curriculum in place, the most important being its nearly unanimous adoption by commercial textbook publishers. The K–6 social studies series and the secondary school United States and world history textbooks of the major publishing companies follow that sequence with only minor variations.

The curriculum scope and sequence described above has a number of inherent weaknesses. In the first place, it lacks a coherent sequence of courses from kindergarten through grade 12. The expanding environments model provides a structure for the early grades, but the sequence ends at grade 6, effectively severing the K–6 curriculum from that of the junior and senior high school years. That model has other failings as well. It does not provide a framework for cumulative learning; the environments expand outward, but not upward. That is, the content prescribed for one level does not help to prepare students for a higher level of learning at the next grade or series of grades. Moreover, the sociology of family, neighborhood, and community life is surely not the most interesting curriculum to offer students in the primary grades. It is better calculated to extinguish than to kindle interest in social studies.

The single most important failure of the present curriculum is its inability to provide a structured foundation for studying history. Each level of instruction ought to help prepare students for the study of history at the next higher level. Material presented in the primary grades should help the students get ready for the formal study of history that usually begins with state history at about grade 4. It should start preparing them to think in terms of time and space—concepts that provide the matrix in which historical development takes place. Building upon this foundation, the elementary grades should offer aspects of historical development selected to cover what young people can most easily understand. The secondary school curriculum should then go on to examine stages of historical development that are still more complex, including the history of industrial and postindustrial societies in modern times. No such developmental sequence undergirds the existing history curriculum. Children begin the study of history with little or no preparation. They proceed through cycles of survey courses in United States and world history that repeatedly cover much of the same ground and that have no sense of coherence and direction.

The curriculum in place today relies far too much on survey courses that limit the opportunity for students to study periods or civilizations in depth. Surveys of United States history are presented usually at three grade levels (5, 8, and 11), with surveys of world history appearing in two grades (6 and 10). While survey courses have value for the purpose of synthesis, by their very nature they sacrifice depth of learning for breadth of coverage. Required to cover too much ground too rapidly, students tend to end up with a superficial historical understanding. The survey format is of most questionable value for the study of world history. Covering whole civilizations in a few days or a few weeks is not likely to lead to any permanent learning. In both

United States and world history surveys, students are wearied by having to skim over and relearn material that has little meaning to them, that was imperfectly taught in earlier courses, and that was quickly forgotten.

The emphasis on survey courses is also partly responsible for an excessive reliance on textbooks. Social studies has a well-deserved reputation for being one of the most textbook-driven subjects in the school curriculum. One would hardly expect it to be otherwise, as helping teachers "cover the ground" is one thing textbooks do well. History textbooks lay out a course of study organized so that each chapter encompasses roughly one week of instruction. A teacher who maintains the pace set by the publisher can expect to cover the sweep of world or United States history in the thirty-six weeks or so available in a school year. To pause for an in-depth look at a topic or period is to risk falling behind and failing to bring students up to the present. The latter, of course, is a frequently heard complaint. Teachers do fall behind and students do graduate from high school without ever having studied modern history.

The enduring popularity of the lecture method in history classrooms is due in some measure to this emphasis on coverage. "History teachers are under pressure to 'cover' a great deal of material," notes Hazel W. Hertzberg, "and the lecture is one way to provide the coverage with the kind of information and interpretations the teacher thinks important. It is a way to ensure that the class has a common body of knowledge other than that gained from instructional materials."[1] Generations of pedagogical reformers have condemned this method of teaching history in the schools, but it continues to thrive. In the mid-1970s, teachers were reported to be using the lecture-recitation method every day in a third of the nation's tenth- to twelfth-grade social studies classrooms, and at least once a week in almost half of the classrooms.[2]

It is even possible that textbooks themselves would be of higher quality if writers and publishers were freed from some of the constraints imposed upon them by the present curriculum. History textbooks have been widely criticized for being blandly written and insensible to the conflict, passions, and turmoil of real life. But the single most important failing, especially of world history textbooks, is the superficial manner in which they treat complex individuals, developments, and events. Individuals who had a decisive impact on their times may be barely mentioned; philosophies, ideologies, and religions often are summarized in brief paragraphs. Complex social processes are given one-sentence definitions that students are expected to memorize. But how much more can one reasonably expect? Required to sweep through world history in eight hundred or so pages, textbooks can provide only superficial treatments that distort and oversimplify the complex reality of the past.

The structure of the curriculum does a lot to account for the perennial complaint of high school students that history is boring. They often associate their boredom with repetition of subject matter, especially in the United States history course, which most students take first in grade 5, then in grade 8, and once again in grade 11. "In high school, American History courses become monotonous," reports a student from Edgewater, Maryland. "They continue to teach the things that have already been learned in previous years. . . . History becomes an empty show that is continually repeated until all interest is soon lost."[3] Or, as a student in Rhode Island explained, "You can only hear about the Civil War so many times. American history does not go back very far, so you have to study the same stuff over and over again."[4] The complaint is not that American history itself is dull but that students are bored because of the way the subject is presented to them. In large part that is a curriculum problem.

Of course, in addition it may be that students also are bored with history courses because of the kind of content that has traditionally received emphasis. "Many students, however, claim that the traditional method of studying history is boring, and that past dates, wars, and government have no relation to their present and future," reports another student. Since history in the schools has a civic as well as an intellectual purpose, the content usually is weighted toward political and institutional history. It is a history of the public rather than private lives of people. "In order to make studying history more enjoyable, and history itself more attractive, students should first be exposed to the things in history which can inspire them," the student quoted above continued. "These things may include famous personalities, their own ancestors, and the ways in which people their own age lived. . . . By stressing the personal and cultural aspects through the new concept of 'social history,' teachers can inspire their students to learn more."[5] Her recommendation, in other words, was to introduce students to the private as well as the public side of the past. The problem is that to do both adequately requires a great deal of time, more time over the course of a school year than the present curriculum permits.

The present curriculum is not cast in concrete. Not only is there an obvious need for change; there is also ample historical precedent for the kind of change being called for here. The history–social studies curriculum has evolved over time, responding to changing social priorities and perceptions of what students need.

The first widely adopted history curriculum in American secondary schools, established early in this century, was based on an 1899 report by the American Historical Association's Committee of Seven.[6] It called for a four-year sequence of courses: ancient history at grade 9, medieval and modern European history at grade 10, English history at grade 11, and United States history and government at the grade 12. This remained the basic menu of history offerings for high schools into the 1920s, when a new wave of curriculum reform swept through American schools.

The new blueprint for curriculum reform was a scope and sequence for secondary social studies introduced in 1916 by the National Education Association. It called for a year of civics at grade 9, world history at grade 10, American history at grade 11, and a one-year course on problems of American democracy in grade 12. The world history course was designed to replace the sequence of European history courses recommended in the 1899 AHA report. By the end of the 1930s the NEA curriculum for secondary social studies had become widely adopted. The present elementary school social studies curriculum also took its present shape in the 1930s, as school districts and textbook publishers embraced the "expanding environments" curriculum, which Paul Hanna at Stanford University had done much to popularize.

The most recent wave of reform—the New Social Studies movement of the 1960s—also had an impact on the curriculum. Led mainly by social science educators, this movement succeeded in replacing the NEA-inspired, twelfth-grade course in problems of American democracy with elective courses in the social sciences. In many schools it also helped to dislodge the ninth-grade civics course and replace old social studies courses with the New Social Studies offerings. The history curriculum remained largely intact, although enrollments in the tenth-grade world history course declined as the course was changed from a requirement to an elective in many school districts.[7]

The effort now underway to revitalize history teaching calls for three fundamental changes in the history–social studies curriculum. In the first place, we need to design a structure that provides for cumulative learning from kindergarten through grade 12. At each grade level, students should be building upon knowledge and skills already learned and should be receiving preparation for the levels yet to come. Secondly, the survey approach should either be abandoned or sufficiently modified to permit students to study in depth various periods, cultures, and civilizations. Finally, learning in depth should help students integrate and understand the varied dimensions of human thought and activity that give richness of texture to the past. That is, courses should integrate social and cultural developments along with the political and institutional history; should incorporate art, literature, and music as well as scientific and technological contributions of a people; and should include the private as well as public side of the past.

Restructuring the curriculum to provide for cumulative learning poses a major challenge. In the first place, it will require a major departure from past habits of thought. Efforts to reform history–social studies education have traditionally focused on single parts of the curriculum, usually the high school grades. That has been true especially for reform movements led by university historians and social scientists, who perhaps feel most comfortable working with students and courses in situations that most closely resemble their own university students and courses. This reform will require history educators to develop a K–12 curriculum perspective. Understandably also, implementing a new K–12 curriculum will be impossible without the support of textbook publishers. Since new textbook series demand a substantial investment on their part, publishers will need assurance that the new curriculum will be widely adopted. That would require endorsement of a new curriculum by a substantial number of teachers associations and other professional organizations, school districts, and state departments of education. Although a major challenge, restructuring the history–social studies curriculum is not beyond the realm of possiblilty.

To develop alternatives to the current history survey courses is a somewhat easier task. A variety of course models exist that would permit greater depth of study if the chronological coverage were reduced. The weighted survey is one variation. It retains the survey format but emphasizes different periods of history in each grade level at which the survey is taught. The idea of giving a different chronological emphasis to United States history courses in elementary, junior high, and high school was first proposed in a 1944 report by a joint committee of the American Historical Association, the Mississippi Valley Historical Association (now the Organization of American Historians), and the National Council for the Social Studies. Entitled *American History in Schools and Colleges*, this report recommended weighting the elementary survey course toward the earliest period of the nation's history, while emphasizing 1776–1876 in junior high and the post–Civil War period in high school.[8] In recent years many school districts and some textbook publishers have moved in this direction. The resulting courses remain surveys, nevertheless, and teachers still are expected to cover the sweep of American history.

An alternative to the one-year survey course that is currently gaining favor is a "period-focused" course in United States or world history that divides the material into periods to be taught sequentially in different years. Such courses cover a more extended period of time than the popular period courses offered in most university departments of history, such as "the Age of Jackson," "Civil War and Reconstruction," or "the Progressive Era." Each course represents a portion of the traditional survey course and typically begins with a review that ties each new period to the one that preceded it. For example, Texas schools divide the United States history survey between grades 8 and 11, with the Civil War as the dividing point. California's recently revised "History–Social Science Framework" (1987) divides the United States history survey as well as the world history survey among three grades.[9] Different periods of United States history are recommended for grades 5, 8, and 11, and world history for grades 6, 7, and 10. The courses are designed to be linked together by introductory reviews that refresh the students' memories about what they have previously learned and by conclusions that foreshadow historical developments that are yet to come. The purpose of both the Texas and California models is to reduce to a manageable period of time the amount of history to be studied each year in order to make time for in-depth study.

The great advantage of such period-focused courses is that they provide the time needed for a study of the past that has both depth and breadth. By sharply reducing the time period to be covered (by one-half or two-thirds), teachers will be able to let students examine the music, literature, religion, and other aspects of cultural life of the period being studied as well as the customary political, economic, and social history. Students thus can become more deeply involved and will encounter a greater number of topics of potential interest than would be possible in the conventional survey course. This can only be done by limiting the chronology to be covered in a one-year course.

What would a history–social studies curriculum look like if it were based on period-focused courses that recognize the importance of cumulative learning? The K–12 scope and sequence that follow represent one attempt to develop such a curriculum.[10] Although it is a sequence that emphasizes history and geography, it also recognizes the importance of preparing students for their responsibilities as citizens in a democratic society—a traditional role of social studies education in the public schools.

The curriculum is divided into three sections: primary grades (K–3), elementary grades (4–8), and secondary grades (9–12). These divisions help to emphasize the point that learning should be cumulative, each stage of instruction preparing the student for more advanced learning at the next higher level. The primary school curriculum begins development of skills and understandings that serve as the foundation for historical study. The elementary years will offer period-focused courses in world and United States history, from prehistoric people through the nineteenth century, providing a historical basis for understanding the modern world. Emphasis in the secondary school years on the study of modern history and civic education helps prepare students for their future roles as citizens of a democratic society in an interdependent world.

THE PRIMARY GRADES

Instruction in the primary grades builds a foundation for future learning in the social studies. It is an essential part of the curriculum, providing children with basic knowledge and skills.

In the primary grades, students first encounter the concept of culture (much too abstract an idea to be used formally at this level) by looking at three of its concrete dimensions. Cultural patterns are most visible in the way people (1) provide for the necessities of life, (2) live together, and (3) enrich their lives and express themselves through the visual arts—storytelling and literature, music, and dance. To learn how people have lived in other places and times helps children develop new vantage points from which to see themselves and the world around them.

An essential step in developing reflective and critical thinking is learning to view the world from alternative perspectives. Social studies instruction in the primary grades contributes in a fundamental way to the development of higher-level thinking skills.

The primary social studies curriculum also helps children begin to think in disciplined ways about space and time, two of the most difficult concepts that students must learn to master.

KINDERGARTEN: THE CHILDREN'S WORLD

The child's first encounter with social studies needs to be a wide-ranging introduction to the way people live, as seen through the eyes of children. Pupils should be introduced to all kinds of children, those who live far away as well as nearby and those who lived in remote times as well as those of the present. They should also get to know children from literature and fantasy. During each encounter, the students need time to compare their own experiences with those of the children they are learning about. Instruction this year should examine children's play, nursery rhymes and children's stories, conditions of family living, and a variety of relationships between children and adults. Kindergarten should also introduce formal instruction in spatial and temporal relationships, concentrating on personal space (school and home) and personal time (daily routines). Students should learn to make simple maps of the spaces around them and to tell time and make simple time schedules. Above all else, social studies instruction needs to help make this an exciting year, filled with mental adventures out in space and back in time.

GRADE 1: ESSENTIALS FOR LIVING

Social studies instruction at grade 1 ought to focus on the most basic elements of human culture, what people depend upon to meet their daily needs—shelter, food, clothing, tools, means of transportation, and, in modern societies, basic services. While from time to time instruction should be concerned with the familiar here and now of the children's own lives, the sense of adventure planted in kindergarten must be expanded by discovering how people in other places and times have provided for basic needs in their own unique ways. Students should compare types of houses, clothing styles, and levels of technological development at various times and places, as depicted in art and literature (especially children's literature) as well as in factual accounts. Also they need to learn about the kinds of work people have done and the music they have composed about work and to help ease the drudgery of work. Even at this age, children should be able to recognize similarities in the human experience despite the great differences in the way people have met their basic needs. Learning about spatial relationships can continue by examining the location of essential places and services in the neighborhood and community; and students can map their way to school or to the shopping center. They may look at time in terms of family or generational time, comparing physical aspects of their own lives with those of their parents' when they were children.

GRADE 2: LIVING TOGETHER

At the second grade, horizons should widen, with attention shifting to the social groups in which people live and to the institutions and customs that groups of people create. Instruction here begins with the family and moves on to examine kinship groups, work groups, social groups, and people grouped into nations. As in the earlier grades, children's encounters with groups of people should be wide-ranging in space and time, although never losing touch with the here and now. In each instance, the focus should be on the human needs that groups help people fulfill—linking this new knowledge to that already acquired in the first grade about the way people meet and have met essential needs. It will be useful also for students to look at customs and traditions developed through group living, including special family days and national holidays. In this respect, social studies at grade 2 ought to be concerned about the quality of life that living in groups makes possible, foreshadowing the qualitative emphasis that will receive major attention in grade 3. Development of the students' understanding of spatial and temporal relationships will be expanded by having them now map spaces related to their own family and kin, including family migration patterns, and by examining the temporal dimensions of family and group experience. Constructing family trees and timelines and finding out about the history of their family are suitable activities.

GRADE 3: LIVING WELL

In third grade, the focus of social studies instruction shifts once again, this time to qualitative dimensions of living. People do more than survive and organize themselves into societies; they also express feelings and aspirations in tangible ways, decorate their surroundings, and have visions of a better life. These dimensions of culture, touched upon briefly in previous grades, now should receive major attention. Students need to look at how styles of clothing and shelter reflect a people's artistic tastes and notions of beauty as well as practical necessity. Also, the ways that groups of people have used literature, folklore and myths, and art and music should be explored to see how these have given meaning to daily experiences and have expressed people's hopes and aspirations; students can compare these to aspects of their own culture today. Introducing children to folklore and myths also helps prepare them for their encounter with the cultures of primitive and early peoples in the elementary grades. The students can continue by making maps that show the relationship of their community to others in the state and region.

THE ELEMENTARY GRADES

The elementary social studies curriculum introduces students to the formal study of history and geography. Equipped with an understanding of the basic components of the concept of culture (an abstraction that most students will not yet have grasped) and with the capacity to think backward in time and outward in space, children are ready to investigate people and culture in historical times. Instruction must still be kept concrete, with many opportunities provided for students to relate the past to the present. Instruction at the elementary level begins to present the historical knowledge needed for understanding twentieth-century societies and cultures, which students will go on to study at the secondary school level.

GRADE 4: EARLY PEOPLES OF THE WORLD

The fourth grade is a transitional year. Instruction here is designed to consolidate the knowledge learned in the primary grades and to prepare students for the formal study of history and geography that will begin in grade 5. The curriculum consists of an examination of primitive peoples and cultures. Much of the time should be spent on native American groups in North and South America, including an investigation of Indian cultures in the students' own locality and region. For comparative purposes, children ought to be introduced also to early human societies in Africa and Europe and to primitive cultures that still exist today. This year of study should challenge students to push back their conception of time to prehistorical eras. In addition they need: practice in viewing cultures in a holistic way, in order to see how one aspect of living relates to another. This is more easily done through examining primitive cultures rather than more complex modern ones.

It is also easier to understand the relationship between human culture and the physical environment by studying primitive societies. Finally, this venture into primitive societies will provide the perspective needed for grasping the significance of the classical civilizations that students will encounter in grade 5.

GRADE 5: CLASSICAL AND MEDIEVAL CIVILIZATIONS

This year marks the formal beginning of the study of history and geography. Students will examine civilizations on three continents: Asia (including Japan), Europe, and Africa. Each unit of study should cover the evolution of one culture and include comparisons of how people of different cultures have responded to their physical environment. The year begins with studying classical Greece and Rome. This should be followed by a unit on China through the Han Empire (A.D. 220) so that students can compare cultural development in the West and East during approximately the same historical era. But these ought not to be static comparisons; each unit must show how the culture developed and changed over time and how Greeks, Romans, and Chinese interacted with other peoples. A third unit presents the expansion of Islam and examines what life was like in Islamic civilization at about the end of the eighth century. Another set of comparative studies focuses on western Europe during the Middle Ages and the emergence of feudal society in Japan. A final unit compares western Europe during the Renaissance with China during the Ming dynasty (1368–1644). Treatment of Renaissance Europe should include the expansion of European commerce during the 16th century along with European voyages of exploration. The year concludes with an investigation of an African culture of the premodern period, such as the Benin kingdom in West Africa during the sixteenth and seventeenth centuries. In each study, the students should examine the multiple dimensions of each culture, observe how the culture changed over time, and view it within a larger regional and world context. Ideally, the focus remains concrete, with an emphasis on social history.

GRADE 6: AMERICAN HISTORY—THE BUILDING OF A NEW NATION

American history should be introduced in this grade, with major attention given to the colonial background, the creation of the United States, and the expansion of the new nation across the continent. Each unit includes instruction in geography, including the physical geography of each region studied and the interplay between culture and environment. Although basically a course in United States history, this year of study also should help to give students a hemispheric perspective. When appropriate, there should be opportunities to examine parallel developments in North and South America, especially European colonization and movements for national independence. Instruction this year will cover United States history up to the end of the Mexican War. A unit on state history may be included at an appropriate place, in order to see larger historical developments in a local context. Despite the emphasis on nation-building, this is not to be primarily a year of political history. The focus ought to be on social history, including the everyday lives of ordinary people, and on the social and cultural diversity of early America. The art, music, folklore, customs, and religious beliefs of the peoples who helped build the new nation need adequate attention.

GRADE 7: WORLD HISTORY—THE EARLY MODERN AND INDUSTRIAL ERAS

Students in the seventh grade will return to a world-history-and-cultures perspective, with the focus on the web of relationships that developed between Europe, Asia, and Africa during the eighteenth and nineteenth centuries. Geographical instruction will continue, with the emphasis this year on world economic geography. The year begins with a review of the social and cultural developments examined in the fifth grade, especially the intellectual awakening of western Europe during the Renaissance. During seventh grade students will examine in depth the following areas and periods: Europe during the Enlightenment (1689–1789); the Industrial Revolution in England (1750–1850); China in transition (1700–1900); the modernization of Japan (1850–1900); Africa under colonial rule (1825–1900); and tradition and change in India and Southeast Asia (1763–1900). Students ought to consider why, during the era of European expansion, some cultures were more successful than others in resisting Western ways. Developments in European art and music and the emergence of modern literary styles deserve special attention.

GRADE 8: UNITED STATES HISTORY—THE MAKING OF AN INDUSTRIAL NATION

At the eighth grade, students will study modernization and social change in a single nation by examining United States history during the period 1789–1914. Geographical instruction will emphasize the changing patterns of land use that accompanied industrialization and the growth of cities. This year begins with a review of early American history, emphasizing the development of trade and handicraft manufacturing during the colonial and early national periods. The eighth grade curriculum focuses on the economic changes that we associate with industrialization and on the impact of these developments on American society and culture. Political history needs more attention now than it did in grade 5, with particular attention given to the growing sectional divisiveness that led to the Civil War. Students should look also at American literature, art, and architecture, especially as these cultural forms reflected social change. Although the course should focus on the United States, American history ought not to be presented in isolation. Subjects covered will include the expansion into Latin America of U.S. commercial influence, territorial expansion in the Caribbean and the Pacific, and the complex web of cultural and intellectual ties that developed between the United States and Europe.

THE SECONDARY GRADES

The focus of social studies in the secondary school years is on the modern world. The historical knowledge about societies and cultures acquired in elementary school will have provided a solid foundation upon which to build a mature understanding of the world of the twentieth century. History instruction during these high school years should consist mainly of the study of modern times. However, both years of historical study (grades 10 and 11) need to begin with a modified survey, to provide students with a historical synthesis that will help them set developments of the twentieth century within a larger historical framework. Social studies instruction in the secondary years (grades 9 and 12) should focus on civic education, preparing students for their role as citizens in a democratic society embedded in an interdependent world.

GRADE 9: COMMUNITY CIVICS

In this yearlong civics course students learn about their community, become acquainted with local public issues, and become involved in community service. The focus this year is on the public life and institutions of the town or city in which the students live. To become more familiar with the community, students are to undertake either a local history project or an investigation calling for a social science research method. This kind of activity also will help develop research, writing, and thinking skills. Students need to study local history as well, and to find out what opportunities are available to involve citizens in contributing to the welfare of the community. This can be done in part through presentations by and interviews with community leaders and public officials. A second major project for the year will require students themselves to become involved in some useful community services; this will also serve as the basis for a reflective essay on the value of civic participation, to be submitted by the end of the year. This course in community civics is grounded on the assumption that good citizenship begins at home.

GRADE 10: THE WORLD IN THE TWENTIETH CENTURY

Instruction will consist of a year of world history, focused on the twentieth century. An introductory unit reviews the knowledge of world history acquired in earlier years; students will look at those aspects of European, Islamic, Asian, and African cultures that have endured over time, as well as those that changed during the process of modernization. This broad synthesis will give students a historical perspective on the world of the twentieth century. During the course of the year, students will examine the growing instability of Europe during an era of world wars and economic depression, as well as the growth of nationalism in areas of the world colonized by European nations. They should look at people and cultures that by midcentury were resisting European influence and should trace the demise of colonialism after World War II. These developments need to be examined within the context of the ideological and political conflicts of the Cold War era, and the emergence of the Third World as a force in world affairs. The curriculum also includes studying patterns of investment and trade and the growing economic interdependence of nations. Aspects of cultural change and cultural diffusion should be explored as well, by examining the impact of mass media and modern communications technology on peoples and cultures in the world today. Geographical instruction in grade 10 emphasizes world cultural geography in the twentieth century and the growing interdependence of the world's peoples.

GRADE 11: THE UNITED STATES IN THE TWENTIETH CENTURY

The year of modern world history will be followed by a course on the United States in the twentieth century. It begins with a survey that traces major threads of historical development that enabled the United States to become a major industrial and world power by 1900. However, the curriculum should be devoted chiefly to the twentieth century. Students will examine the emergence of the modern corporate economy and the changing social structure and ethnic composition of American society, as well as changes in the family and in other social institutions. Instruction in political history will cover the expanding role of government in American life and the success of American political institutions in adapting to change. Cultural history ought to be studied too, defined broadly enough to include popular culture and the mass media as well as art and literature. Geographic units should focus on the twentieth-century cultural geography of the United States, with particular emphasis on the American people's changing perceptions of environmental resources.

GRADE 12: AMERICAN CITIZENSHIP IN THE MODERN WORLD

The capstone of the social studies curriculum is a year of national and world civics designed to help students define their role and responsibilities as citizens of a modern democratic society in an increasingly interdependent world. The course begins by looking backward to the roots of American political culture and the original meaning of citizenship in a democratic republic. Students should examine those assumptions about the inalienable rights of human begins that date from the eighteenth-century Enlightenment and that were embodied in the Declaration of Independence and protected by the Bill of Rights. Also they need to consider implications for American foreign policy of the nation's commitment to republican government and to human rights, as well as the responsibilities of American citizens in the world community. During the course of the year students will engage in two projects. One will require research leading to some course of action on a public issue of national importance; for the second, an issue of international significance will be examined. While we assume that good citizenship begins at home, we do not assume that it ends there.

This scope and sequence are presented as one alternative to the present history–social studies curriculum. It is not the only possible alternative that could satisfy the basic requirements for curriculum reform described earlier in this chapter. Any chronologically developed history sequence that provides for cumulative learning, in-depth study, and investigation of a period or culture in sufficient breadth to permit students a glimpse of the rich texture of the past is a curriculum that deserves consideration. Unless the current movement for reform in history education includes such a fundamental reform of the history curriculum, it is unlikely to have significant or lasting impact on the teaching of history in the schools.

NOTES

1. Hazel W. Hertzberg, "Students, Methods, and Materials of Instruction," in Matthew T. Downey, ed., *History in the Schools* (Washington, DC: National Council for the Social Studies, 1985), p. 35.
2. Ibid.
3. Kimberly R. Kilos, "An Optimal Course: American History," *Magazine of History* 2, special teaching supplement (1987): 21. This was one of four essays by students published in a special section of this issue entitled "From the Other Side of the Desk: Views from Students."
4. Quoted in Barbara Tucker Cervone, "Student Attitudes Toward Studying History," *The Clearing House* 57 (December 1983): 164.

5. Gail Magenau, "Making History More Interesting," *Magazine of History* 2, special teaching supplement (1987): 23.
6. The following historical account is based largely on Hazel Whitman Hertzberg, *Social Studies Reform, 1880–1980* (Boulder, CO: Social Science Education Consortium, 1981).
7. For a fuller account of the status of history in the public schools in recent years, see Matthew T. Downey, "The Status of History in the Schools," in his *History in the Schools*, pp. 1–12.
8. *American History in Schools and Colleges*, The Report of the Committee on American History in Schools and Colleges of the American Historical Association, The Mississippi Valley Historical Association, The National Council for the Social Studies (New York: The Macmillan Co., 1944), 68–72.
9. "History–Social Science Framework for California Public Schools, Kindergarten through Grade Twelve, Field Review Draft, March 1987" (California State Department of Education, Sacramento, CA, 1987).
10. The following course descriptions were originally published in Matthew T. Downey, "Time, Space, and Culture," *Social Education* 50 (November/December 1986): 492–497. Reprinted by permission.

Chapter 13

Another Look at Community History

KAREN JORGENSEN-ESMAILI

"History, like charity, begins at home,"[1] proclaimed Johns Hopkins University professor Herbert B. Adams in 1885. This comment appeared in the revised edition of the first American book on methods of history teaching. For the next century, discussions about the importance of using local sources in the classroom appeared in leading educational and historical journals. Educators showed particular interest during four periods: 1885–1897; the years of the Great Depression; 1945–1965; and the second half of the 1970s.

This paper will explore the history of educational interest in local sources during these periods and also will address the following contemporary questions: What special contribution does community history make to the history–social studies curriculum? How can community history be integrated into the existing program? What types of teaching strategies work best for today's students? How can we reform our pre-service and in-service teacher training so that it adequately prepares teachers to use local sources in the classroom?

THE DEBATE OVER LOCAL SOURCES: 1885–1986

During the 1880s and 1890s interest in community history was part of a larger debate over the nature of the emerging public high school. Educators of the period struggled with the question of how to articulate the high school and college curricula. They sought to define how modern disciplines such as history and science could be integrated into the high school course. Not the least of their concerns was the question of methodology: What were the most effective techniques for teaching history to secondary students?

Mary Sheldon Barnes of Stanford University led a group of educators who advocated that students should not be taught by traditional textbooks but rather should study history primarily through a care-

214

ful investigation of original sources. Barnes saw the community as the richest repository of these materials.[2]

The "source method" was soon criticized by a number of prominent historians in the American Historical Association (AHA). While admitting that sources provided useful supplemental material, AHA spokesmen attacked the method as a "shallow imitation of the German seminar."[3] In 1899, the AHA Committee of Seven put to rest this fledgling community history movement by declaring that they were "unable to approve a method of teaching sometimes called the 'source method,' in which pupils have in their hands little more than a series of extracts."[4] As Robert Keohane suggests, the committee reaffirmed the legitimacy of the "textbook . . . and ready-made conclusions, guaranteed as pure by historical authorities."[5]

During the social turmoil of the thirties, community history found new advocates. Foremost were the proponents of the community-centered school. This group, composed primarily of social studies teachers, believed that the work of the school should be united with the activities of the community. The community offered "raw materials for an understanding of our total culture" and helped students develop "an understanding of our evolving culture, . . . a wholesome framework of (democratic) values," and "social competence necessary to participate effectively in the action of our culture."[6]

But by the end of the Great Depression, despite the enthusiasm of community-centered school advocates, relatively few teachers were using local sources.[7] In the early postwar years, however, another community history movement came to the fore, led primarily by state historians and state historical societies. Mary E. Cunningham of the New York State Historical Society was an important spokesperson for this group. In 1946 she suggested that the new interest in community history was rooted partly in the increased acceptance of local sources by the American Historical Association. Cunningham cited the AHA's 1944 Wesley Report on history teaching as an example of this change in attitude. She also contended that new developments in learning theory showed educators how "the natural progression was from the near to the remote, from the known to the unknown, and from the locality to the state and nation."[8] Further, she suggested that the postwar revitalization of many state historical societies was itself a major factor in the new movement.

Throughout the fifties and sixties, new proponents of this postwar movement emerged, such as Clifford Lord of Columbia University, who edited the "localized history" series published by Teachers College Press. Major titles in the series included Lord's general introduction to local history and additional volumes for thirty-eight states.[9] Among these was

Andrew F. Rolle's *California: A Student's Guide to Localized History,*
published in 1965.

The most recent period of interest in community history began
about 1975. As Metcalf and Downey point out, the current revival is
partly a creation of the decentralized celebration of the bicentennial,
which stimulated student and teacher interest in classroom projects.[10]
Continued acceptance of local sources in academic circles is another
factor. During the last few decades, a new generation of social historians
has built a significant body of professional literature that uses local
sources to explore the dynamics of family and community life.

Given the history of the local sources movement, two inevitable
questions come to mind: How long will the current interest last, and how
deeply will it affect actual classroom practice? It is my impression that
community history remains a marginal component in the social studies
curriculum and, if major changes do not occur, it will be lost to another
generation of teachers. There is some evidence to support this view.
According to the semiannual indexes of the Educational Resources
Information Center for the 1974–1986 period, the number of papers
and articles written on the subject peaked in 1975 and slowly declined
over the next nine years.[11]

This historical pattern persists for several reasons. First, despite
recent changes in attitudes toward local sources, professional academic
and amateur local historians continue to view each other with suspicion.
Academicians dismiss amateur historians as parochial and untrained;
amateur historians view academicians as isolated and esoteric. The gulf
between these groups weakens the movement for community history
in the schools because teachers need the cooperative support of both
camps to make it work. The professional historian offers the broad
perspective, while the amateur local historian provides vital local color
and access to rich collections of local source materials.

A second factor inhibiting the community-history movement is the
teacher's dependence on textbooks. Community history invites non-
textbook teaching strategies. The preeminence of the history textbook,
however, has not been seriously debated during this century. Further,
pre-service and in-service teacher training programs have not prepared
teachers to evaluate textbooks critically or to develop strategies for integrating source materials into their history teaching. Under the press
of daily program demands, teachers have not been prepared to consider
the reforms suggested by several generations of community history advocates.

If the current wave of interest in local sources is to become more
than a passing fad, educators first must address the teacher training
issue and second clarify a number of central questions. These questions
will be discussed in the remainder of this paper.

COMMUNITY HISTORY: WHAT DOES IT ADD?

A history curriculum should provide students with knowledge, skills, and an enthusiasm for further historical study. The knowledge objective has three components: mastering factual material, developing an understanding of social processes, and nurturing empathy. Specifically, students must be able to identify significant groups, events, and institutions from the past. They need to understand the dynamics of such fundamental social processes as immigrant assimilation or the diffusion of technological change. It is equally important for students to develop a sense of empathy with the struggles of people who have lived in other times and in other places.

Ultimately, students should be able to use this knowledge to understand the relationship between past, present, and future. As Herbert Adams suggested in 1885, "History is not a record of dead facts [and] pupils who fail to realize the vital connection between past and present do not grasp the essential idea of history which is the growing self-knowledge of a living, progressive age."[12]

How can local sources enrich the history curriculum? Local sources provide a powerful tool for evoking empathy and building a solid foundation of knowledge. As Lord pointed out in the sixties, abstract generalizations and complex social processes can be examined in a manageable way when the community is used as a case study.[13] And there is another advantage: when they study their own community, students are much more likely to identify with historical actors and their problems.

Skill development is another important objective of the history curriculum. A well-designed history program includes effective teaching of map reading, research, oral and written communication, critical thinking, and other basic skills. As Mary Barnes pointed out, the best way to develop these skills is to engage students in investigating original sources. The local community provides the richest and most accessible repository of materials. Integrated with other readings, such a study will "bring the pupil face to face with all the sources and give him the best training that history has for him in accuracy, the weighing of evidence and the sympathetic interpretation of the past."[14] As New Social Studies advocate James Banks reaffirmed in the early 1970s, "The community offers an excellent laboratory for students to use in their search for answers to historical queries."[15]

A third essential objective of the history curriculum is to cultivate enthusiasm for continued historical inquiry. To develop this enthusiasm, students need to experience the excitement of discovering how historical understanding helps unravel the complexities and paradoxes of everyday life. This process must begin as early as possible: history in the elementary school years should motivate students to want to study history at the secondary level. Because of the familiar and tangible nature of local sources, no approach works more effectively than community history to achieve this goal.

INTEGRATING COMMUNITY HISTORY INTO THE CURRICULUM

Making a case for the educational value of community history is easier than devising strategies for integrating local sources into the history–social studies program. How do you add this material without destroying program continuity? Do you use local sources to illustrate concepts throughout the school year, or do you set aside a larger block of time to explore the community in depth? How early in the elementary grades should these materials be introduced? At the secondary level, should community history be offered as an elective or used as supplemental material in courses on state and United States history?

Let us address the question of program continuity. In the elementary grades, only a limited amount of time is devoted to history–social studies. Indeed, the average teacher spends only two or three hours each week exploring this curricular area. On the other hand, state and local authorities issue numerous directives regarding what should be taught at each grade level. Community history should not be introduced into this program as another add-on unit, squeezed into an already crowded agenda. Local sources have to be thoughtfully integrated into existing curricula.

One potentially useful approach is to treat community history as a case study.[16] By case study, I mean a sequence of learning activities in which a small unit of a larger entity is studied in depth. In this instance, the entity is the state or national history unit. Key themes selected from these programs can be explored through a systematic investigation of local sources.

Because it links the local area to larger units of analysis, this approach is appealing. As Gerber suggests, the case-study strategy prevents community history from becoming parochial and ethnocentric and "affords us the opportunity to use the 'little' picture as a means to achieve empathy and to discover the 'big' picture."[17] The study of the community also, as a direct extension of an existing program, gives students an opportunity to view the dynamics of social processes in depth. The community, as Banks observed, is the laboratory in which hypotheses and generalizations are tested and evaluated.

This approach works well in California, where educators are grappling with the implementation of the 1981 California Framework for History–Social Studies.[18] For example, the setting for grade 3 is "People as Members of Communities." In this curriculum, pupils learn to define the concept of "community," locate their community on a map, identify its diverse peoples, and understand the basic processes of group cooperation and conflict. In addition, boys and girls can compare and contrast their own community with others—in the United States and in other parts of the world. Clearly, this entire grade 3 unit can be approached from a historical perspective. Later, the local case study serves as the basis for a comparative analysis of communities around the world.

The grade 4 setting is California history. In this program students learn to identify major immigrant groups, understand their contributions to the state, and learn when, how, and why they settled in California. This immigration theme makes an excellent basis for a community history case study in which local immigration patterns are contrasted and compared to those in other parts of the state.

The foregoing discussion implies that local sources can be effectively integrated into the curriculum as early as grade 3. But we need to consider why we teach history to eight-, nine-, and ten-year-olds when decades of research in learning theory show that, before the age of eleven, most students have only a limited understanding of chronology and historical reasoning.[19] Given these findings, the purposes of the elementary program should be to introduce students to time concepts, nurture appropriate thinking skills, and stimulate an early interest in historical study. To achieve these goals, history must be taught in a very tangible and concrete way. This is the special strength of local sources; educators, therefore, should consider developing an articulated elementary-secondary program that introduces students to local source materials during the midelementary years.

THE QUESTION OF CLASSROOM STRATEGIES

Once teachers have decided to integrate community history into the curriculum, the next step is to design effective learning activities for the classroom. Teachers should begin with the child's own experiences and build, as Mary Cunningham suggested, from the "known to the unknown." This principle has at least two implications for the sequencing of activities. First, history study in the elementary grades should begin with an exploration of personal and family history. Personal time lines, family birthplace charts, interviews with family members, letters to grandmother, and biographical and autobiographical sketches all help students organize personally significant but jumbled data from the past into a logical sequence based on the passage of time. This experience prepares students to understand the more remote time concept embedded in the study of community, state, and national history.

Beginning with what students already know has a second implication for designing the history curriculum. For the young child, the "known" is the present and the "unknown" is the past. Through learning about their own world, students come to understand periods of time that they cannot directly experience. In the classroom, this means that teachers should use comparative studies of past and present whenever possible. A successful community history case study, for instance, includes activities in which students compare historic photographs with contemporary scenes of the same area or subject.

The second principle that should guide the development of activities concerns the use of primary source materials to investigate the local community. These materials lend themselves to certain types of teaching strategies and, unlike textbooks, invite hands-on experiences and inquiry methods of teaching. Because these materials are so diverse, classroom activities can address the needs of a wide variety of students: photographs fascinate visual learners; oral history interviews appeal to auditory learners; architectural walks and artifact explorations engage kinesthetic learners.

At the elementary level, several types of local sources are particularly appealing: historic photographs, memoirs and firsthand accounts, oral history interviews, and local architecture.[20] Historic photographs, obtainable through local libraries and historic museums and organizations, probably offer the richest resource. In general, successful photographs should be prints of clear originals, rich with details of social life. Students are particularly fascinated with images of children, families, schools, and early transportation systems. Effective photographs also contain some frame of reference, such as a recognizable structure, extant in the modern community. Slides or mounted prints of these images can form the basis of rich comparative studies of social life.

Firsthand accounts and memoirs provide another important source material for classroom use. Like photographs, they richly describe the social milieu of another time. Available in local history collections, such diaries, letters, memoirs, and oral history transcriptions provide vibrant stories for classroom reading and writing experiences. As Downey suggests, accounts of childhood are particularly appealing and are "a primary resource for involving students in the process of history on a personal level."[21]

A related source material is the oral history interview. In the elementary grades, an interview consists of an individual project conducted with a neighbor or family member or a group interview conducted in class with an invited guest from the community.[22] Interviews are an effective teaching strategy for several reasons. Because students have to ask questions, interviews enhance inquiry skills. Also, the personal quality of an interview underscores the concept that ordinary people participate actively in the historical development of a society.

Local architecture gives teachers another important medium for exploring the past with students.[23] In the study of community history, the principal purpose of teaching children about architecture is to provide them with tools for reading the history around them. Architecture in a history program—beyond the usual goal of sensitizing students to structural form and design—teaches students to recognize shapes and details so that they can identify important styles in the community, learn when these styles were popular, and use this knowledge to help piece together the social and demographic history of the area. The geographic distribution of styles, for instance, contains clues to help students understand how population changes affected various parts of the community. Also, the size and construction of houses tells a lot about the socioeconomic composition of the area.

Students often raise questions about preservation when they see older houses torn down or remodeled—appropriate but thorny issues for classroom discussion. Many preservationists look with horror at the sight of asbestos shingles nailed to the original drop siding of a Queen Anne cottage. For the family that resurfaced the house, however, the shingles may represent an economical and practical solution to the problem of modernizing the deteriorating exterior of that home. If the purpose of studying architecture in the history program is to teach students to use the built environment as a tool for understanding the past, then both the asbestos and the drop siding are part of the community's history. Teachers do not need to decide whether the preservationist view is right or wrong. They do have to teach students to learn to use what they know about their material culture to help answer such queries.

REFORMING TEACHER TRAINING PROGRAMS

Clearly, every community contains ample classroom resources, and adding these materials to the curriculum could measurably strengthen history teaching at all grade levels. As the previous discussion has suggested, however, many obstacles have kept community history out of the curriculum. These obstacles cannot be removed without reforming areas of pre-service and in-service teacher training programs.

We must address a number of critical issues: How do we use the skills of professional academic and amateur local historians to strengthen our training programs? How do we prepare teachers to evaluate history textbooks? How do we design programs so that teachers feel comfortable about integrating source materials into the history curriculum?

Professional, academic, and local historians have differing but complementary roles to play in a community history teacher training program. Professional historians can offer courses in local and state history to provide teachers with an understanding of the broad issues that help shape the curriculum. Too little of this is currently being done. According to a 1979–80 survey, the history departments of our four-year colleges and universities offer few courses in local history.[24]

Professional historians also should participate in cooperative programs with teachers and local historians from the community. In these programs, teachers would receive training in the general use of sources in historiography and develop an understanding of the important types of resources found in most local history collections. Hands-on training on how to convert these materials into practical classroom activites is another essential ingredient for a successful program.[25]

The textbook issue, which cuts across curricular areas, should be addressed by teacher training programs regardless of interest (or lack of it) in community history. The textbook market is lucrative, and commercial publishing houses use sophisticated techniques to sell their products. Teachers, administrators, and curriculum specialists need training in the critical evaluation of these resources. This training should focus on the selection and use of stimulating, well-written, accurate textbooks that can be easily supplemented with source materials. With these skills, teachers, who also receive the support of cooperative programs in local history, will be well equipped to integrate community history into elementary and secondary social studies programs.

NOTES

1. G. Stanley Hall, *Methods of History Teaching*, vol. 1 (Boston: Ginn, Heath, and Company, 1885), p. 125.
2. Mary Sheldon Barnes, "The Teaching of Local History," *Educational Review* 10 (Henry Holt and Co., December 1895): 482.
3. Robert E. Keohane, "The Great Debate over the Source Method," *Social Education* 13 (National Council for the Social Studies, May 1949): 213.
4. Ibid., p. 216.
5. Ibid., p. 217.
6. Ruth West, ed., *Utilization of Community Resources in the Social Studies* (Washington, DC: Ninth Yearbook of the National Council for the Social Studies, 1938), pp. 9–10.
7. Fay Metcalf and Matthew Downey, *Using Local History in the Classroom* (Nashville: American Society for State and Local History, 1982), p. 4.
8. Mary Cunningham, "General Aspects of the Problem: A Survey of Current Practices in the Teaching of State and Local History," in George Oeste, ed., *Teaching Local History in Today's World*, vol. 44, part 2 (Annual Proceedings of the Middle States Council on the Social Studies, 1946–1947), pp. 3–4.
9. See Clifford L. Lord, ed., *Teaching History with Community Resources* (New York: Teachers College Bureau of Publications, 1964).
10. Metcalf and Downey, *Using Local History*, p. 2.

11. *Semiannual Indexes,* Educational Resource Information Center, January 1974 through July 1986.

12. Hall, *Methods,* p. 132.

13. Lord, *Teaching History,* pp. 8–15.

14. James A. Banks, *Teaching Strategies for the Social Studies* (Reading, PA: Addison-Wesley Publishing Company, 1973), p. 186.

15. See Lord, *Teaching History,* for more details on the case-study approach.

16. David Gerber, "Local and Community History: Some Cautionary Remarks on an Idea Whose Time Has Returned," *History Teacher* 13 (Society for History Education, November 1979): 26.

17. See the *California Framework for History–Social Studies in the K–12 Program,* Department of Education, State of California, 1981.

18. The literature on this topic is fairly extensive. See Roy Smith, "The Development of Children's Constructions of Historical Duration," *Educational Research* 19 (June 1977): 3; Michael Zaccaria, "The Development of Historical Thinking: Implications for the Teaching of History," *The History Teacher* 11 (May 1978): 3; Ray Hallam, "Logical Thinking in History," *Educational Review* 19 (June 1967): 183–202; Gustave Jahoda, "Children's Concepts of Time and History," *Educational Review* 15 (November 1962): 87–104.

19. See David Weitzman, *My Backyard History Book* (Boston: Little, Brown and Company, 1975) for some interesting family history activities.

20. Good discussions of local sources are contained in Metcalf and Downey, *Using Local History,* and in David E. Kyvig and Myron A. Marty, *Nearby History* (Nashville: American Association for State and Local History, 1982).

21. Matthew T. Downey, "Childhood: The Way It Was," *Teacher,* (October 1980), p. 59.

22. The best resource for planning a secondary oral history project is George McHaffey, Thad Sitton, and O. L. Davis, Jr., "Oral History in the Classroom," How To Do It Series, National Council for the Social Studies, Washington, DC (1979).

23. See Catherine Taylor and Matthew Downey, "Using Local Architecture as an Historical Resource: Some Teaching Strategies," *History Teacher* 11 (February 1978): 175–192.

24. V. Ben Bloxham, "Training History Teachers to Teach Family and Local History," World Conference on Records: Preserving Our Heritage, Salt Lake City, Utah, August 12–15, 1980.

25. Ibid.

Part V
CONCLUSIONS AND REFLECTIONS

The ability to learn from the past, to be able to envision alternative futures, to be able to exercise prophetic wisdom, is an outcome that all of us seek, to some degree or other, when we study history. Why, then, is it the case that so many of us who have assiduously studied our history books make such poor prophets about the course of future events? This is one of the issues that Ernest R. May, a long-time member of the Harvard history department, addresses in his essay. May argues, as have others in this collection, that in the hands of both the weak and the powerful, the haves and the have-nots, the presence or absence of historical knowledge and understanding has some important behavioral consequences. What makes May's views illuminating, however, is not his message, but his method of reasoning, his rationale, and his approach to this obvious truism.

I requested Professor May to prepare this essay specifically for use as an epilogue for *History in the Schools*, because he is unique among historians for the thoughtful attention he pays to the use (and abuse) of historical arguments by elected officials and influential policy makers in the formulation and explanation of public policy initiatives. However, May has not limited his field of vision to the use of historical reasoning by the influential. He has also written widely and wisely about how ordinary individuals make everyday decisions on the basis of their understanding of the lessons of history, only to discover that whatever lessons they thought they might have learned turned out to be poorly learned, or worst yet, erroneous. As May points out, knowing when history has important lessons to teach, when history is useful for helping us to formulate the proper questions to investigate, and when history is useful as an aid to the imagination, is no small challenge. His contribution will help us meet this challenge by helping us to better understand when we are demanding too much from history, and when we are ignoring its obvious lessons.

Chapter 14

The Dangerous Usefulness of History

ERNEST R. MAY

All teachers face students asking, "Why study *your* subject?"

Some teachers have ready answers. Most history teachers do not. Unlike reading or arithmetic, history is not a basic skill. Unlike auto mechanics or accounting or engineering or a science related to one of the health professions, history does not lead obviously toward a job. Simply as fun, history has a hard time competing with literature, music, or art.

When asked why rabbis always answer questions with questions, a rabbi allegedly responds: "Why do you ask?" To the skeptical student, the history teacher should probably reply: "What happens if you *don't* study history?"

At a very abstract level, one can argue that there are only two ways of thinking—one mathematical; the other historical. Mathematical thinking uses pure logic—preferably with symbols rather than words, so as to escape all ambiguity. Historical thinking uses experience. (This happened. Therefore, it may happen again. Etc.) In varying degrees, the physical and social sciences are both mathematical and historical. They build logical formulae, then test them experimentally. The arts tend to be one or the other. Composers and painters think more or less mathematically, novelists and playwrights more or less historically.

While a history class is certainly not the only place where someone learns historical thinking, it is not a bad place to do so. The more history a person has studied, the more readily he or she can bring to bear on questions that really matter the experience of others drawn from distant times or places. As the Spanish humanist Juan Luis Vives says, in the lines quoted earlier by Diane Ravitch, "Where there is history, children have transferred to them the advantages of old men; where history is absent, old men are as children."[1]

Consider black Americans. As recently as the early 1960s, many lived in legally enforced segregation. The majority were meanly paid, meanly housed, meanly treated, and meanly educated. Large numbers accepted their lot not only because they were powerless but also because they had no experience of any other kind of life.

A movement for change was led by men and women who knew otherwise. These men and women, black and white, knew—from history—that conditions had not always been as they were; that they could be different; and that they could be changed.

It was W. E. B. Du Bois, a professional historian, who jarred awareness that black Americans were African-Americans. While they had mostly come unwillingly, as slaves, they were in many respects similar to other immigrants. The cultures from which they came were at least as rich as those of other immigrants. Their contributions to a distinctive American culture were, as Du Bois argued in *The Souls of Black Folk* (1903), second only to those of English-Americans. "Here," he wrote,

> we have brought our three gifts and mingled them with yours: a gift of story and song—soft, stirring melody in an ill-harmonized and unmelodious land; the gift of sweat and brawn to beat back the wilderness, conquer the soil, and lay the foundations of this vast economic empire; . . . the third, a gift of the Spirit. . . . Actively we have woven ourselves with the very warp and woof of this nation. . . . Would America have been America without her Negro people?"[2]

No one exposed to Du Bois's writings could help but wonder why Afro-Americans suffered greater discrimination than other immigrant groups, or how it came to be that, as Du Bois commented in the beginning of his book, it was difficult "for a man to be both a Negro and an American, without . . . having the doors of Opportunity closed roughly in his face."[3]

In *The Strange Career of Jim Crow* (1955), C. Vann Woodward, another professional historian, awakened understanding of the comparative newness of legalized segregation. The Southern states' Jim Crow laws forbade blacks to eat with whites, sit beside them on streetcars and buses, use the same public lavatories, or even drink at the same fountains. Du Bois had already pointed out that such segregation had not existed in the South before the Civil War. "There were bonds of intimacy, affection, and sometimes blood relationship, between the races," he wrote. "They lived in the same home, shared in the family life, often attended the same church, and talked and conversed with one another."[4] It was nevertheless widely assumed, in the North as well as the South, that Jim Crow laws had been somehow "natural"—a means by which the society preserved order once slavery had been forcibly abolished. Woodward produced evidence that, on the contrary, blacks and whites had continued to mingle freely for a quarter-century after the Civil War. Jim Crow laws had been put on the statute books in the

1880s and 1890s by demagogues exploiting racism in a period of economic depression. There was an imperfect but not wholly farfetched analogy to the later use of antisemitism by Hitler and the Nazis.[5]

Analyses of past experience by Du Bois, Woodward, and other historians helped to shape the views of Martin Luther King, Jr. King's thought about what to do was further affected by knowledge of another body of experience—that of Indians, led by Mohandas Gandhi, who achieved national independence through nonviolent resistance. King took specific as well as general guidance from study of Gandhi. He justified occasional tactical retreats by reference to Gandhi's similar action during the Punjab riots of 1919.[6] Nor was King alone in drawing lessons from the experience of Indians. When blacks in Montgomery, Alabama, boycotted the city's buses rather than continue obeying the Jim Crow laws, Juliette Morgan, one of their leaders, wrote that they were imitating Gandhi's "salt march." (She also likened their use of alternative vehicles to the French mobilization of taxicabs for the first battle of the Marne in 1914.)[7]

Of course, many others besides historians contributed to discrediting segregation. Many who were less well read than King or Juliette Morgan contributed to its outlawing. A sense of history was nevertheless an important, perhaps even indispensable, element in the civil rights movement that made racial segregation unlawful. Without it, blacks and whites alike might have continued even longer to tolerate Jim Crow laws.

Consider, as a second example, the national economy. Students in colleges, high schools, and even junior high schools talk a good deal about what work they are going to do later in life. Unless they know some history and have learned to think historically, they fail to reflect on what conditions may exist when they actually enter the job market. Such absence of foresight is common among people older than they. There is a regular pattern, for example, in the engineering professions. In one year, there will be a shortage of engineers. Jobs go begging. Four or five years later, predictably, it will be the other way around. There will be more engineers than jobs. The reason is that when jobs are plentiful many college freshmen sign up to be engineering majors. When jobs are less plentiful, fewer do so. Not many freshmen seem to think four or five years ahead.[8]

Any student, at any age, can think more constructively about career plans if he or she takes into account the possibility that the world may change. This is not to say that anyone can prophesy with assurance. It is to say, however, that awareness of change can open new prospects. Someone who starts to think about the skills that may be most in demand five or ten or fifteen years from now is a long step ahead of someone who merely asks what is in this week's want ads.

The ability to envision alternative futures is greatly affected by knowledge of the actual past. Anyone who has studied any American history knows that the boom of the 1920s ended in the Great Depression. Stocks and bonds lost most of their value. Suddenly, a quarter of the labor force was unemployed. With that knowledge alone, someone thinking of the future has at least some starting questions. Will prosperity continue? Is there likely to be another Great Depression? The more someone knows about the real Great Depression and what was subsequently done to prevent its recurrence, the better the questions he or she can formulate.

The wider one's knowledge of history, the larger is the set of potentially instructive questions. In the past, Americans have periodically been fearful about the economy's future. During the 1890s, steel mills and factories sat idle. It was commonly said that the United States had overbuilt its smokestack industries. Then came, unexpectedly, the age of the automobile and of turbine-generated electricity, and demand for industrial products far outstripped existing capacity. New factories went up. There followed the Great Depression and renewed pessimism. But the airplane and the vacuum tube provided the basis for another unexpected industrial boom. And when that boom seemed about to peter out, the microchip provided the basis for another. While the pattern of the past certainly does not justify any predictions, it does, equally certainly, prompt one to keep in mind the possibility that new ideas or new technologies may give the economy an entirely new turn.

The study of history is not going to *answer* questions about the future. The first lesson learned by any serious student of history is that things are never the same. Knowing that changes have taken place in the past does, however, make one aware that the future will almost certainly not be like the present. Knowing what actual changes took place in the past can be helpful for imagining the range of futures ahead.

The principle of fair disclosure requires any preachment about the usefulness of history to be accompanied by a warning against misuse. Knowledge of past experience can build false expectations or beliefs. It is easy to draw wrong lessons from seeming precedents. Martin Luther King, Jr., may have decided wisely when he acted on the analogy with Gandhi in 1919, but there are many examples of analogies wrongly applied.

The history of international relations teems with such examples. After World War I, many people thought that the war's lessons were plain. One lesson was that governments should be prepared to make concessions to the passions of nationalism: Austria-Hungary's failure to accommodate the nationalism of South Slavs was thought to have been a prime cause of the war. Second, statesmen should go to great lengths to avoid any armed conflict. The fighting between 1914 and 1918 had taken more than ten million lives, and almost no one could find arguments to justify their deaths. Hence, in the 1930s, when Adolf Hitler demanded that all German-speaking Europeans be incorporated in Nazi Germany and hinted at war as the alternative, French, British, and American leaders followed a policy of appeasement. They made concessions to Hitler in order to stave off war. Since Hitler kept taking territory, even where the population was not German, and war came—with Germany better armed than earlier—appeasement was condemned as a ghastly mistake. The presumed lesson of the 1938 Munich conference and the war of 1939–1945 was that the lessons drawn from World War I had been wrong.

"Munich" then became the catchword for a new lesson: don't appease dictators; show them from the outset that any territorial demands will bring war. Americans applied this lesson to the Soviet Union. It was, after all, a totalitarian dictatorship. Many Americans looked on the Soviet Union as a counterpart to Nazi Germany. Hence, Americans expected reckless expansionism like Hitler's in the 1930s. It became the keynote of United States foreign policy to create conviction in Moscow that any adventurous Soviet move would bring on a war. The American government therefore adopted uncompromising and even threatening positions with regard to a number of issues that might conceivably have been subjects for mutually satisfactory diplomatic compromises.

The error was by no means all on the American side. Josef Stalin, the Soviet dictator, was probably much more cautious than Americans assumed. But Stalin seems to have been in the grip of analogies from the First World War. He expected the United States to retreat into isolationism and to go through another Great Depression. He expected the war-damaged countries of Western Europe—including Germany—to revive quickly, and he probably foresaw the British organizing, as they had in the 1920s, a European concert that excluded the Soviet Union. Hence, Stalin, too, was slow to seek negotiated compromises. Some of his actions encouraged the American belief that he should be dealt with as if he were another Hitler. One example was his cutting off Western road and rail access to Berlin in 1948—the so-called Berlin blockade. He may have meant only to protest forcibly against the Western powers' dealing with West Germany without consulting Moscow, but what he did was construed in the West as a trial move in preparation for a military attack on West Germany. Analogies from the interwar period partially blinded both sides.

The image of Munich, carrying the supposed lesson that it was crucial to avoid any "appeasement," remained a powerful force in American thinking for a quarter century after World War II. During the Vietnam War of the 1960s and 1970s, American leaders constantly invoked

"Munich" in partial explanation of why they were reluctant to negotiate an end to that increasingly unhopeful and unpopular conflict. When explaining his decision to send large numbers of American soldiers to Vietnam, President Lyndon Johnson said in 1965 that failure to do so "would encourage and spur on those who seek to conquer all free nations within their reach. . . . This is the clearest lesson of our time. From Munich until today we have learned that to yield to aggression brings only greater threats."[9]

After the Vietnam War, less was heard about "Munich." But that war itself became a potentially imprisoning analogy. Probably fortunately, it did not become the catchword for a single alleged lesson. Some Americans cited Vietnam as teaching the unwisdom of involvement in other countries' internal wars. Others saw as its lesson the danger of incremental or small-scale involvement, if dependent on persistent public support. In the 1980s, with regard to Central America, the first group took the view that the United States should not actively participate in operations against guerrillas assisted by the Nicaraguan Sandinistas. The second group held that, if the United States acted on any substantial scale, it should strike against Nicaragua itself. If it acted on a small scale, the action should be taken by the executive without Congress or the public having knowledge. Legislation by Congress reflected the former view. For practical purposes, it forbade American military personnel to give direct advice on counter-guerrilla operations. Activities secretly undertaken by members of the National Security Council staff reflected the second view. These activities came to light in the "Iran-Contra Affair," which marred the final phase of the Reagan Administration. In retrospect, both readings of the lessons of Vietnam seem at least as simplistic as were the earlier readings first of World War I and then of "Munich."

Nor is it only history in the small—the single-incident analogy—that can mislead. History can be grossly misinterpreted or misused. The long persistence of legalized segregation, including Jim Crow laws, owed a great deal to the power of racist interpretations of historical trends. In the nineteenth century, historians and would-be social scientists borrowed Darwinian biology. Without thinking much about the huge differences between bugs and humans, they hypothesized struggles for survival among races of humankind, wherein "the fittest" prevailed. English and German-speaking nations seemed at the time to be on top—so histories were written as success stories of Caucasian or Teutonic or Aryan races. Undeserved acceptance of these absurd interpretations had much to do with making segregation acceptable. Woodward concluded that the demagogues' success in enacting Jim Crow laws was due less to their own persuasiveness than to the fact that opposition melted away.

The continuing force of this nineteenth-century racism was nowhere better illustrated than in a college-level survey of American history published in 1930 by the eminent Harvard and Columbia historians Samuel Eliot Morison and Henry Steele Commager. Writing of the Southern states after the Civil War, Morison and Commager justified certain provisions of their "black codes" on the ground that freed slaves were not the equals of whites. "Owing to their well-known aversion from steady work," the pair wrote, "they were required to have some settled occupation, and subjected to penalties for violation of labor contracts."[10] Since their textbook is widely and not unreasonably regarded as the best United States history survey ever written, its example reinforces the argument repeatedly made in this volume against excessive reliance on textbooks.

Blinkered reading of historical trends is, however, a common failing, not confined to textbook writers or those who rely on them. Du Bois's reportage on the rich African inheritance of Afro-Americans helped correct stereotypes such as those of Morison and Commager. His work encouraged black pride. He went on eventually, however, to argue his own version of racism, claiming that history demonstrated the superiority of blacks over whites.[11] Similarly, writers and teachers addressing Hispanic-Americans can easily go beyond merely calling attention to the great role of Spain in world history or the majesty of such empires as those of the Incas, Mayas, and Aztecs. They, too, can become racist. Alternatively, they can encourage the kind of belief in a distant, never-to-be-recaptured golden age that in turn discourages hope and enterprise.

If misknowing history can be as much a handicap as not knowing it, how should teachers deal with the students' second question: "How do we learn the *right* history?"

As this entire volume testifies, there are no clear-cut answers. The essays by Hazel Hertzberg and Diane Ravitch show that there never have been such. In the United States, teachers and writers of history have debated what students ought to be taught and how. As they and others suggest, elements in the debate echo disputes visible in biblical and classical texts. Contributors to part 2 of this study identify subjects that deserve attention—the civic good, the nature and evolution of science, the immigrants' experience, and the multiplicity of American cultures. Contributors to part 3 speak more of perspectives than of subjects—seeing world history as a whole and as a process; looking at the histories of humans and their day-to-day lives and associations rather than primarily at the histories of nations and governments; and considering American history as, among other things, the history of a nation with a distinctive set of laws and legal processes.

In a book of greater length, still other subjects and perspectives would have been introduced. Government and business are examples. The essays by R. Freeman Butts, William M. Sullivan, and Harry N. Scheiber concern politics and law. They suggest questions much more interesting and important than those usually raised in history courses that proceed president by president. But they do not deal with the governmental apparatus—the myriad federal, state, and local agencies that, among other things, employ about 20 percent of working Americans. If students read newspapers or see television news, they are told a good deal about the Pentagon, the CIA, the FBI, the Drug Enforcement Administration, federal health and safety organizations, state insurance commissions, state and local police, etc. History courses do not often help them to understand where these organizations came from. They should.

Similarly, history courses could well give students better understanding of corporations and business firms. It is in such organizations that many students' parents spend their working days. It is there that they themselves are likely to spend a large part of their lives. Despite the growth of government and many other changes, there remains a good deal of truth in Calvin Coolidge's dictum, "The chief business of America is business." Yet students of history seldom learn how American business evolved. Indeed, from textbooks and history courses that mention only "robber barons" brought to heel by Progressives, American students can leave school with hardly a clue as to what entrepreneurship means or why their country has a Gross National Product approaching four trillion dollars (or, indeed, what Gross National Product *is*).

The essays here, and others that the Clio Project may eventually inspire, can help teachers at all levels see facets of history to which students might be exposed. But the conditionality should be stressed. It is *might*, not *ought*. As the Hertzberg and Ravitch essays indicate, and the essays on teaching strategies illustrate, the content-versus-method debate is largely sterile. History cannot be taught without content. But the point most often made in all these essays has to do with the importance of questions. A major reason for questioning reliance on textbooks is the fact that even the best textbook is largely a book of answers. Not only are the answers sometimes wrong, as in the Morison-Commager example cited earlier, but they are answers to the textbook writer's questions, not to the questions of students. The teacher who presents history as a set of propositions to be memorized is acting as a human textbook and very likely does not do the job as well as do printed pages. The teacher who poses questions and who then tests answers not as "true" or "false" but only as logical or consistent with evidence available helps students discover the history that *they* can use, whatever their backgrounds or prospects.

The central aim of this brief essay is, however, not so much to reinforce points made by others as it is to emphasize how important is the work of history teachers and how careful they ought to be in doing it. Their students need history—indeed, are crippled without it. On the other hand, history misunderstood or misapplied can do at least as much harm as medical knowledge misunderstood or misapplied. Jim Crow laws were—and military cemeteries are—among proofs of this proposition. History teachers at all levels need to remember that they are helping students learn the use of a powerful, potentially valuable, but also highly dangerous tool.

NOTES

1. Chapter 2.
2. W. E. B. Du Bois, *The Souls of Black Folk* (Chicago: A. C. McClurg, 1903), pp. 262–263.
3. Ibid., p. 4.
4. Ibid., p. 183.
5. C. Vann Woodward, *The Strange Career of Jim Crow* (New York: Oxford University Press, 1954), especially chapters 1 and 2. Woodward himself, it should be noted, does not make explicit use of this analogy. He only refers to "the psychologists['] . . . hypothesis that aggression is always the result of frustration." (p. 63).
6. David Levering Lewis, *Kind, A Biography*, rev. ed. (Urbana: University of Illinois Press, 1978), pp. 162–163.
7. Ibid., p. 64.
8. Richard B. Freeman, *The Market for College Trained Manpower: A Study in the Economics of Career Choice* (Cambridge, MA: Harvard University Press, 1971), pp. 55–75.
9. *Public Papers of the Presidents: Lyndon B. Johnson, 1965* (Washington, DC: Government Printing Office, 1966), vol. 1, p. 449. The misuse of analogies is a major theme of Ernest R. May, *"Lessons" of the Past: The Use and Misuse of History in American Foreign Policy* (New York: Oxford University Press, 1973), and it is a theme picked up again in Richard E. Neustadt and Ernest R. May, *Thinking in Time: The Uses of History for Decision-Makers* (New York: Free Press, 1986).
10. Samuel Eliot Morison and Henry Steele Commager, *The Growth of the American Republic* (New York: Oxford University Press, 1930), p. 622. By 1937, when their text went into a new edition, Morison and Commager had amended this passage to the extent of substituting "alleged" for "well-known."
11. For a generally sympathetic portrayal of this evolution, explained in part in terms of Du Bois's justified sense of persecution, see Manning Marable, *W. E. B. Du Bois, Black Radical Democrat* (Boston: Twayne Publishers, 1986).

Contributors

R. FREEMAN BUTTS, William F. Russell Professor Emeritus in the Foundations of Education, Teachers College, Columbia University, received his doctorate in history, philosophy and education from the University of Wisconsin, Madison. Dr. Butts is currently a member of the Kettering Foundation Associates Council and of the board of directors of the Center for Civic Education and of the Council for the Advancement of Citizenship. He is also a member of the National Advisory Committee for the National Bicentennial Competition on the Constitution and the Bill of Rights to be conducted in schools throughout the United States from 1987 through 1991. His most recent book is *Civic Education for America's Third Century: Perspectives for the Public and the Profession* (1988).

MATTHEW T. DOWNEY, formerly a professor of history at the University of Colorado, is a visiting professor and history curriculum specialist in the Graduate School of Education at the University of California, Berkeley. He received his doctorate in history from Princeton University. Dr. Downey is the author of books and articles on history teaching, including *Using Local History in the Classroom* [with Fay D. Metcalf] (1982), and was editor of *History in the Schools* (1985), a report on the status of history in the public schools. He is a member of the National Commission on Social Studies.

BERNARD R. GIFFORD has been chancellor's professor and dean of the Graduate School of Education, University of California at Berkeley, since January 1983. A Ph.D. in radiation biology and biophysics from the University of Rochester, where he was also elected to *Phi Beta Kappa*, Gifford also studied at Harvard University, where he was a Kennedy Fellow at the John F. Kennedy School of Government, as well as a Loeb Fellow at the Graduate School of City and Regional Planning. Before becoming a full-time academic in 1981, as vice president and professor of Political Science and Public Policy at the University of Rochester, he served as program officer and resident scholar at the Russell Sage Foundation (1977–81) and as deputy chancellor of the New York City Public Schools (1973–77). Widely published in a number of disciplinary areas, ranging from applied physics to public policy, in recent years, Gifford has devoted most of his scholarly efforts to thinking and writing about the process of educational change and reform and the gulf between the sciences and the humanities.

HAZEL WHITMAN HERTZBERG is professor of history and education at Teachers College, Columbia University, where she is in charge of the social studies program. Her books include: *Social Studies Reform, 1880–1980* (1981); *The Search for an American Indian Identity: Modern Pan-Indian Movements* (1971); and *The Great Tree and the Longhouse: The Culture of the Iroquois* (1966). She is currently writing a history of the social studies in American public secondary schools for which she has received fellowships from the Guggenheim Foundation and the Woodrow Wilson International Center for Scholars at the Smithsonian Institution.

NATHAN I. HUGGINS is professor of history and Afro-American studies at the DuBois Institute, Harvard University, where he received his doctorate. He is the author of *Protestants against Poverty* (1971), and *Slave and Citizen: The Life of Frederick Douglass* (1980). A former Guggenheim fellow, Professor Huggins has been a Ford Foundation travel-study fellow and a fellow at the Center for Advanced Studies in Behavioral Sciences. He serves as vice president of the Howard Thurman Educational Trust.

KAREN JORGENSEN-ESMAILI, professional expert, Berkeley Teachers Center, in the Berkeley Unified School District, received her doctorate in education at the University of California, Berkeley. She is the author of *A Teacher's Guide to Primary Resources on Berkeley History* for the Berkeley History Project (1983). Dr. Jorgensen-Esmaili also serves as coordinator of the Berkeley History Project.

ERNEST R. MAY is Charles Warren Professor of History at Harvard University. He has written several books on American history and the history of international relations. His most recent book, written jointly with Richard E. Neustadt, is *Thinking in Time: The Uses of History for Decision-Makers*.

WILLIAM H. MCNEILL, Robert A. Millikan Distinguished Service Professor of History and former chairman of the Department of History, University of Chicago, received his doctorate from Cornell University. His numerous publications include: *The Rise of the West: A History of the Human Community* (1963); *Plagues and Peoples* (1976); and *Pursuit of Power* (1982). Professor McNeill is a former Fulbright research scholar for the Royal Institute of International Affairs in England and the recipient of numerous grants, including awards by the Ford, Guggenheim, Rockefeller, and the Carnegie Foundations. He is past president of the American Historical Association.

DIANE RAVITCH is adjunct professor of history and education at Teachers College, Columbia University. A former Guggenheim fellow, Dr. Ravitch is the author of a number of books and articles on American education, including *The Great School Wars, The Troubled Crusade,* and *The Schools We Deserve.*

HARRY N. SCHEIBER, professor of law, Boalt Hall School of Law, University of California at Berkeley, is also a member of the Department of History. He is former chairman of the university's program in jurisprudence and social policy, and he has served as director of the Berkeley Seminar on Federalism, an annual international conference. He received his bachelor's degree from Columbia University and holds a doctorate in American history from Cornell University. He has held Guggenheim, Rockefeller, and National Endowment for the Humanities fellowships. In 1983 he was Distinguished Fulbright Scholar to Australia. His numerous articles and books include *Ohio Canal Era: A Case Study of Government and the Economy* (second edition, 1987), *American Law and the Constitutional Order* (1978), and *American Economic History* (1976). He is former chairman of the College Board's Committee on Advanced Placement in American History, and in 1986–87 was chairman of the National Assessment of Educational Progress academic committee for the assessment of education in American history and government.

JOHN ANTHONY SCOTT teaches at Rutgers University and has taught for many years at Fieldston High School of New York. He received his doctorate in history and political science from Columbia University. Among his numerous articles and books are *Hard Trials on My Way: Slavery and the Struggle Against It, 1800–1860* (1978) and *The Story of America* (1984), a National Geographic Society book. A former fellow of the Commonwealth Foundation and the Social Science Research Council, Dr. Scott serves as cochairman of the Committee on History in the Classroom, an affiliate of the American Historical Association.

PETER N. STEARNS, Heinz Professor of History at the Carnegie-Mellon University and editor of the *Journal of Social History,* received his doctorate from Harvard University. Author of numerous books and articles in professional journals, he has recently written *Old Age in Preindustrial Society* (1983) and *Anger: The Struggle for Emotional Control in America's History* (1986). A former Guggenheim Fellow, Professor Stearns serves as a member of the board of directors of the Public History Association and is past chairman of the Council on Academic Affairs for the College Board.

WILLIAM M. SULLIVAN, professor of philosophy at La Salle University in Philadelphia, is the author of *Reconstructing Public Philosophy* (1982).

He is coauthor of *Habits of the Heart: Individualism and Commitment in American Life* (1985).

CHARLES WOLLENBERG, instructor of history at Vista College in the Peralta Community College District, received his doctorate in the history of education from the University of California, Berkeley. His publications on California social history include *All Deliberate Speed: Segregation and Exclusion in California Schools* (1978) and *Golden Gate Metropolis: Perspectives on Bay Area Regional History* (1985). Dr. Wollenberg, a past president of the Laney Faculty Senate and the Peralta Federation of Teachers, served on the board of trustees for the California Historical Society.

INDEX

Index